Starmaker

the untold story of Jimmy Murphy

Brian Hughes MBE

EMPIRE
PUBLICATIONS

First published in 2002

EMPIRE PUBLICATIONS
1 Newton Street, Manchester M1 1HW
copyright Brian Hughes 2002

ISBN 1 901 746 26 7

Front cover photograph courtesy of Paul Windridge
Jacket design: Ashley Shaw
Edited by Ashley Shaw and Stuart Fish

Front Cover: Jimmy and Matt survey a rebuilt Old Trafford.
Back Cover: (centre) Jimmy in a typical pose gets to grips with his many proteges (clockwise from bottom left): Dennis Viollet, Roger Byrne, Bobby Charlton, Duncan Edwards, George Best and Nobby Stiles.

Printed in Great Britain by:
Bookcraft
Midsomer Norton
Radstock
BA3 4BS

Contents

Contents

Introduction

First of all, can I start by saying how proud and honoured I was when Brian Hughes asked me if I would like to write the foreword for his book, a tribute to Jimmy Murphy. I consider it a privilege to write about a great man. I first met Jimmy in the early 1950s when I joined Leeds United. Jimmy, as you know, was already with Manchester United and I, like many others in football, heard all about the great work he and Matt Busby were doing with young players at Old Trafford. I became very close to Jimmy, very close. We would often meet and have a few drinks and discus football, the Welsh team and other players.

When Jimmy became the Welsh team manager all the Welsh players were delighted. The players didn't call him 'Boss', 'Gaffer' or whatever - Jimmy was just known as Jimmy! He was magnificent, bringing the players together as a team. At our first team meeting he gathered us all into a room in the hotel we were staying in. "We don't want disturbing," he told the hotel reception. Usually at a team meeting players admit they get bored listening to the manager twittering on about 'marking space', 'playing in the hole', and other such phases and some would fall asleep, pick their noses and be distracted by other things. Well, there was none of that at this first meeting I can assure you. Jimmy stood up and spoke and the room fell into a respectful silence. He was a fervent patriot. He first of all welcomed everybody and then spoke about his hopes and desires for the Welsh national team.

"We're lucky, lads," he said. "We're involved in football for a living. Think of those poor coal miners working their fingers to the bone down the pit. Remember those hard-working people in the valleys who've hardly got two pennies to rub together. Here you are, representing your country. When you run out onto that pitch, play with pride, lads, play for your country." He was absolutely brilliant. He spoke passionately and everyone was rivetted to their seats - spellbound. The hairs on the back of my neck stood to attention. I had never heard a manager speak the way Jimmy spoke that night. After what seemed a matter of minutes, but was actually over an hour, he looked at his watch, apologised for keeping us so long and said: "When I get talking I forget time, I'm sorry for boring you," as he finished. The whole team and officials stood up and applauded. If that speech was boring then Jimmy could bore me any time was the general consensus of opinion.

He was without question the best motivator I ever came across in football. He was loved and respected by all the Welsh team and I do mean all of them. He was fair and totally honest with them. He treated everyone equally - no matter what club they played for. After giving someone a dressing down he would order drinks and tell the offender to pull up a chair and join him.

Jimmy didn't have things easy when he first became the Welsh team manager, taking over from Wally Barnes in 1957. People wouldn't believe some of the things that went on - at times there seemed to be more selectors and committee men than we had players, but Jimmy eventually changed things. To him, the players were the most important people and had to be looked after. Obviously our success in the 1958 World Cup in Sweden was the pinnacle and sadly Wales have never equalled that success since. Qualifying for the World Cup was down to Jimmy Murphy, he worked tirelessly for Wales and the players selected. I was playing for Juventus at the time and there were problems with them allowing me to play for my country. Can you imagine this sort of situation happening today? Jimmy had no illusions about our chances in Sweden - he knew it was going to be a monumental task.

It was an even more incredible achievement to take us so far for it had only been a matter of a few months since the Munich air disaster and Jimmy was obviously still distraught, although he kept his feelings under wraps. When I think of the heroic job he did in keeping Manchester United going and taking them to the FA Cup final against Bolton, then turning his attention to the Welsh quest for glory in Sweden I have nothing but admiration for him. It was astonishing! A lesser man would have buckled under all that pressure and responsibility. He would play the piano in the team hotel, have a sing-song with the players and he relaxed everybody. "Let me do the worrying," he would tell us. "Any problems you have, no matter how big or small let me know and I'll do what I can to help." A genuine, loveable, down-to-earth man.

Our 2-1 play-off victory over Hungary was our finest hour. In the dressing room after the game Jimmy was unusually quiet, going around shaking hands with all the players and thanking them. It should have been us thanking him. However, later that night in the hotel he relaxed, enjoyed a few drinks, and was the life and soul of the party when he suddenly got up on stage and started singing *Land of Hope and Glory* with everyone joining in. A great man!

I desperately wanted to play in the quarter-final against Brazil but I had received troublesome injuries in the two games against

Hungary and couldn't play. Jimmy kept encouraging me leading up to the game but in reality he knew I had no chance of playing. In fact, so bad was the injury that I was sidelined for two months and missed the start of the 1958-59 Italian League season, nevertheless the record shows how close our team came to winning that game.

It was after this game that Jimmy was offered a coaching job with Brazil. I was also asked to sound him out by officials of Juventus regarding him becoming their manager. He was offered £20,000, a fortune in those days. He wasn't interested. He thanked them and explained to me his reasons for turning the offer down. "I've got to help Matt pick up the pieces and start all over again, we have to rebuild after losing ten players at Munich. Besides John, how can you put a price on loyalty?"

In later years I still kept in touch with Jimmy. If he liked you, you were friends for life. After coming out of the services after the war he devoted his entire life to Manchester United's cause. The large number of players he produced for United are legendary, he loved Manchester United. Jimmy was a reticent man, and introspective. He was a truly warm, honest, sincere person with a wonderful sense of humour, I shall never forget his valued help and encouragement. I am delighted that this book is paying tribute to a great human being and my friend. Characters like Jimmy come around very rarely.

John Charles OBE
Freeman of Swansea

Foreword

My father, uncle and brother were rabid Manchester United supporters so it was only natural I suppose that I also followed United's progress. In Collyhurst where I was born and brought up you were either a Red or a Blue, there was no in-between. Mind you, it was Manchester City who were the most talked about club then. The area was sports mad, football and boxing being the district's main interest. As a kid my dad and uncle would take me to watch Manchester United's 1948 FA Cup team. What great players they were: Carey, Chilton, Mitten, Cockburn, Rowley and Pearson, to name but a few. I idolised them. In my spare time, and we had plenty of that, I spent hours playing football on those cobbled street corners or on the crofts and tips that were littered all around the Collyhurst area due to the bombing from the German air raids. And they were full of half bricks, tin cans, and broken glass. Yes, there were no grass fields in Collyhurst, yet those derelict sites to us kids were like Wembley Stadium. Like hundreds more I learned how to control the ball, tackle and look after myself. I would join in with dozens of other kids of all ages and sizes and play till our hearts content, pretending we were either

United or City.

When I was old enough I played for my school St Pat's. and represented Manchester, Lancashire and England Schoolboys. Several clubs made approaches for me to join them, but there was only one club for me and that was Manchester United. Joe Armstrong, the United scout, used to watch me on the red, bone hard Monsall Rec, (there was no grass but red shale and if you fell on that you had to be taken to Monsall Hospital for a tetanus injection) would often call in at our house on Rochdale Road. Joe wanted me to join the Reds, he didn't know it but I would have crawled on all fours to be part of this great club.

In September 1957 I signed amateur forms and joined the groundstaff. Old Trafford was vibrant, exciting and breath taking, it was the Busby Babes era. But apart from those great, great players there were brilliant youngsters being groomed for the first team and I wanted to be a part of this set-up. After meeting the boss, Sir Matt Busby, I was put under the supervision of Jimmy Murphy and Bert Whalley, two fabulous men. When I first joined United, my wages were £3 5/ (shillings) a week. I was a small, scrawny lad, I stood just over 5 feet tall and weighed in at about 6 stone wet through, and many of the other young players looked at me in disbelief. I played at inside-forward until I switched to wing-half. "Don't worry about Nobby," Jimmy would tell them. "He's a Collyhurst lad. They breed great boxers and footballers there. He can take care of himself."

Mass public adulation is not usually reserved for modest, unassuming family men and Jimmy Murphy was in this category. However, he was the main reason why from the 1940s through to the 1960s Manchester United produced so many world-class players who later became legends. He was a tireless worker, out on the training field morning, noon and night. Next to his family, his only other interest and love was United. I have him to thank for making me into the player I became. I'm not the only one either, Sir Bobby Charlton, Wilf McGuinness and George Best would tell you the same thing.

One of my first impressions of Jimmy was funnily enough on my first day at Old Trafford. He stood next to me near the pitch at a deserted Old Trafford. "This, son," he said, with his arm around my shoulder and full of enthusiasm and bulldog tenacity, "is the greatest club in the whole world and when you pull on that famous red jersey and run out of this tunnel onto that pitch you'll feel a special sensation in your whole body, there is no other thrill like it. You'll be happy here and we want you to enjoy it with all your heart and soul. Nobby, son, you'll never regret joining us - there is no other club in the world like us."

On another occasion after a hard training session he told a group of us new comers: "This is the place to be, lads, you'll all get a chance here. Show me you can play and before you know it you will be playing in the first team." We kids used to like hearing Jimmy saying things like that, it encouraged us. There was a great camaraderie throughout the club. Jimmy taught us the fundamentals and to play for each other. He would soon sort out the players who acted like prima donnas. "You win together and lose together," he told us. From the day I joined the club, Jimmy instilled in me that special club spirit. He never told you things you couldn't do but emphasised the things you were good at. He made a great impact on me and gained legendary status throughout the club. With a twinkle in those Welsh eyes of his he would have a laugh and a joke with the lads. He was a larger than life character and sometimes he rubbed some players up the wrong way with his brash talk. However, having said, that there was never any malice with him, he did it for our own good. There is no doubting it - Old

Trafford was a more exciting and vibrant place when he was around.

Like Jimmy, we all loved and respected Sir Matt but it was Jimmy who made it possible for me to achieve all the things I have in football. Jimmy gave me an insight into what could be achieved in football by 'thinking' about the game. He had the wisdom and ability to make players believe in themselves, he taught good habits. It was Jimmy who worked on our defensive system and taught me how to time my tackles. He would often play in practice games and knock us flying, ankle tap, obstruct, trip us up, pull our shirts and foul. This was all done for a reason, and that was to let us know that these sort of things would happen to us during games. "Play it simple, son," he would yell. He might have taken a liking to me because I was small like he was and played in a similar fashion but that didn't stop him from giving me a rollicking. All the players at Old Trafford will testify that they owe Jimmy Murphy a great debt and a great deal of gratitude for making them into the players they became. He never got tired of talking football and discussing different players and teams.

There was a little incident that sticks in my mind. After we won the European Cup in 1968 the club went on a tour. We played in Scotland, then went over to Germany. Myself, Bobby [Charlton] and Shay [Brennan] went for a walk and stopped at a little bar. There were three days to go before we were playing a game against Munich. We were sitting outside having a quiet drink when we spotted Jimmy walking toward us with Denzil Haroun, a United director. We slumped down in our seats trying not to be noticed and Jimmy walked straight past us. A couple of minutes later he came rushing back - he had noticed us, but continued walking with the director. He left him to go shopping and hurried back and sat down with us, ordered the drinks and started talking football. That was Jimmy, football mad!

The 1960s Manchester United had great players, Bobby, George, Denis, but we had a sound defence as well. Shay Brennan, Tony Dunne, Paddy Crerand, Big Bill Foulkes and myself. We worked as a unit.

Sir Matt preached attacking football - he loved flair players and always wanted us to entertain the spectators. "Go out and enjoy it," he would tell us and didn't we just and at the end of it all we were part and parcel of that fabulous night in 1968 when we won the European Cup. It was a great decade. Like I said, Sir Matt loved to see us attacking while Jimmy would emphasise the importance for us defenders to have a good understanding between ourselves, pointing out in his own inimitable manner that from a strong foundation we could attack.

I feel very blessed that I was a player at the greatest club in the world, Manchester United! I was also extremely fortunate and privileged to have been guided during my career by Sir Matt Busby, Bert Whalley and Jimmy Murphy and all the other warm-hearted, loyal people at Manchester United.

Jimmy Murphy was the heartbeat of the club - he is an unsung hero and I hope this book enlightens the new breed of United supporters as to exactly who Jimmy Murphy was and his great contribution to the club. Pull up a chair and read about the exploits of one of the greatest teachers and characters it has been my good fortune to have been associated with.

God bless Jimmy!

Nobby Stiles MBE

Acknowledgements

Collyhurst and Moston Lads Club would like to thank Richard Shepherd for the photographs of Jimmy Murphy and for his help; Mario Risoli, author of 'When Pele Broke Our Hearts'; Sean Kelly, a Manchester United Memorabilia collector; Nobby Stiles MBE for writing the foreword for this book; and John Charles OBE who, in March 2002, was honoured with the Freedom of his hown town, Swansea. We would also like to thank John Donagh for his unfailing help and advice, the *Manchester Evening News* and their wonderful readers for their help and assistance and last but by no means least to Ashley Shaw and Stuart Fish of Empire Publications who were supportive and helped in every way possible. Anyone I have forgotten please forgive me - it was not intentional I can assure you.

Jimmy Who?

It was a bitterly cold, bleak and dismal November morning in the early 1950s. A party of overseas soccer enthusiasts were on a visit to Manchester United's old training ground, the Cliff, which was situated in the Lower Broughton area of Salford. The visitors watched intently as Dennis Viollet, Duncan Edwards, Mark Jones, David Pegg and other young United stars of the period went through a training session. Even in their formative years, these players were exceptional and being fashioned into stars of the future - a collection of youngsters who would go on to become the 'Busby Babes', effectively football's first superstars.

Although the party were thrilled to be watching the United fledglings in action, it was the muddy little fellow wearing the baggy tracksuit caked in mud who caught their eye. He organised the training session like a musical conductor. Full of vigour and enthusiasm, he shouted out instructions to the young professionals on the pitch. One of the visitors turned to the guide and asked in awe: "Who is that man? He is brilliant!" The guide thought the guest meant one of the players and asked: "Which one do you mean?" When the visitor pointed to the man organising the training session, the club official smiled broadly and replied: "Oh, that's Jimmy!"

The speaker was right, of course, because the coach he was referring to was known by football insiders as 'The Starmaker'. This was the man who helped Matt Busby assemble and mould the greatest array of soccer talent ever seen at one club. With a mixture of Welsh and Irish blood flowing through his veins Murphy was indeed a soccer genius. His name, given to him by his father, William, who came from Kilkenny, was James Patrick Murphy, a name as Irish as the Mountains of Mourne, but he was born in Ton Pentre, in the Rhondda Valley, South Wales in 1910, of a Welsh mother named Florence. This man's contribution to the long-term success of Manchester United cannot be emphasised strongly enough.

As a footballer his career with West Bromwich Albion appeared to be going nowhere until a slice of luck won him a starting place as a wing-half with both the Baggies and later Wales. However despite a lengthy career Jimmy never scored a goal in competitive football - not one.

To say that Jimmy Murphy was instrumental in laying the foundations of the club's popularity is an understatement. While Matt Busby was the suave, silver-tongued architect who planned the building of a dynasty, Murphy did the spadework, sowing the seeds of United's unprecedented youth policy.

These two masterminded a football empire. While Busby was quite comfortable speaking to the press, Murphy hated the spotlight and preferred to be out on the pitch, coaching United's stars of today and tomorrow. Jimmy was highly respected by everyone at Old Trafford but swapping quotes with the press pack was an anathema to him - Murphy was a brilliant man in many senses, but it was as a teacher that his greatness shone through. Jimmy was a loyal, articulate, intelligent and honest man and more perhaps than his boss Busby, Murphy came to personify Manchester United's trademark style of play - honest, open, attack- minded and daring.

Murphy the Welshman

"My entire life was changed by that mere chance of another player being injured...but for that I might have been a failure in football and never continued in the game after my playing career"
JIMMY MURPHY

Jimmy's mother was widowed with six children when she married Billy Murphy for the second time. Jimmy would be their only child. That very Irish name in the Rhondda was like putting a red rag to a bull. It caused young Jimmy no end of trouble with his school friends and other youngsters but with a mixture of Welsh and Irish blood coursing through his veins he was more than capable of taking care of himself during schoolboy skirmishes. His parents brought him up to be honest and forthright, with loyalty high on the agenda. They also sent him for piano and the organ lessons - Jimmy learned quickly and as a teenager he played the organ in Treorchy Parish Church.

But as much as he loved music, the young Murphy loved football more. He attended Ton Pentre Village School, learning the game on the concrete schoolyard with the help and encouragement of teachers Arthur Hanney and George Tewkesbury. They certainly toughened him up and in 1924, with their help and guidance, Jimmy became a Welsh schoolboy international, making his debut against England Schoolboys in the pouring rain at Ninian Park, Cardiff - Wales winning 2-1. He was an aggressive little whipper-snapper - a schoolboy Nobby Stiles - and soon learned to give and take the hardest of tackles without complaint. As a schoolboy and teenager he played as an inside-forward. In time he became a ferocious tackler and as hard as nails. His ambition as a schoolboy was to play for Cardiff City. His mother always told Jimmy that to succeed in life he had to become a good listener, and not to speak unless he had something sensible to say. And he kept to his dear mother's principles to the letter.

Many years later, when talking about his schooldays, Jimmy remembered: "I came from a little Welsh village in the Rhondda Valley. I played for Wales as a schoolboy and they were unforgettable times for me, I was passionate and extremely proud to have been selected. Wales at schoolboy level at that time were really a nonentity, but in the year I played we beat England 3-2 in Cardiff and then drew 2-2 with Scotland at Hampden Park. Those results fired my imagination and brought me to the attention of English League clubs."

After his second schoolboy international against Scotland, West Bromwich Albion asked his parents if they could sign him. At 14, Jimmy left Wales for the West Midlands club. This was a terrible wrench for young Murphy who had hardly travelled further than the confines of his own valley. So going miles away from home was an ordeal for him. He soon became homesick, but he stuck it out and through his enthusiasm, hard but scrupulously fair tackling and an unquenchable spirit, forced his way into West Bromwich's first team. Jimmy was still playing as an inside-forward at this time. He had talent but it was never developed, and while playing in the reserves he was frequently barracked by a section of the Baggies support.

"I was determined to make the grade as a professional footballer," said Jimmy years later. "After two years, I appeared to be getting nowhere when a stroke of luck fell upon me. All players need that little bit of luck at the start of their careers. I had run out of goals as an inside-forward and one day in a reserve game we had a player injured and I dropped back to the wing-half position and happened to play exceptionally well." He played so well that he kept this position when, two weeks later, he was selected for his first team debut against Tottenham at White Hart Lane. Spurs were top of the league table and West Brom drew 2-2 with them. "Can you imagine how I felt," asked Jimmy. "I was a boy of 19 playing in front of over 60,000 people when I had only been used to appearing in front of a few hundred spectators in reserve matches."

Jimmy enjoyed himself at West Bromwich Albion and he appeared in the 1935 FA Cup Final which the Baggies unfortunately lost 4-2 to Sheffield Wednesday. Nevertheless, an example of the Murphy spirit came when a deflated West Brom trailed 4-1. With just a few minutes of the game left, the Midlands side scored to make it 4-2. The crowd thought the game was over. Murphy, however, never gave up hope and chased the ball into the net, picked it up and sprinted back to the centre circle before screaming at the referee to restart the game. This was Jimmy to a T - he just never knew when he was beaten.

Murphy learned valuable lessons from his own career which would stand him in good stead when later he became Manchester United's architect in developing younger players. Despite his early difficulties, Murphy eventually became West Brom's regular right-half. Interestingly, Matt Busby had a similar experience with Manchester City. A failure as an inside-forward, he too became a wing-half but only by accident.

"There are two morals to this experience," said Jimmy. "The first is that no matter how bad things seem, a young player should stick to his guns and never give up. The second is that my entire life was changed by that mere chance of another player being injured. But for that I might have been a failure in football and never continued in the game after my playing career finished."

In 1933, he became the youngest player in the Welsh team at just 21. It heralded the start of a glittering international career. During his six years as an international, he went on to captain Wales and win 22 caps.

It was a great Welsh team - Wales' golden era. They won the Home Championship three times including the Triple Crown in 1933/34 when they beat England, Scotland and Ireland and were joint winners on another occasion. He became one of his country's finest pre-war players. "And I would have won at least another eight or nine caps if West Brom had always released me to play for my country," added Jimmy.

During his playing career, he often played against Matt Busby, when the Scotsman played for Manchester City and Liverpool. Although Busby and Murphy had completely different styles of play, they admired each other's ability and later became close friends. Jimmy was forever telling friends and colleagues what a wonderfully talented player Busby was. "The way Matt could shield the ball was brilliant," said Jimmy. However, it disgusted him that Busby had received only one peacetime international cap. He had a good idea why his friend received such scant recognition from the Scottish selectors: bigotry! Busby, like Murphy, was a Roman Catholic. However both men, along with hundreds of other players throughout the leagues, had their football careers cut short by the war.

To Jimmy Murphy, football was the greatest game in the world. However, he realised that only in the post-war years could it become a profession in the best sense of the word; a career offering opportunities and experience unrivalled elsewhere.

Compare today's coaching practices with the period when Jimmy Murphy started his career in football. In the late 1920s, few clubs signed on boys straight from school. They relied instead on getting hold of players when they were 17, 18 or 19. Few clubs had coaches. Young players like Murphy had to fend for themselves and pick up what advice they could from older players. In any case, the young player would never receive any attention from anyone until he was considered first-team material. The trainer would be the sole source of advice or help for a young player - the manager would hardly be seen. Jimmy remembered that at West Bromwich Albion, as with almost every other club, there was hardly any practice with the caseball or any other ball for that matter. And certainly no coaching as we understand it today. For this reason among others, Murphy was determined that the lot of apprentice footballers must be improved, that schoolboy talent was all too often wasted.

*

Not for nothing was Jimmy referred to as 'the genius behind the Busby Babes' in later years. In his role at United, Murphy discovered a wealth of exciting footballing talent, the like of which had never been seen before and rarely seen since. The players he nurtured would go on to dominate the British game and become priceless on the transfer market. The list of world-famous players he helped through his coaching is endless. Duncan Edwards, who, 44 years after his death in the Munich disaster, is still regarded as the greatest English footballer ever produced; Dennis Viollet, Mark Jones, David Pegg, Roger Byrne, Albert Scanlon, Billy Whelan, Eddie Colman, Bobby Charlton, George Best, Wilf McGuinness, Alex Dawson, Nobby Stiles, Brian Kidd and Johnny Giles, were among the diamonds he helped polish. Tommy Taylor, Denis Law, Albert Quixall, Paddy Crerand and others, though costing the club transfer fees, still had Murphy to thank for polishing their skills and making them into world-class players.

Even in his seventies, Murphy was spotting talent for United: Peter Beardsley, Gary Lineker, Steve Coppell, Stuart Pearson and Gordon Hill were all recommended to the club by the man who became known as 'The Starmaker'.

The great thing about Jimmy Murphy was his wisdom and his ability to listen and learn, especially from his own mistakes. He was never one of those coaches who constantly told the kids under his care how great it was in his day, or how he used to do certain things. He was quite the opposite in fact. Murphy would tell them, whenever he thought it served a purpose, just exactly how hard it was, compared to the state of the game when he played.

When Murphy became assistant manager at Manchester United, the club had good, honest and reliable people helping out with their young players and no effort was spared to teach the willing pupil everything that could be learned. Manchester United had initiated a youth policy before the outbreak of the Second World War under caretaker manager Walter Crickmer. Under the acronym MUJAC (Manchester United Junior Athletic Club) and with the guidance of Louis Rocca, the club had intended to build on the success of their Colts and 'A' teams. Unfortunately, the Second World War ended MUJAC's short-term success, but youth was put high on the agenda by United's enterprising board and became a key element in Busby's appointment.

Under MUJAC a young player's career was closely monitored from the start so that the best possible use could be made of his talents. However, from the moment Busby and Murphy assumed control at Old Trafford, a more professional attitude towards youth football was taken.

The same could also be said for the first team. The majority of United's first team regulars had seen their careers abruptly interrupted by the war. However, Jimmy and Matt created a spirit closer to a family than mere business. The older players were really great people as well as being great players. They also liked a laugh and a joke, which created a good environment. United had been managerless since the resignation of Scott Duncan in 1937, so with the arrival of the dynamic duo, a much happier atmosphere surrounded the club.

Both men knew how they had suffered during their own playing days and were determined it would never happen to youngsters under their care. At Old Trafford they prided themselves on their family spirit and the way in which everyone was made to feel they were an important part of a big organisation. As Jimmy once told a group of United youngsters: "When players of my generation wanted to see the manager about some matter, they had to first make an appointment with the secretary, then they would be told to meet the manager in his office at a precise time. That doesn't happen here, our door is always open."

Murphy always wore a tracksuit during training. Whether coaching at Old Trafford or at the Cliff, Jimmy shunned the flashy designer styles of today's tracksuited managers - Jimmy's was the old-fashioned baggy type. As often as possible, Matt Busby would put on his tracksuit and get working with the players. Along with their more open style, Busby and Murphy brought more democracy to the club - but at the same time they were held in higher respect because of it. Of course they knew that not every lad could reach the top but they would make sure that he received every opportunity to develop and offer him every encouragement, aware that in their day virtually nothing was done to help or advise kids.

Matt and Jimmy often said that even the kids who didn't make it with United would leave with a better understanding of life because of their experience with the club. The expectations of a young player had been raised, because they encouraged and tried to develop character. They preached that from football, players could get self-assurance and a breadth of mind which would serve him throughout his life and equip him to take a better job after he had finished playing - it was all there for the taking. The only stipulation they made was that the youngsters had to be willing to listen, work hard and always be willing to learn.

A Coaching Revolutionary

"He had us all transfixed. He was wonderful. It was as if he had put everybody in a hypnotic trance. It wasn't a speech, it was more like a rousing sermon. I visualised what good he could do for Manchester United"

MATT BUSBY

From 1946 until the late 1960s, Jimmy Murphy was regarded as one of the greatest soccer coaches in the world, and the best motivator in football. However, Jimmy admitted that at one time he saw no future beyond his playing days with West Bromwich Albion. Earlier in his life, his mother wanted him to become a schoolteacher. Football was a dead-end job in the 1930s with little or no future beyond a brief playing career. However, Jimmy Murphy's thinking changed dramatically while in Paris with Wales for an international against France in the 1930s.

I will digress for a moment. The name Jimmy Hogan is not familiar to many football followers today, but to Jimmy Murphy, this man was regarded as the most famous, and perhaps the most important of all football coaches. To Murphy, Hogan was a soccer revolutionary. "If any one man taught the continentals, and especially the Austrians and those magical, brilliant Hungarians, how to play football that person was

Jimmy Hogan," said an enthusiastic Jimmy Murphy when discussing how he began thinking about a career as a football coach. The admiration Murphy felt for Jimmy Hogan came shining through as he spoke about his old friend.

Murphy met Hogan briefly in the 1930s. Hogan was a Lancastrian, from Nelson to be precise. No more than an average player, he ended his career with Fulham. At Craven Cottage, Hogan met several Scottish players who were exponents of the classical Scottish style of controlled short passing, and they aroused his interest in the technical side of football.

However, it took a meeting with Hugo Meisl, the great figure of Austrian football, before Hogan could embark on his biggest triumphs. The Lancastrian also spent time in Hungary and when war broke out in 1914, he was thrown in prison as an enemy alien. When he was later released, he spent the war years in charge of Budapest club MTK, laying the foundations for the later success of the Hungarians. After the war, Hogan was in joint charge with Meisl of the great Austrian international team of the 1930s before returning to England in 1937-38 to manage Aston Villa. These were the days when continental ideas of any kind were regarded with cynicism and a great deal of suspicion in England.

Hogan believed in the European-style attacking centre-half. His mistake was in trying to introduce this and other continental ideas too quickly in England. Jimmy Murphy remembered playing against Villa while Hogan was in charge. "He played with his attacking centre-half and square defence," recalled Murphy. "We beat them 7-1. I felt deeply sorry for Jimmy because I knew that basically his ideas were ahead of their time in England. Villa won promotion and reached the FA Cup semi-final, but his contract was not renewed. I was great friends with him by now and had found him digs in Birmingham. I knew how disappointed he was." After the Aston Villa debacle, Hogan became a sort of wandering coach, giving demonstrations in schools or on film. He was eventually given a job coaching youngsters, at Aston Villa of all places.

Now back to Paris in the 1930s for the France v Wales international and the first time Jimmy Murphy met Jimmy Hogan. The day before the game, Murphy took a walk down to the Colombes Stadium to watch Hogan conduct a coaching session. "I was a fully-fledged professional player and an international, yet this was the first time in my life that I had ever seen a coach at work. What interested me more was that all his teaching was based on use of the ball, an object we never saw from one Saturday to the next," remarked Jimmy. This in itself is sufficient condemnation of the insularity of English football in this period.

Murphy was eager to learn more from Hogan and they struck up a close friendship. Hogan told Jimmy that within a few years the continentals would overtake us. Murphy didn't believe him. Events, however, proved that Jimmy Hogan was right. The moral of Jimmy Hogan's career and far-seeing ideas, and of the football he inspired on the continent, was that the basic thing was mastery of the ball. "I saw him," added Jimmy, "white-haired and fitter than most men half his age, performing miracles of ball control. He once drove a ball through wood panelling with his bare foot. He could hit a mark at 30 yards distance, ten times out of ten. Whatever basic skill of ball control he was teaching, he could perform it to perfection."

Jimmy concluded his praise for Jimmy Hogan by saying that he was a good judge of a player and an excellent manager of continental teams playing the kind of football he had taught them - the kind that was being copied around the world from the 1950s onwards. Murphy also said that he had learned a great deal from watching and listening to Hogan. "After our first meeting I always tried to break away from the British custom and sneak out with a ball. Experience as a player, coach and team manager has shown me his ideas were right. Mastery of the ball and of the simple way of doing things were the basis of football. I used a lot of Jimmy Hogan's ideas when I joined Matt Busby at Manchester United. He was a very influential coach."

The Passion and Pride

Bill Shankly was, without a doubt, among the greatest football managers of the post-war era. He remains a Liverpool legend. Shankly had a very high profile and was very quotable. Pressmen bent over backwards to get him to appear on their programmes and hung on to his every word. It is folklore throughout football about how volatile and passionate Bill Shankly was about the game - most famously describing it as more important than life itself. But believe me, as great and as committed as he was to Liverpool's cause, Bill Shankly was a Boy Scout compared with Jimmy Murphy.

Murphy's love affair with United started in the summer of 1945 while in Bari, Italy. Murphy was an NCO in charge of a Services sports centre. He had seen plenty of action in the war and had been involved in heavy fighting in the Far East. He had also spent over four years with the Army in the desert. "I was a Desert Rat," Jimmy would recall. "I served in the Royal Artillery and I went through the North African campaign before becoming involved with football again. It was the war that really ended my active playing career."

As the war in Europe was ending, Sergeant Murphy had taken over from Stan Cullis. He organised cricket matches, swimming galas, donkey rides, cycle races and polo but the most popular events by far were Jimmy's soccer coaching clinics.

One boiling hot afternoon Murphy was giving a talk in his usual enthusiastic Welsh way to a crowd of servicemen. On the fringe, listening intently, and liking what he heard, was Matt Busby, an old footballing friend and rival. Jimmy's talk had Busby and the large gathering absolutely fascinated. They seemed spellbound by the Welshman who was speaking with gusto using extravagant hand gestures. Busby himself was absolutely captivated and totally absorbed as Murphy was giving his talk. Jimmy spoke with a fervour and a passion that had the troops hanging on to his every word. All of a sudden, he would pitch his voice with a passion, a little like one of those old-fashioned church ministers. His oratory would be full of fire and brimstone, mixed with a little comedy and, of course, those endless gestures. Nobody present on that day could have failed to be enthralled by him. It was a brilliant and fascinating speech and he received a tremendous ovation once he'd finished.

Immediately, Matt Busby walked over to congratulate Jimmy on his talk. Both men's playing careers were virtually over. A smiling Busby told the Welshman that he was taking the manager's job at Manchester United once he got back home. "There's a job waiting for you as my assistant. Get in touch when you are demobbed," said Busby. "We shook hands on the deal. He was the first and the best signing I ever made for Manchester United," Busby said later.

Years later, Busby was speaking to his close friend Paddy McGrath, a former professional boxer and member of the world- famous Brown, King, McAvoy boxing stable from Collyhurst, North Manchester. Paddy was also the owner of the Cromford Club, in the centre of Manchester. This was a private and prestigious establishment where Matt Busby and his players would often gather for social events. Telling McGrath about how he came to offer Jimmy Murphy the job with Manchester United, Busby said that after listening to Jimmy Murphy address his audience in Italy at the end of the war, he knew in his heart that he had to have Murphy alongside him. "He had us all transfixed. He was wonderful. It was as if he had put everybody in a hypnotic trance. It wasn't a speech, it was more like a rousing sermon. I visualised what good he could do for Manchester United," said Busby. A few years later, Peter Doherty, the great Irish player and manager, echoed Matt's sentiments when they were discussing Murphy. "When Jimmy starts talking about football and Manchester United, he not only paints the lily - he fills in all the details like Michelangelo or Raphael."

These two former international players proved that two heads were better than one. Their deeds are etched in the history of Manchester United. Busby often said that his assistant was a player you would like on your side. "He never knew when he was beaten; he played the game as though his life depended on the result. He was a wonderful man for a crisis. He was my best friend, companion and right-hand man. No manager could wish for a finer coach and motivator, especially for youngsters just starting out in professional football," remarked Sir Matt.

On the surface, Matt and Jimmy were as different as night and day. They hardly ever socialised together away from football. Though both men were steeped in football tradition, Busby was an establishment person with the mind of a classical scholar. He was at the top, presiding over everything connected with Manchester United. Quietly spoken, sound in judgement and experienced and with an incredible flair for public relations, Busby was the debonair front man, a pressman's dream. Murphy, on the other hand, while educated, was more outgoing and inspiring when dealing with the young players at the club. Jimmy shunned the limelight and preferred his own company. But both men cared about soccer excellence, not just about winning, but winning with flair and excitement.

The pair came from similar backgrounds, and had similar modest tastes and the same ambitions for United. Busby and Murphy were the best double act in football. Before a game, Matt would speak to the players in a quiet, dignified tone and tell them to go out and enjoy the match. Jimmy would sit listening, not saying a word. Once Matt had excused himself and left the changing room, Murphy would rise to his feet and speak - his talk would be like a rousing, rallying call to the troops in the trenches. Secretly, the players loved it. He would use industrial language and become animated and extremely passionate, always ending his talk by telling them: "Remember, you're wearing this Red Jersey. And don't forget, bloody well get stuck in." Of course, Matt knew Jimmy's talk would be completely different from his own but that was their chemistry working as one.

During the early years, Murphy's contribution had yet to be appreciated outside Old Trafford. Busby was the tactician, Murphy the motivator. Matt was the quiet officious type, Jimmy the emotional extrovert but in United's cause they acted as one. These comrades marched shoulder to shoulder for over 25 years, through triumph and tragedy, thick and thin with one common ideal: to make Manchester United the best club in the world. And how well they succeeded!

The Untold Story

Sadly, Jimmy Murphy's work for Manchester United seems to have been largely forgotten by the club and its officials. On a Saturday afternoon radio talk-in programme in late 1995, Jimmy Murphy's name cropped up in a discussion about Manchester United's new stand. "We have the Sir Matt Busby Way and plans are underway for a permanent commemorative statue of Sir Matt to be situated in Old Trafford," said one caller. "Why not something to recognise Jimmy Murphy?" Many older supporters of the club were urging the club to name the new stand 'The Jimmy Murphy Stand'. No snub or disrespect to Sir Matt Busby was intended.

Guests Wilf McGuinness and Pat Crerand agreed with the caller's comments but added: "Though we fully agree with your sentiments, many people have forgotten who Jimmy is." To be fair to Manchester United, there is the Jimmy Murphy 'Young Player of the Year' trophy, which is awarded at the end of the season to the most deserving reserve player. Also, in the past two or three years, a bust of Jimmy has appeared in the United Museum. However, there is no large public monument or recognition of one of the most influential figures in United's history at the ground.

Let me digress again, and start from the beginning of Jimmy Murphy's career with Manchester United. It wasn't all roses, far from it. In the spring of 1946, when a smiling, whistling Jimmy Murphy arrived at Old Trafford, he looked at the stadium and gasped at the sight of it. He couldn't believe his eyes. The ground, once the pride of pre-war Manchester as the north's answer to Wembley, had been hit by German bombs and almost demolished. There were no facilities to speak of, there was grass on the terraces and far from looking like a football stadium, Old Trafford looked more like a disaster area.

The scars inflicted by that terrible war could be seen all over the British Isles - nowhere more so than in Manchester. Life was grey and dour, extremely hard and difficult for everyone. Practically on United's doorstep stood the giant industrial centre of Trafford Park, where thousands commuted daily to work in the hundreds of factories, foundries, engineering works and other firms. From the grass-filled terraces you couldn't miss the hundreds of huge chimneys belching thick smoke into the surrounding atmosphere from the furnaces and coal fires of Trafford Park.

The 'smog' this created made clothes and homes filthy, often causing the deaths of old people and leading to countless sufferers of lung disease. Working-class folk were still living in slums and squalor, homes had no hot water, electricity or outside toilets. People were becoming resentful. The war was over, yet National Service and rationing for food and clothing were still in force, while authority was in its zenith and was to be obeyed at all costs. Times were indeed grim and deprivation appeared to be the norm in industrial Manchester.

But none of these apparent setbacks deterred an enthusiastic 35-year-old Jimmy Murphy. "We had no money and the players used an old Nissen hut for changing. The way ahead was very hard," Murphy recalled. Resurrecting this burnt-out club was going to be an uphill fight for all concerned. This was where Matt Busby and Manchester United were extremely fortunate, because no man was better equipped for a fight than Jimmy Murphy.

'Spud', as he was known throughout football circles, had always been a grafter, a fighter. A tough, tenacious wing-half for Swansea, West Bromwich Albion and Wales, Jimmy was a character of unflagging drive and enthusiasm, a man of tremendous personal loyalties. If you were a friend of his, no man dare cast even a shady glance in your direction. Over the coming years, nowhere in the football world would you find a more honest atmosphere than at Old Trafford and this was down to Murphy and Busby. Jimmy had received many offers for his services, but he had shaken hands and given his word to Matt Busby, and as time would record, he never wavered in his devotion to Busby or the club.

Stocky, with brushed-back hair; the fast-speaking, chain-smoking soccer disciple Jimmy Murphy wore a perpetual frown. This look gave people the wrong impression of him because beneath the serious looking face he had a terrific sense of humour. He played the piano, loved a good old-fashioned sing-song, a pint of beer and a good conversation. He was down to earth. He and Matt Busby were the first track-suited managers in British football. Murphy was never one to seek the limelight or personal glory, but he lived and breathed football.

The main problem in rebuilding Manchester United after the war was the stadium. The damage to Old Trafford meant United had to use Maine Road for their first team games - Manchester City's directors had kindly agreed to help them out until Old Trafford could be renovated and made safe, which wouldn't be until August 1949.

"We had no proper training facilities when I joined United in 1946," said Jimmy. "The players used an old piece of spare land at the back of the stand for practice matches. They wouldn't be allowed to play on that kind of surface today. It was a rock-hard, stony surface. Believe me, you had to be both tough and extremely clever to play on that ground. But for all that, those crude, basic facilities built up the camaraderie and team spirit that served the club well over the proceeding years."

During those austere, post-war years United were a wonder to behold. They swiftly established themselves as the most exciting team in the country, playing football as if to entertain. United had some brilliant individuals and these great players were Busby and Murphy's greatest assets, because they gave them time to build for the future. With players such as Carey, Aston, Cockburn, Rowley, Pearson, Morris, Mitten, Chilton and Delaney, United finished runners-up to Liverpool in the First Division in 1946-47. Many pundits in those days maintained that this United side were by far the best team in England and should have won the title but said that they were so busy playing attacking football and entertaining vast crowds that they left gaps in defence which allowed other teams to steal a goal and grab the two points.

Nobody, though, could ever forget this team. Though they failed to win the League Championship, Johnny Carey's side touched perfection when they won the 1948 FA Cup Final against Blackpool in what is still described as the best-ever final. In that 1947-48 season, United nearly won the double, finishing runners-up to Arsenal by one point before they won the Cup.

"Thousands were watching us all over the country because we were so exciting," added Jimmy. But although this brilliant team missed the fabulous League and FA Cup double by a single point, they won the Cup in amazing fashion, 4-2 against Blackpool.

The team at Wembley that day read: Crompton; Carey, Aston; Anderson, Chilton, Cockburn; Delaney, Morris, Rowley, Pearson, Mitten. What a host of memories those names conjure up! They were characters of the highest order and made United into a club recognisable throughout the British Isles.

Many critics said that Matt Busby was very fortunate in that he inherited these superb players. This of course was utter nonsense! The war had taken its toll on every player and, as Jimmy stated in later years, no matter how great players are, they need moulding into a team and this is what United's management team did with tremendous results.

Once things at the club got established, Jimmy took charge of the reserves and the young players the club had recently signed, although he also helped Busby with the first team squad. In this period, training was conducted at various places like the YMCA ground and the Cliff. Once Old Trafford had been suitably repaired and renovated and the pitch re-seeded and cleaned up, the players would train there. Jimmy and Matt would play in practice games with the team but on opposing sides. Jimmy would play alongside the defenders while Matt played with the forwards and wing-halves. Both managers would encourage or cajole a player they wanted to make a point to. With such sensitive, volatile players like Rowley, Morris and a few others it was only to be expected that sometimes tempers would become frayed. During these sessions there were many flare-ups and heated moments as Murphy would whack a player from behind, or trip him up, push him off the ball, obstruct him and various other little niggly things. This was done for a reason.

"They will have to encounter this kind of treatment in competitive matches," said Murphy. He loved it, however, when the player concerned would pick himself up and tear into him. "That's the spirit son!" he would shout at the offending player. There were never any lingering resentment or grudges. He loved footballers like Rowley, Morris, Mitten, Cockburn and the rest, because though they possessed brilliant skills in great quantities, they all had bags of 'bottle'.

Jimmy's only failing at this time, if you can call it a failing, was his over-enthusiasm when talking about the young prospects under his wing. Despite all the mythology and legend which followed post-war United, and having read many books concerning that period of United's history, the reader could be forgiven for thinking that for every first-teamer there were several world-class youngsters waiting to claim their place in the first team. The fact was that United's youth team in the immediate post-war years was a failure in comparison to what came later.

In fact, for all his tireless efforts, Jimmy failed to produce any top-class youngsters in those early days. Murphy, though beavering away on the training field morning, noon and night, was more than a little disappointed when certain young players he firmly believed would make the grade failed to develop or fulfil their early potential. Because of his exuberance and enthusiasm, Jimmy believed he had unearthed some exceptional lads but the players concerned lacked that little 'spark', the certain something that separates the great from the ordinary. In reality, it wasn't until the start of the 1950s that young players of note were ready to make their mark.

Despite his obvious disappointment, Murphy never allowed it to bother him. Busby hated people with gloomy faces and negative outlooks. Jimmy was his ideal companion because the Welshman would arrive at the ground whistling and smiling, a cheery character who made everyone feel better no matter what the circumstances. If any problem regarding the players cropped up, Jimmy would try and sort it out before it could get to Matt Busby. If a player was discovered drinking excessively or gambling heavily, Jimmy would also sort this out. As a result, there were a great deal of things that Matt never heard about because Murphy quietly dealt with the players involved, which is why the club ran so smoothly. An important aspect in a team as worldly wise as Manchester United's in the immediate post-war period.

Breaking the Mould

"They were like mechanics building a car from scratch... I started my career at Inside-Forward but within weeks of them moving me to Centre-Forward I was capped for England"
JACK ROWLEY

A successful football club has to have a long-term plan if it is to prosper. The following points are worth mentioning. To build Manchester United up from the post-war shell Murphy and Busby inherited took the combined talents and abilities not only of these two men but their assistants. For instance, someone has to be able to spot potential in young schoolboys, to be persuasive in convincing them to sign for Manchester United, to instill the basics of professionalism into 15- and 16-year-olds and to enhance and develop those basics and take them on to the Youth and Reserve teams. They are then required to make the grade at First Division and, possibly, international level.

They also need to instigate tactics, strategies and vet opposition teams, recommend new players who will strengthen the team and manage the club in times of pressure. Some clubs are lucky to have someone who can combine several of these very different abilities and talents. Jimmy Murphy was unique and a genius in that he did all these jobs during his years at Old Trafford and was renowned for his work in these areas.

Jack Rowley, or the 'Gunner' as he was known to fans and reporters, had signed for United in October 1937 from Bournemouth for a £3,000 fee aged 17. He turned out to be a bargain buy for the Reds, going on to play 422 games and scoring 208 goals. Rowley was famed for his bluntness and fiery temper. Over the years he proved himself a loyal and honest player for the Red Devils and one of the finest centre-forwards of his time. When one also takes into account that his best years were lost to the war, his record seems all the more remarkable.

In 1948, Rowley made his England debut. He played six times for the national team, scoring four times in one game against Ireland. In six matches he scored six goals, not a bad record at all. However, it was said he only received six caps because of his outspoken views and the establishment's dislike of Jack's combative, vicious streak and confrontational nature. Yet it must also be said that the likes of Tommy Lawton and Stan Mortenson were also fighting for places during this period. Once Jack returned to United, after the hostilities, he was obviously a much more mature man, although still obstructive and outspoken. It is perhaps an indication of Jimmy Murphy's personality that Jack and Jimmy got on very well and often worked together in training.

Years afterwards Rowley said: "It's always a pleasure to meet Jimmy Murphy. I was an experienced player when he and Matt Busby came to United after the war had ended. All the players were a bit sceptical about them. Players always are about a new manager and coach. Jimmy was one of the great characters of football, whenever he spoke he illuminated the proceedings with his conversation. You might not always agree with him but you would most certainly never be bored listening to him. Sometimes he could be controversial, but his heart was in the right place. I joined United as a left-winger and it was only after the war that Matt Busby switched me to centre-forward. I watched

Murphy with the kids and he was good, very good in fact. When they first came and football got back to normal they would both be out on the pitch training with us, but a few years later we saw less of Matt, this was because he was busy with his duties as manager."

Another stalwart of that 1948 team, Henry Cockburn, joined United before the war and won FA Cup and First Division Championship winners' medals with the Reds. When discussing the early days of Busby and Murphy at Old Trafford, he said: "Jimmy Murphy didn't really have much to do with the first team lads. Yes, he helped us, but we were an experienced team and we could play brilliant stuff on the park. Jimmy and Matt played in practice matches with us regularly. Jimmy would help us with individual coaching, but he mainly worked with the kids. One thing you couldn't fail to notice about him though, was that he could really motivate players. I never realised it at the time. I'm talking about the late 1940s and early 1950s. He used to 'gee' us up. A few of the older, established players didn't really appreciate his total enthusiasm for the game. It was funny really. Although Murphy was a devout Roman Catholic, and went to mass every morning before making his way to training, once he got out on the pitch he was forever effing and blinding, he swore like an old trooper. He was a genuine character and everything he did was done for a purpose and a love for Manchester United.

"Myself and several other players were already at Old Trafford before he and Busby arrived. In fact I had signed for the club as a junior player in 1944 but the likes of Carey, Pearson, Rowley, Aston, Chilton and one or two others had all joined the club before the war started. It was an education at times, because Jimmy and Matt liked tinkering with players, putting them in different positions. They were like mechanics building a car from scratch, putting this plug here, that part there etc. Few people know it but I started my career as an inside-forward. They switched me so I was facing the ball and within weeks I was selected for England. So in that respect they were far-sighted."

Just to emphasise what Henry and a lot of the other United players said about the way Matt and Jimmy would switch players to other positions than the ones they were established in, there are managers today, some very successful, who would shudder at the thought of playing a player out of his recognised position, and yet Busby and Murphy were doing this regularly with their players in the 1940s. There are others of course who have tried it with it disastrous consequences both for the clubs (or countries) they were in charge of. But for Busby and Murphy this was no mere guesswork, they used their intuition to reinvent players, knowing instinctively where they could make best use of their talents.

Allenby Chilton had been a full-back and wing-half before being converted into one of the best and most reliable centre-halves of the period. Johnny Aston joined United as an amateur in 1938 and a year later signed professional forms. An inside forward before war was declared, John returned to Old Trafford as a wing-half and later moved to full-back where his pairing with club captain Johnny Carey became one of the best in the country. Indeed, so good was he in the new left-back position that he won 17 England caps. The duo switched him to centre-forward with great success and in the 1950-51 season from 22 games as leader of the attack he netted 15 goals. How about that for conversions!

Another player who was tried in other positions was Ray Wood. Ray joined United in September 1949 as an 18-year-old goalkeeper. He would go on to establish himself as first choice goalkeeper in the 1953-54 season and was later capped by England. Ray remembers his early days at Old Trafford with a great deal of affection: "Yes, Matt and Jimmy put me in the 'A' team at centre-forward," said Ray smiling broadly. "It's perfectly true - I had a few games leading the attack and I scored a few goals. Jimmy knew I was a keeper though, but it was interesting the way they would experiment. What about Jack Rowley? He was an outside-left, yet they moved him to centre-forward where he was capped for England. He was then moved to a couple of other positions. In the 1960s they had problems on the left wing, moved Bobby [Charlton] there and he was that good he was picked several times for England. And don't forget what they did many years later with Bill Foulkes. He was a right full-back, got selected for England in that position but they moved him to centre-half where he stabilised the team and was unfortunate not to be selected for England again. There was a great atmosphere throughout the club in those days. It was enjoyable."

Henry Cockburn said that Matt Busby was the first football club manager who actually put on a tracksuit and went out on the pitch and practised with the players. According to Cockburn, both Matt and Jimmy brought a more caring approach to Manchester United - they went out of their way to get to know each player individually. They had been through the mill themselves as players and knew how managers and directors could treat players. So Busby was determined to do things differently at United.

"Players from other clubs told me that their manager was always in his office sat at his desk. They saw him perhaps once a week. All the day to day work was done by the trainer," Jack Rowley said many years later. "They both genuinely seemed to care about us. They brought into Manchester United a more personal touch. Every player was important to them and made to feel that they were. They had to contend with some difficult characters, many people said I was one. But they tried to understand the players' point of view. Matt would discuss things about our play and he would listen to our points of view about certain aspects. He might not always agree but he listened. You certainly would never get that with other managers, not at all. You did what you were told."

Those were the days when, if a player was a full-back, wing-half, inside-forward or winger, then he usually stayed in that position for the remainder of his career. Of his era, Henry Cockburn said: "Yes, that 1948 team had great players who could play scintillating football. We were the first of the great pre-war teams for Manchester United but, I fear, many people seem to have forgotten the fact."

In their first season in charge of United, Busby and Murphy did exceptionally well. The first team finished runners-up in the First

Division Championship race, while Murphy's second team squad ended the season as Central League champions. This was a truly magnificent feat. Most other clubs would deem that as a huge success. However, Busby and Murphy were striving for absolute perfection. Nevertheless the directors were happy enough and a reception was held to which the players and their wives were invited. Matt was doing the rounds, moving from table to table, having a kind word with the guests and thanking the players for what they had done for the club. From the corner of his eye, he spotted his usually cheerful companion failing to enjoy himself. After a while Matt sat next to Jimmy and asked him what was wrong.

Murphy explained that although it was indeed a tremendous achievement for the first team to have done so well and for his team to have ended as champions, in his humble opinion there wasn't one player in his team capable of being promoted into the first team and strengthening it. Matt gave a deep sigh, looked at his friend and replied: "In that case, Jimmy, we must double our efforts and go out and find our own youngsters and develop them into our system - the Manchester United style." From that moment on Matt and Jimmy decided that they would build a dynasty, around a style of play particular to Manchester United, that would attract the greatest footballing talents in the country.

After finishing runners-up in their first season, United held the same position in the following two seasons. Though they failed to win the League championship, the brilliant, exciting football this team played had fans all over the country drooling and laid the foundations for an all-out attacking style particular to the club. 1952 saw the crowning triumph of this marvellous team when they became First Division champions. The ultimate honour, this was the first time in 41 years that United had won it but the cheers of success on that never-to-be-forgotten April day had turned sour by October the following season. United were languishing at the foot of the First Division table, the once-great side was spluttering along, the fluency gone because the players were growing old together. They ended the season in eighth place, the lowest in Busby and Murphy's time at the club. Despite this, Matt and Jimmy, although disappointed, kept preaching their gospel of simple football: "Give the ball to a red shirt, lads!"

*

From the moment Busby and Murphy formed their partnership, the Manchester United players and especially the younger ones coming to the club, were among the most fortunate in football. They had men looking after them who were first-class teachers because of their vast experience and knowledge of the game. They also had men helping them who were totally honest and sincere, full of decency, compassion and loyal to the core. As Jimmy often said: "A great football club is the product of many people directed by the manager." These stalwarts of the United backroom staff were upholders of the system Busby and Murphy designed.

These men included the legendary Louis Rocca who had been associated with the club for years and the man who invited Matt Busby to become manager of Manchester United. Bert Whalley, a former United centre-half whose career had ended abruptly following an eye injury, had been with the club since 1934 and after his injury in the 1947-48 season he assisted Murphy. Tom 'Tosher' Curry and Bill Inglis had joined the club in 1934. Arthur Powell, Joe Travis, Bert Fishburn and 'genial' Joe Armstrong worked together with Jimmy Murphy who was, of course, the chief coach. They were the soul of the old club. There was no fuss or glamour about them.

Busby and Murphy also recruited a select band of landladies from neighbouring areas where they could safely place youngsters signed from outside Manchester. These ladies were vetted very carefully indeed. This was all part of building the club from the bottom upwards.

It was Murphy who decided which players were ready for promotion into the reserves and first team, while each coach had a responsibility and got on with the young fledglings in their care. The one thing in common among them was that no swearing was allowed and the players were taught discipline.

Jimmy put in hours of work for the Manchester United cause. At lunchtime he would eat his sandwiches in an old hut beneath the stands which he called his office. He sat with his pals Bert Whalley, Tom Curry, Bill Inglis, Arthur Powell, Joe Travis and little Joe Armstrong. They would discuss all topics but mostly football. Even in later years when the club became one of the richest in the world and directors entertained people from the worlds of showbusiness, politics and celebrities from all walks of life, Jimmy rarely ventured 'upstairs' into the boardroom or the swanky restaurants. "Those people talk a lot but say very little," he would often say. Jimmy preferred a quiet drink with his pals rather than the limelight of the boardroom.

Jimmy was the one who dealt with the younger players on a day-to-day basis, he was charged with the responsibility of preparing youngsters for life as a Manchester United player. Newcomers quickly found out that self-importance, exaggerated self-esteem, arrogance and conceit were not qualities that would be tolerated at Old Trafford and the individual would have to change his ways very quickly or be shown the door. On arrival at the Cliff, familiarity was not allowed to breed contempt. The most noticeable characteristic here, as players, coaches, groundsmen and manager shuffled around the place, was a respect and love for Manchester United.

There was humour: banter, jibes, loads of fun, but the whole interaction was conducted with an underlying recognition of authority. The longer one observed United at work at this time, the more obvious it became that they had mastered all the ingredients of making a big football club run smoothly, efficiently and successfully. Long-winded lessons on playing football were avoided, so the players were never left standing around bored. The theoretical approach was frowned upon. In each training session the 'little things' were taught. Watching Murphy supervising his players was both an enlightening and chastening experience. His eyes rarely left the field of play, he would kick every ball, make every tackle, head every centre. Jimmy used to say: "There's a lot of nonsense talked about how to play football. Blind side runs, decoy runs, track back, dig in, why do they make it so complicated? Good coaching is about common-sense and ideas."

You wouldn't find what Jimmy Murphy did in any coaching manual. Everything he coached was based on the game itself. He saw no sense practising things that would not be much use during a game. Jimmy loved training with the players, he got involved passionately and many a session would see him leave with beads of sweat dripping from his head, his voice hoarse from shouting. Jimmy taught the young United lads that football was quite simply a passing game, that there was no need to dribble around everyone and that the ball moved faster on its own. And the sooner they learned that the better. He got to know the players' strengths and weaknesses, also playing and training with them meant he could give advice and ideas.

"Too many instructions are no use either," Jimmy would say. "The players will keep looking to the dugout before they do anything. No, decisions have to be made in a split second." Jimmy sometimes had to bawl out certain players, not very often, but when he did it was sorted out there and then. He was firm but fair and invariably honest. He would drum it into the players that they were only as good as their last game.

"Football is so simple it becomes difficult to achieve," Jimmy would preach. "Doing the simple thing takes years of practice, it really does. Players have to do it automatically and not clutter up the pattern of the team."

In those days there was no such thing as coaching in English football - everyone believed that great players, or even good players, were born and there was no way anyone could improve upon God-given talent. Jimmy and Bert ingrained in the United youngsters a belief that practice could improve skills as well as tactical knowledge. What they taught was simple and basic. Jimmy succeeded in making the kids understand that they could improve individual and collective skills, and in turn improve the performance of the team and achieve better results.

Breaking the Mould

In any sport it is very unusual for a coach to allow other coaches to work with their athletes. It was to the Manchester United players' extreme advantage that they were being helped by such loyal and unselfish men. All the United backroom staff worked in close co-operation with each other in order to help the players fulfil their potential. Without these dedicated people, many famous names might never have matured as they did.

Football can be a cruel and precarious occupation for the unlucky ones. United's staff would monitor and assess a player's chances. If they were doubtful about a certain lad making the grade as a United player, his parents would be invited for a friendly chat about the boy's future. Matt Busby would make the final decision. Often he tended to give a lad who was not showing the necessary progress, but who was the right type of individual, an extra year to see if he could do better. However, he would emphasise that he would not be kept on the books unless the coaching staff were satisfied that he was good enough.

It was the personal touch the club employed which created goodwill. On many occasions Matt would leave Jimmy to be the bearer of bad tidings when a player had to be released. Jimmy never complained - he did it as compassionately as possible under the circumstances.

The United Revolution

"Joe (Armstrong) and Bert (Whalley) could spot future stars on a foggy day. The spirit we fostered was second to none... it was like one big happy family"
JIMMY MURPHY

Manchester was still overshadowed by war in the 1950s. The recovery from the upheaval and heartbreak brought to families throughout the country could still be seen in Manchester and beyond as buildings remained dilapidated while shabbily dressed people shuffled the streets. Almost five years on from the war there were still gaps between buildings caused by bomb damage. There were few cars on the roads and folk used bicycles and public transport to get to and from their destinations. The Labour government had been in power since 1945 and had brought in much-needed welfare reform. They had also tried to tackle the shortage of houses but much had yet to be done. Many families lived in small, dank, rotten terraced houses that were heated by a solitary open coal or coke fire which had to be laid, lit and cleared out daily.

Others lived in 'prefabs' which had been thrown up as temporary accommodation but remained for years to come. The country was up to its eyeballs in debt and food such as butter, bacon, meat, tea and sugar were rationed and would remain so until 1954. It was still rare for people to eat in restaurants because the five-shilling (25p) limit on meals wasn't removed until May 1950. Meanwhile, there was little choice in clothing, especially for women; nylon stockings remained scarce while most men wore drab 'Demob' clothes. The average wage was eight shillings (40p) a week and out of that there was little to spend on entertainment. City centres were usually deserted at night - an evening out for young people typically involved the pictures or a dance.

In 1951, the Festival of Britain brought a bit of colour into this grey world. Young men still had to do National Service and as if families hadn't had enough of war, many saw service in Korea, the Canal Zone, Cyprus and with the British Army of the Rhine. The 1950s also saw a change in what used to be called the British Empire, now the Commonwealth, and the gradual realisation that Britain was no longer one of the world's leading powers and that our future lay with America and Europe.

Football was still a working class game. Flat caps and overcoats, with the occasionally trilby was the dress mode. There were no team shirts, no flags or club merchandising; a red and white scarf or a rosette, a bell, whistle or a rattle sufficed. There was never any concern about youngsters attending games; kids as young as nine or ten would go with their pals to the game. Sometimes, those like us who lived in Collyhurst, had to cross the city on foot because they could not afford public transport. It was a big day out for us. Going to the game was the highlight of the week for most fans. People worked five-and-a-half-days a week and Saturday afternoons were something we looked forward to all week. Sundays were sacred and sacrosanct; nobody did anything, so the fans, the match was the highlight of the week.

Despite all this gloom, football was about to see a revolution take place. Jimmy Murphy and Matt Busby had a dream; to create a world-class football empire where they would take lads who had just left school and coach them into world-class football players for club and country. There was no doubt that, at the turn of the half-century, English football was not in good shape. The reasons were several but most could be blamed on the Second World War, which extinguished serious football for six whole years. Clubs had a minimum of staff. Because playing fields were used as sites for anti-aircraft guns and other implements of war, the coaching of kids had disappeared from schools and youth clubs, while the established stars were growing older. However, in Manchester a football revolution was underway.

*

At the beginning of the 1950s, United signed a number of brilliant schoolboy prospects and Murphy was in his element coaching them. Jackie Blanchflower, Mark Jones, Dennis Viollet, Jeff Whitefoot, Eddie Lewis, Cliff Birkett and Geoff Bent were among the first. These were quickly followed by Albert Scanlon, John Doherty, and a little while afterwards, Eddie Colman, Duncan Edwards, Bobby Charlton, Ronnie Cope and Wilf McGuinness.

In the glory years that followed the team was quickly dubbed the 'Red Devils' and later the 'Busby Babes'. In truth, they might just as well have been called 'Murphy's Marvels' or 'Whalley's Wonders' because it was these two stalwarts who spent those vital formative years grooming this new wave of players for United. During this period, Busby, Murphy and the United coaches worked overtime at Old Trafford and at the Cliff training ground. These youngsters became close to both Murphy and Busby, but it was Jimmy who had the day-to-day contact with the kids, so he got to know them much better, while Matt was held in respect. The older players noticed how much Murphy was excited by the talent now at his disposal.

One of Murphy's strengths was his knowledge of how young footballers developed. At this stage United had signed some exceptionally talented young players from around the British Isles. They all started as equals; all of them had skill or they would not have been signed by the club, but how they progressed to the various levels was mainly down to the individual. Jimmy knew if he could get perhaps get two or three lads into the first team, that was enough. But with such latent talent at his disposal he schemed to get them all into the top grade and this was why he strove so hard for perfection.

Murphy knew that between the ages of 15 and 20, most young players reach their peak. After that, most of them stand still - they mature, but don't improve. Players like Dennis Viollet, Bobby Charlton, Duncan Edwards and much later, George Best were the exceptions who proved the rule. Those great players went on improving long afterwards. Talking about this subject in the 1960s to Joe Travis, United's 'B' team trainer, Jimmy told him that in his opinion a lot of youngsters were at their best as schoolboys. By that he meant that they were early developers but never matured. As an example, Murphy mentioned David Cliss. A brilliant youngster, some southern newspaper reporters had acclaimed him as the greatest schoolboy footballer of all time. Jimmy didn't agree with that assumption: "What about Duncan Edwards? What about Bobby Charlton?"

In a televised game watched by thousands, young Cliss scored a spectacular goal. It was a goal in a million - people were going wild. Here, they said, was someone special, a player head and shoulders above his contemporaries. There would be no holding him back according to the experts. The lad had the football world at his feet. He signed for Chelsea and they groomed him but he never made the grade. "What those people watching him playing on television saw, was David Cliss at the peak of his footballing ability; he never improved. This is the hazard with youngsters," Murphy concluded.

After the 1952 championship success, United entered a period of rebuilding. The foundations were already in place and solid enough. Busby and his coaches were delighted at the progress of their young, brilliant footballers. It was just a matter of time before these lads would take their places in United's first team.

United's star search had begun in 1947. Following on from the success of MUJAC, Busby and Murphy had decided on a more professional approach to scouting. The system was expanded and reorganised, with the express intention of filtering off the cream of the crop to turn them into Manchester United players.

In 1952, at a meeting of shareholders held at Old Trafford, Busby stunned his audience when he told them there was no need to panic. The club had talent worth at least £200,000, he said, and they would soon be writing a new and more glorious chapter in the history of Manchester United. Of course, Busby's bold statement was splashed all over the following day's newspapers.

With Busby's proclamation, the nationwide search for the very best schoolboy and youth footballers was widened. Matt and Jimmy planned their own football academy. It was a great idea and put into immediate action. The British Isles was a potential goldmine of wonderful all-round footballers. The dynamic duo decided to try and find their own nuggets, then polish and groom them into the United system. Their aim was not just to build a First Division Championship winning team, as most club managers would have been more than happy to accomplish; both Busby and Murphy envisaged building five or six teams, all playing in an identical manner, with the summit being the first team. The idea was that every player in their teams could play in the same system and when called upon for promotion to the next rung of the ladder they would be accustomed to that system. They were years ahead of their time - Ajax famously adopted this pattern with huge success in the 1970s.

Experienced footballers tend to be clannish and don't appreciate the idea of younger players stepping into their position in the first team. Busby's post-war United team was no different. After all, they were only human and we must remember that many of United's 1948 team had lost their best years to the war. As things were progressing at Old Trafford they could be forgiven for looking anxiously over their shoulders at the influx of young players arriving at the club. Jimmy himself was still in his thirties, and he understood their concerns. He also understood that the older players nearing the end of their careers were afraid of the future. But Matt Busby had told Murphy to do a specific job - coach, develop and polish the gems of United's future and there was nobody better suited for achieving that goal than the Welshman.

The search begins

"There is no substitute for skill and character," Murphy told the United scouting staff charged with travelling hundreds of miles to scour the parks and recreation grounds where schoolboy, boy scout, youth club and boys brigade matches were played.

"There were three men most instrumental in putting Matt's ideas into swift action," Murphy once recalled. "They were known as the Three Musketeers; one was myself, then there was Joe Armstrong and the other was Bert Whalley. Bert was my assistant and a brilliant coach. He had bags of patience with youngsters.

"Bert was a Methodist lay-preacher: a quiet, serious type who had been with United for twenty years until an eye injury put paid to his playing career. Matt took him on the staff as soon as he had recovered and Bert never forgot this act of kindness. Joe Armstrong was a lovely person. He had retired from the Post Office and done some scouting for Manchester City before joining us. Only small, with a thatch of snow-white hair, the parents of the kids we wanted to sign loved him. He had a wonderful, honest, down-to-earth and friendly disposition. Joe and Bert could spot future stars on a foggy day. We travelled thousands of miles in search of the right youngsters to bring to the club. The spirit we fostered at Old Trafford was second to none. It was like one big happy family."

Many jealous observers claimed that United had a monopoly on young players because they had scouts in every city, town and village throughout the British Isles. This was nonsense. In fact, they only had one full-time scout and that was Joe Armstrong, who had taken over from Louis Rocca. The other eight or nine scouts were part-time: men such as Bob Bishop in Northern Ireland and Billy Behan in Eire. Some clubs employed as many as 40 scouts. Where United had an advantage over their rivals was their gracious and impeccable behaviour, their honesty and the known fact that they looked after youngsters. There was also the cache of playing for Manchester United who, in this period, had overtaken Arsenal as England's premier club.

As a result, the United staff gained the respect of schoolmasters and youth club leaders up and down the land. Several times these people would contact the club recommending certain lads who they thought capable of making the grade. Murphy didn't always go to a prospective young player's home. Joe Armstrong, Bert Whalley or Busby would make the initial approach. They would charm the parents. Jimmy was an excitable fellow who wore his heart on his sleeve. He tended to be too enthusiastic - he would visit later if required.

The Thinker

One day while in his little office under the Old Trafford stands, Murphy sat talking to his journalist friend Len Noad. During the conversation the two friends started discussing the merits of the great Sir Stanley Matthews and Sir Tom Finney. "If Stanley Matthews was one of our players we would make better use of his talent," claimed Jimmy.

Len was puzzled, believing Matthews was essentially a right-winger. He asked Jimmy what he meant. "Sure he's a great winger," Jimmy told him, "but often he is wasted out there on the flank. We would try him out as an inside-forward or at wing-half where his unique skills and footballing brain would be of more benefit to the team. Stan has so much more to offer to football than being stuck out on the wing." The two men made comparisons: "What about Tom Finney then, where would you play him?" asked Len. Jimmy smiled: "Tom Finney can already play in two or three positions. He can play on both wings, centre-forward and he would also make a great inside-forward. We would also like to see how he performed as an attacking wing-half. My honest opinion is that because he is such a brilliant footballer with such a sharp brain he could play anywhere," confirming what the older players had said about the experiments Busby and Murphy often made with players.

Football was Murphy's life. He wasn't interested in the latest jargon or complicated moves. Instead he had a marvellously creative mind for football. He taught the basics, instead of doing the difficult and spectacular, he preached the theme of keeping it simple. He knocked the bad habits out of players, almost brainwashed them if you like. The basics without which all the talent in the world counted for nothing.

As Lawrence Cassidy, former headmaster of St Patrick's School in Collyhurst who played for United in the 1940s, points out: "Jimmy was a one-off, he had his own theories on how football should be played and taught. 'Do it simple,' he would say. He had his own way of expressing his psychology and ideas. He never stopped talking about football, even if you wanted to discuss something else. He was so interesting when talking about the game that you ended up listening diligently.

"For instance, he urged his players not to keep the ball but to lay it off first time. The time would come in games where a player would have to do the difficult things. 'Give it to a red shirt,' was his mantra to the youngsters. He taught them that when taking throw-ins they should throw the ball down the line instead of across the pitch. These small things meant the difference between playing the game and being professional about the game. Turning talent into professionalism was a matter of mental strength - often it seemed like nothing, but football is all about this kind of professionalism. Everyone recognises brilliance but football was also about the unspectacular: 'Concentration is so important. Do the simple things, which is basically common sense. Mark your man when you have to, lose him when your team has the ball. Get the ball and make it hard for the opposition when you have it. And make it harder for the opposition when they have it'."

I will digress for a moment and give a little example. During the 1960s Shay Brennan and Tony Dunne were United's first choice full-backs. They were very neat and clever on the ball. When clearing the ball, Tony and Shay would gently poke the ball out of play for a throw-in to the opposition. Jimmy used to tell them: "Put that ball high up into the stands and give yourselves extra seconds to get organised for the throw-in. If you just touch the ball out of play they will take a quick throw-in and attack you straight away and put the whole defence under pressure." Agreed, it was quite simple but the change of approach proved highly effective.

Captain of the Busby Babes

Roger Byrne became the outspoken and fearless captain of Manchester United during the Busby Babes era. However, were it not for a trick of fate, he might never have starred with United or England at all.

Roger was born in the Gorton district of Manchester in 1929, the only child of Mr William (Billy) Henry and Jessica (Jessie) Byrne. Roger's father was a crown green bowling champion besides being a student of football. Roger was a studious lad who attended Burnage Grammar School. Although an all-round sportsman at school, showing promise as both a footballer and a cricketer, Roger had little ambition of becoming a professional at either discipline.

Roger did his national service in the Royal Air Force where he played football, rugby and cricket for his unit besides being a fair gymnast - so much so that the RAF requested that he sign up for a further period of service to become a physical education instructor. Roger didn't fancy staying on in the services and once he was demobbed he starting playing football for Ryder Brow Youth Club.

United's scouts had been monitoring his progress and later invited him to Old Trafford where they eventually signed him. Roger studied and learned by watching and training with United's fabulous 1948 team. In his early days with United, Byrne was a left-winger, not really outstanding in many respects, more a steady type of player. What Jimmy Murphy and other members of United coaching staff discovered was that Roger was very outspoken and regarded by some as a rebel. However, according to Billy Wootton, Byrne would have been lost to United were it not for a simple twist of fate.

Billy was a friend of Matt Busby's and had been managing non-league Northwich Victoria for seven years when he was appointed manager of Oldham Athletic in 1947. Billy was a cheery character who used to travel with Busby to the League meetings and they often had a drink together. Billy, Matt and Andy Beatie, Stockport County manager at the time, and a couple of other managers would meet on a Monday lunchtime outside the Queens Hotel in the city centre and proceed to Mere Golf Club. One day, Billy was visiting the Cliff training ground, watching one of United's junior teams in a game, with a view to signing Laurie Cassidy. The fee was agreed but after speaking to Laurie, Wootton was told in no uncertain terms: "I would sooner play in United's third team than play in Oldham's first team." That was the end of the matter as far as Billy was concerned.

A short while later, he sold his left-winger to Liverpool for a fee in the region of £7,000, which was a great deal of money in those days. Oldham had to sell their best players in order to survive and Wootton's job was to look for bargain buys - he got a tip that United were prepared to sell a left-winger called Roger Byrne for the small fee of £1,000.

Wootton agreed to buy him and arranged all the necessary documents and registration forms and it was arranged that he would meet Jimmy Murphy that evening to conclude the deal. Roger Byrne knew nothing about his impending transfer to Oldham at this stage. That night, United had a Lancashire Cup match away to Accrington Stanley. Billy travelled to the game, after which it had been agreed that he would speak to Byrne and settle terms. However, on the coach journey from Manchester, the first choice United left-back fell ill and obviously couldn't play. Jimmy Murphy was forced to juggle the team around and he pencilled Byrne in at left full-back.

"He had a blinder," declared Billy. "He was absolutely brilliant playing in the left full-back position. I knew instinctively that my hopes of signing Roger Byrne had vanished."

At the final whistle Billy looked at Murphy and coyly asked him if he should follow him into United's dressing room in order to speak to

Byrne. Jimmy, who could be very terse when the occasion called for it, gave Wootton an icy stare and rasped: "He's not going anywhere. So don't bother."

The Oldham boss was disappointed but added: "I didn't blame him really. I wanted Roger as an out-and-out left-winger but later Roger proved his class. He had greyhound speed and he played like an accomplished and seasoned full-back. And look what he achieved."

Dennis Viollet

Dennis Viollet was one of the original Busby Babes. A former captain of Manchester, Lancashire and England Schoolboys, Dennis signed for United in 1950 to the utter dismay of Manchester City who thought he was a certainty to sign for them because Dennis and his family were committed 'Blues'. Viollet made his League debut in April 1953 and went on to play in over 250 first team games. He will forever be part of English football history because he was the first Englishman to score a goal in the European Cup and remains the holder of United's single season goalscoring record of 32 goals from 36 league games in the 1959-60 season.

A frail-looking player, Dennis had superb balance and awareness and was one of the most skilful players ever to pull on the red shirt. He was, of course, confident as well as an exceptional footballer. He could play as a winger and look as if he was born to play in that position. On other occasions, he was used as a wing-half and spectators could see he was one of the great thinkers of football playing there, while he also possessed the ability to make things easier for his colleagues because of his creative ability. Dennis was always looking to set United on the attack and his perception was magnificent. He had few peers when it came to ball control and running into open spaces. He was immaculate! He could dribble, was an accurate passer, a brilliant schemer and he not only made goals, but could also take them, as his final record of 179 goals from 294 games testifies.

When he arrived as a teenager, Dennis came under Jimmy Murphy and Bert Whalley's wing.

"Jimmy Murphy and Bert Whalley were like father figures to us young players," said Dennis, many years later. "Dear old Tom Jackson, who wrote about United for the *Manchester Evening News*, wrote an article in the early 1950s in which he named us the 'Busby Babes', that was the first time I had heard that phase used. We had some great young players at the club in the early fifties and every close season they would sign more schoolboy internationals. The competition for places in the teams was tough, extremely tough. Matt Busby would be seen now and again training with the youngsters or the first team but he was very tied up with running the club so the main coaching was done by Jimmy and Bert. They would spend hours and bags of patience and understanding with us kids. Bert was like a kindly uncle whereas Jimmy could be gruff, strict, and had a no-nonsense approach. He would play hell with us when he thought we needed it, then, he would give us a little sugar. By that I mean he would put his arm around your shoulder and quietly explain what he wanted you to do.

"In 1952 the FA Youth Cup began. I was slightly too old to play in this competition. I was gutted because it was a great platform from which to get noticed and a great many of United's first team players came through from that competition. Jimmy Murphy made me the footballer I later became. He was the person who told Matt Busby when a young player was ready for a run out in the first team. He talked sense and everything he told you was aimed to make us professional. He taught me that football had always been, and should always be, a game to be enjoyed. He also believed that young players would improve by simply listening to older, more experienced players. There was no kidding him either. Like one or two of the lads, I liked my nights out, I liked a drink, but Jimmy knew when we had overdone it and would give us a dressing down, although he never went telling tales about us to Matt Busby.

"We were all friends at Old Trafford, there was no animosity between anybody. When I was 18, I had to do my two years' National Service - everyone had to serve his two years. This was a bind for everybody, especially to professional footballers, but it had to be done. I was playing in United's 'A' team and occasionally in the reserves at the time and needed the experience. Jimmy used to advise me about what I should do while at camp. When I made my debut against Newcastle, Jimmy was as pleased as punch for me and his enthusiasm at my promotion was genuine. It was funny really, when we were having a teamtalk before a match if any of the players started swearing Matt would tell them to cut it out. He didn't like profanity in any respect. He would speak calmly about how he wanted us to play and he would mention certain things about the opposition and wish us luck and tell us to go out and enjoy it. Matt would then excuse himself and leave. Contrast this with Jimmy's talk. He would walk in the dressing room full of enthusiasm, all fire and brimstone, his face expressive and his eyes bulging out of their sockets. He would look around and start spitting out his words like machine-gun bullets, geeing us up. He would be effing and blinding about the opposition. He was the complete opposite to Matt. Of course Matt knew this, he knew Jimmy would be more expressive and passionate and that was the chemistry that made them a great partnership. Jimmy was brilliant, the lads loved listening to him.

"Another great asset Jimmy possessed which people never mention, perhaps they're not aware of it, was his ability to make players perform way above their own expectations. Just think for a moment about the team that reached Wembley after Munich to understand what I mean. A good coach doesn't necessarily need to inspire great players, they do that automatically because they have a special kind of ability. It's the ordinary player that needs somebody as dedicated and as inspiring as Jimmy to give them this special kind of motivation in order to play above themselves. Jimmy was unique in this and did it often.

"He was a chain-smoker and it was funny when he'd cadge cigs, he did it to me regularly. He was different to most football managers and coaches of that period because he would have a pint with the players, have a laugh and a joke and listen to your problems and never divulge things you asked him not to. Jimmy was a wonderful coach and a warm-hearted, sensitive human being. One of the things I truly regret in my life is that I never told Jimmy how much I owed him for all the consideration and help he gave me."

Tommy Taylor - The Smiling Executioner

Towards the end of 1952, Matt and Jimmy decided they had to look for a young centre-forward they could groom into a player of substance Their own home-reared centre-forwards didn't look to be making the progress expected and Jack 'Gunner' Rowley was nearing the end of his brilliant career, so the two men decided to look elsewhere for the final piece in their particular jigsaw. Every United scout was alerted to look out for a young strapping leader, someone they could fit into the United system without any disruption. It was at about this time that United Reserves played Barnsley Reserves away in Yorkshire. As usual Jimmy took his seat in the dugout along with first reserve Albert Scanlon. As the referee blew his whistle and the game started, United began playing lovely football. However, this big, dark, curly-haired youngster leading the Barnsley attack caught Jimmy's eye and Murphy asked the Barnsley trainer his name.

"Tommy, Tommy Taylor," came back the answer in a thick Yorkshire accent. Tommy played a 'blinder', scoring a hat-trick despite United eventually winning the game. Taylor had given the young United defence, especially goalkeeper Gordon Clayton, a torrid time.

Albert Scanlon remembers how irate Murphy was when Tommy was plundering his goals. "Charging the goalkeeper was permitted in those days," recalls Albert. "All through the game this big, athletic-looking centre-forward was shoulder charging poor old Gordon. I had to admit that he looked really impressive and seemed to have springs in his heels as he jumped for high balls at corners. Jimmy was in raptures about him. 'That's him, that's him, he's the one,' he kept saying. I didn't know what he meant of course, that he and Busby were looking for a centre-forward. Saying that, he was still annoyed at our lads for letting Tommy treat them with such disdain and allowing him three goals. Very few teams or players did that to us in those days. Murphy was screaming out instructions to our lads, it was comical really but I dare not laugh openly. At the end of the game Jimmy flew out of the dugout like a rat up a sewer, out on to the pitch. He went up to our defenders. 'What did you think of their big feller?' he was shouting. I could see that our lads didn't know what to say really. Fearing Jimmy's wrath if they praised Tommy too highly, or wondering what sarcastic comments he would make if they said he wasn't much good.

"Finally, before coming off the pitch, he grabbed hold of Gordon Clayton. 'Gordon, son, what did you think of their centre-forward?' I could tell from the look on poor Gordon's face that he was in two minds as to what answer to give, he didn't know which way to answer. 'Oh, he wasn't bad Jimmy,' he responded. Jimmy's face was a picture. 'Not bad, not effing bad. Eh? Well he effing knocked you all over the area and you let him get away with it, he scored three effing goals and you tell me he's not bad.' Coming back to Manchester on the coach Jimmy was in his usual seat near the front. He had a contented look on his face and I have often thought about that day and with hindsight all these years later I'm certain it was because he had found the jewel in the crown - Tommy Taylor!"

The following morning, Albert, who was on the groundstaff, was sweeping the dressing rooms when he saw Jimmy rushing about in an agitated fashion. Deciding to make himself look busy, Albert swept a little brisker. Matt Busby walked into the room and Jimmy, his face lit up like a Christmas tree, blurted out: "Matt, I've found him, I've found the centre-forward we've been searching for. He's ideal for us Matt, about six foot tall, superb physique, solid, fantastic in the air and (banging his heart), bags of ticker, he can run for the whole 90 minutes. He's just the type we've been looking for."

Albert heard the full conversation and said Jimmy was as excited as a little boy with a new toy. "I didn't realise it at the time, but many years later when I was at another club I remembered that particular match at Barnsley and Jimmy being so certain that Tommy Taylor would be the ideal centre-forward for Manchester United. He'd only seen him play that once but he backed his judgement. Was he right? Well the record book tells you the answer. Tommy Taylor became the best centre-forward England had had for years. A great player and a lovely man."

It is folklore how Matt Busby sent Johnny Carey and several others to watch Taylor play. When Joe Richards, the Barnsley chairman, alerted the football world that they were willing to sell big Tommy, sixteen clubs were said to be keen on his signature. Busby and Murphy spent three or four nights in Barnsley until they secured the deal. Jimmy, through the help of his newspaper pal Len Noad, had been visiting Tommy regularly before Barnsley announced they were willing to sell. Eventually United got him for £29,999. Busby didn't want to saddle the youngster with a whopping £30,000 price tag round his neck - but what a bargain he turned out to be. In 189 games for United in the League, FA Cup and European Cup, he scored 128 goals. In 19 games for England he notched 16. What more can anyone ask from a centre-forward?

"Tommy was an artistic centre-forward who thrived on hard work," Jimmy was fond of saying whenever discussing the many virtues of Tommy Taylor. "Once he moved to Old Trafford he blossomed. He seemed to move much more quickly and with a far greater sense of urgency. Tommy played a very big part in Manchester United and England's success. He was a shy lad and kept a level head on his shoulders, accepting praise and criticism in the same easy vein. He scored goals with great consistency. Tommy was a dedicated footballer and, in my opinion, the perfect example of a footballer reaching the top because despite all the problems and difficulties he remained cool, never rushed, and appreciated the help of his colleagues."

A Cup Made for Murphy

The FA Youth Cup, or to give the competition its proper name, the Football Association Youth Challenge Cup, was first introduced in 1952. Jimmy Murphy was delighted. It was a competition for under 18s and both Jimmy and Matt were hoping that their young players would do well in the competition in order to vindicate their proclamations at the shareholders' meeting about the quality of their youth system. Jimmy would now be able to gauge the progress of his youngsters against the cream of the crop from other clubs. The United youngsters were used to playing against mainly local teams and he wanted to broaden their outlook. Murphy recognised the opportunity to test his youngsters against opposition from the length and breadth of England.

Jimmy would be in his element in these matches. All his tremendous Welsh fire and fervour would boil to the surface. In time, the United youngsters would play in front of crowds of over 20,000 which was incredible as quite a few First Division clubs could only hope to draw that many for important games.

United's first game in the competition was against Yorkshire rivals Leeds United. In the dressing room before the match, Jimmy gave his usual rousing team talk. On these occasions there would be complete silence, not a sound could be heard except the sound of Jimmy's rasping voice vibrating around the room as he outlined his strategy and told his players what was expected of them.

"You're wearing this famous red shirt, lads," he bellowed, holding up the United strip. "Wear it with pride." After Murphy's inspirational and rousing team talk, the kids felt ten feet tall and were ready to play until they dropped. During the warm-up, before the referee's whistle blew to start the game, Jimmy emerged on the pitch for a word with key individuals: "You are one of the greatest young players in the country," he would tell them. The lads would feel as if the game was already won. "Keep it simple. Pass to a red shirt and plenty of movement off the ball," ending with his favourite remark: "And don't forget, get bloody well stuck into them, have pride." When he spoke, nobody else would utter a word until he had finished. Just as the team were lining up, Arthur Powell, the trainer, added: "By the way lads, the boss is out there watching you." This brought an extra check on their kit to make sure they were turned out clean and smart for Busby's shrewd eye.

Duncan Edwards was made captain of the team and he inspired a 4-0 thrashing of Leeds' lads. Some of the names in United's team would become household names: Albert Scanlon, Gordon Clayton, Ronnie Cope, David Pegg, Eddie Lewis, John Doherty. Scanlon scored United's first goal of the competition with a spectacular cross-shot, David Pegg notched the second playing at inside-forward while a tall, gangling Jack Charlton put through his own goal before Scanlon made it 4-0.

The United coaching staff were thrilled with the youngsters' display and eagerly anticipated the next round against non-league Nantwich. The game should have been played in Cheshire, but Nantwich decided to forfeit the advantage of playing at home in favour of an evening kick-off under floodlights at the Cliff. The result: United Youths 23, Nantwich Youths 0. Yes, 23-nil! This, to my knowledge, is still the highest score in the competition's history. David Pegg and Duncan Edwards scored five goals apiece. United led 8-0 at half-time but as the youngsters trooped into the changing room they were met by an angry, stern-faced Murphy. He demanded they wipe the smiles off their faces, roll up their sleeves and win the match as decisively as possible. The team looked shocked at this outburst from Jimmy. After all, they were winning 8-0. Murphy proceeded to pace up and down the room urging his defenders not to concede any silly goals. As if to make his point Jimmy turned to Duncan Edwards and barked: "I don't know what you're looking so smug about. Now listen, Dunc son, I want to see you making those winning tackles, win the ball, give it to a team-mate and then go for the return!"

"The way he [Murphy] carried on, you'd have thought we were just in front by the odd goal, instead of winning by a landslide," one of the young players told his waiting parents after the game.

"Murphy was always seeking perfection," said Johnny Aston senior. "He was never satisfied with merely winning. He preached the gospel of perfection."

"He would never, ever tell one of his players to go out and deliberately kick another player," said Henry Cockburn, adding, "he did, however, expect one hundred per cent commitment from all of them. Even the dainty ball players were expected to drop back and win the ball if the opposition had it. He implored them to drop deep and help the defenders and make it tough for the other team."

Before every Youth Cup game, Jimmy would be beavering about the dressing room chatting to individuals before giving his team talk. Bobby Charlton recalled that when the United Youths were facing a team from Birmingham, Murphy would seem angry and agitated and tell the lads: "'You've got to beat this lot, I hate this place, everything looks grey. I can't stand the way these Brummies talk.' When we travelled to play Yorkshire teams he'd tell the team that Yorkshiremen were clannish and tight-fisted so they had to beat them. And when we played in the North-East, he would tell us that it was always cold and miserable and full of snow up there. 'Let's get a good result here and get back home lads,' he would say." It seemed to Bobby and the other United youngsters that Jimmy couldn't stand anyone from outside Manchester. "He could have been accused of being one of the most prejudiced men alive - he wasn't of course, it was just his way of geeing us up."

Alex Dawson recalls Jimmy's constant praising of anything Welsh. "According to Jimmy, the Welsh had the best boxers, the best opera singers, pop artists, poets, comedians, rugby players and footballers. When United had a match in Cardiff we were all expecting him to sing the virtues of the Welsh team, instead he came bounding into the dressing room shouting: 'No messing about up here lads, I can't stand these bloody Welshmen, and those bloody sheep, they're everywhere.' Everyone burst out laughing."

The FA Youth Cup proved a wonderful breeding ground for Murphy's youngsters. From its inception in 1952, the United youngsters went 43 games unbeaten, winning the trophy for five successive years. The first game they lost was to Southampton in a two-legged semi-final in 1956. In the first leg at Southampton, United ran out 5-2 victors. However, in the second leg at Old Trafford, the young Reds lost 3-2 to an excellent Saints team that included Terry Paine and John Sydenham - two players who went on to greater honours. For the record books, only five Manchester United players went on to win three FA Youth Cup winners medals: Eddie Colman, Duncan Edwards and Bobby Charlton in 1953-54-55, and Wilf McGuinness and Tony Hawksworth in 1954-55-56.

In Jimmy's mental make-up there was no such thing as a one-horse race; there was no easing up. If you had a team on the run, you hit them with everything you had. John Charles, the Welsh legend, believed that Jimmy's tactical talks were out of this world. He said that when Jimmy took over as Welsh team manager for the first time he gathered the players for a chat. John recalled that it went on and on. The team were usually bored to tears with these team talks from the managers at their respective clubs, but here they sat transfixed as Jimmy spoke. After over an hour Jimmy realised he had gone on longer than he anticipated. "I'm sorry if I've bored you lads, I talk too much. Off you go." Big John Charles stood up and quietly replied: "Bored us nothing, Jimmy. I've learned more from that talk than I thought possible. If that's boring, you can bore me anytime." With that, every player and official in the room gave him a standing ovation. This was unheard of in football circles but that was the kind of impact Jimmy Murphy had on senior professionals. So imagine what it was like for the youngsters he coached day after day.

Geoff Bent

Geoff Bent was a player Jimmy had a great deal of time for. A Salford lad, Geoff was one of the first Busby Babes and was United through and through. He joined the Reds in 1948 around about the same time as Roger Byrne, Bill Foulkes, Dennis Viollet and Jackie Blanchflower. He had captained Salford Schoolboys in 1947 when they were winners of the highly prestigious England Schools Trophy. Standing 5ft 11in and weighing nearly 12 stone, Geoff was solidly built and was considered a left-back but he could also play centre-half which he sometimes did for the juniors. He only played 12 times for United's first team but this was because Roger Byrne was the regular left full-back who occupied the first team berth.

Geoff could have chosen several clubs but settled for United because they were closer to home. He liked dancing and was a nice, pleasant, friendly, easy-going person, well liked by everyone at Old Trafford. "Geoff was a loyal player for Manchester United," Jimmy used to say. "Geoff and Roger Byrne were full-backs with a difference. They were confident on the ball. When Geoff matured and reached his 20s there were many clubs after him but he stayed loyal. You had to feel a little sorry for him really because Roger Byrne was the England left-back and we were covered for every position at United in the fifties."

Geoff was a regular in United's Central League side and was excellent. That's no cliché either. Many people asked why he didn't move to another club when he knew his first team opportunities were so limited. Well, Jimmy always said that if he had joined another club he wouldn't have been much better off financially because every player at that time was on the same basic wage. Another factor was that he married in 1953, he loved his home and did not want to uproot his wife Marion and daughter Karen. Geoff was liked and respected by all the staff and players at Old Trafford. He played in practice games against Jimmy and learned a great deal about how to handle himself physically.

"Yes, of course Geoff could have walked into any other First Division team," said Jimmy after Munich. "Geoff could look after himself and was a great tackler. He knew how to use the ball as well. We had players in every position, so if a so-called first team winger was injured, we would just bring the Central League winger in to take his place. Not that we had such things as first team players mind you. They were all Manchester United players. Roger [Byrne] was a consistent player and very brave - that was the reason Geoff got so few games, but really like I said, he was good enough to hold a regular place in any team."

Liam 'Billy' Whelan

In May 1953, the United youth team were appearing in the FA Youth Cup final against deadly rivals Wolves. Regular inside-right John Doherty had just turned 18 and had been called up to serve two years' National Service in the RAF, stationed at Padgate. The final was a two-legged affair with the first leg played at Old Trafford on May 4th, with the second leg due to be played on Saturday May 9th. Doherty was injured and subsequently required a cartilage operation in an RAF hospital, and Jimmy desperately wanted United to beat Wolves. He knew Stan Cullis, the Wolves' no-nonsense manager, from his playing days and just like United, the Midlands club pinned a great deal of hope on their youth system.

Jimmy wanted to show Cullis how much better United's youngsters were compared to his. He looked at his own lads for a replacement and wasn't happy. Jimmy contacted United's Irish scout in Dublin, Billy Behan, and asked him about a young Irish player who scored a lot of goals. Bert Whalley was asked to go over to Dublin and check on the lad. "If he's any good", Bert was told, "bring him back to Old Trafford." When Bert arrived in Dublin, he was met by Billy Behan, who told him to forget about the player Murphy had sent him to check on. Bert wasn't happy about that, but Billy explained to him that Jimmy was given the wrong information about the player concerned. "He's a big strapping lad," said Behan, "but he's a centre-half really, a lot bigger than the other schoolboys, that's why he's getting plenty of goals. Liam Whelan is the lad for United, take my word for it."

Bert had been given a specific name by Jimmy and politely told Billy he would go back to Manchester and explain the situation to Jimmy and let him decide. Eventually Liam Whelan came to Manchester. He went straight into the team and became an overnight sensation. In the first leg, the young Red Devils, in front of over 20,000 at Old Trafford, thrashed Cullis's lads 7-1. The Wolves prodigies had scored 29 and conceded none in the six ties leading up to the final. But here they met their match - Whelan scoring on his debut. The second leg was played at Molineux on a glorious sunny day in front of over 20,000 fans. Wolves scored first after six minutes, having twice hit the woodwork. But Lewis and Scanlon scored twice for United in a matter of minutes - Eddie Lewis headed home the equaliser before seconds later Liam, now 'Billy' to his team-mates, scored to put his side in front. Wolves pulled another goal back to make the final score 2-2 but United triumphed 9-3 on aggregate. Billy Whelan had made his mark.

Billy Whelan was another young player to whom Jimmy gave extra, one-to-one coaching. He handled the shy Dublin lad with kid gloves. "Billy Whelan was an absolute genius with a ball at his feet," Jimmy said. "If he would just believe in himself a bit more he would be sensational. They talk about these Continentals and South American players and what great ball jugglers they are, well Billy Whelan could do what they did only better. He did it in competitive games in all kinds of conditions."

As a youngster in Dublin he would spend hour upon hour playing with a tennis ball until he could almost make it talk. He was a member of the famous Home Farm club and a prolific goalscorer. He had amazing skill and his close control had to be seen to be appreciated. He was calm and unhurried which made critics describe him as slow but Jimmy said he wasn't slow up here, tapping his forehead. "He could think faster than those cowboys in the Wild West in their 'shoot-outs'," he used to say. Often he would bring the young Dubliner back in the afternoon for extra coaching sessions. Jimmy knew Billy was a quiet, inoffensive type of person who never swore, so he would never use any profanity in front of the lad. "If you weren't such a great player, you'd make a smashing priest," Jimmy would often tell Billy. What Jimmy was trying to get Billy to do was to become more assertive in his play, but it just wasn't in the lad's nature to be aggressive. But that didn't stop

Murphy from trying to make him a better player.

Albert Scanlon often watched as Jimmy would try and goad Billy while they practiced. "Billy would never retaliate, no matter what stick Jimmy handed out. People would get agitated with him sometimes because they knew he was a brilliant player, but he never seemed to display his full range of skills. He was a magician with a ball at his feet, I really don't think he knew how good he was and how much better he could have become. A world-class forward, there is no doubt about that. You had to play with him to appreciate how good he was. His vision and passing was sheer class. He was a lovely, quiet, sensible person who suffered a lot from homesickness. At the time I couldn't understand that because I was a Manchester lad, not living in digs. He shunned the limelight and preferred a quiet night at the pictures. Jimmy was forever telling him how great he would become, trying constantly to make him an even better player."

As with all the players, they had a good relationship with each other. Jimmy would always be encouraging the Irish youngster and emphasising his good points. "Our inside-forward trio of Whelan, Taylor and Viollet scored double figures every season. You won't find many trios doing that!" Murphy told his newspaper friend Len Noad. After the Munich disaster, Jimmy was reminiscing about Whelan. "In his early years with us he won two League championship medals," said Jimmy. "He played enough games to qualify for a First Division medal and had been a regular in our Central League side that won the league so he got another medal. He only played four times for his country but he would have eclipsed whoever held the record for appearances. He only had a brief fling in the limelight but in 96 first team matches in all competitions he scored 52 goals. A marvellous record and, I honestly believe, it would have been much better, but he was a lovely laid-back sort of person."

A first taste of Europe

In May 1954, Jimmy, Matt Busby, Bert Whalley and trainer Arthur Powell plus 15 youth team players left Ringway Airport for a week in Zurich where they were due to appear in two friendly matches at the International Youth Tournament, later called the 'Blue Star' Tournament. Among the kids were Gordon Clayton, Bobby Charlton, David Pegg, Albert Scanlon, Eddie Colman, Billy Whelan and Wilf McGuinness. Duncan Edwards teamed up with them later. All the youngsters were deliriously happy. For most, this was their first-ever journey beyond English shores and as a result, this was a learning trip for all concerned.

Busby and Murphy wanted United's youngsters to sample European tactics and techniques. In the first game against Young Fellows of Zurich, they drew 0-0. In their second match, the youngsters defeated Berne Boys 2-0, the two scallywags Eddie Colman and Albert Scanlon getting the goals. In the third game, it looked like the young Reds were on their way home before Eddie Lewis scored in the last few seconds to put his team through to the last four. After another victory, the Old Trafford 'nursery' team won the competition by beating Red Star of Zurich 4-0. Albert Scanlon got a goal while Duncan Edwards slammed in a brilliant hat-trick.

Of course, the United officials were overjoyed and celebrated in style. A couple of days later, in a friendly against local Swiss team Bienne, United triumphed 9-2, with Whelan five, Charlton two, Scanlon and Edwards the scorers. The following day, the lads were back in Zurich to face the Swiss National Youth team. The match was played before a full international game between Switzerland and Holland. The United team won 4-0, Pegg scoring two goals, with one each for Whelan and Edwards. This ended a marvellous tour in which besides playing superb soccer, the kids were feted and paid glowing tributes from European coaches and newspapers, much to the delight of Busby and Murphy. English football certainly needed the boost given by the United youngsters. Their brilliant attacking football and unique teamwork vindicated Jimmy and Bert Whalley's claims for the team. They knew they were on the right track in building a dynasty for United and they also knew that European jaunts would become a regular event in the coming years.

Albert Scanlon recalled his early days at Old Trafford and the trip to Europe. "Jimmy had an insatiable appetite for the game, he talked about it non-stop. We loved listening to him describe players and teams. One of his favourite players seemed to be Peter Doherty, because he never stopped talking about him. It appeared that while playing for Wales against Ireland in an international Jimmy had flattened Doherty shortly after the kick-off. The great Irish player got to his feet gingerly and yelled: 'Bloody hell, we've only just started the game, Jimmy!' To which Murphy replied: 'I'm sorry old chum, but there's still nearly 90 minutes to play and that's a long time and I don't intend chasing you all over the pitch.' Jimmy would be in raptures when discussing him. 'Peter was a great player, lads,' he would say. 'He had quick feet and a razor-sharp mind and he practised day and night and it paid off for him. A great player, a great man.' The trip to Switzerland was fabulous. Jimmy would organise little kickabouts and loved playing. Of course, even in these games he was preparing us for the future. He would push us in the back, knock us off balance, pull our jerseys, trip us up, obstruct us and do everything we would face later in our careers."

A Tidal Wave of Talent

"Any manager lucky enough to have
big Dunc had half a team"
JIMMY MURPHY

"Matt Busby was the general, he was the 'boss' all right," said Johnny Aston senior, "but he picked the best lieutenant any officer could wish for when he signed Murphy. Don't get the wrong idea Jimmy wasn't a yes-man for anybody. They complemented each other. Busby was quiet, charming, and very diplomatic, whereas Murphy was harder, more open and full of enthusiasm. But he stood for no nonsense."

Jimmy regularly put in 80 hours a week in the service of Manchester United. Fortunately, his wife Winnie and his six children, Patricia, John, Philip, James, Nicholas and Anne understood his dedication. In the close season, Jimmy would make up for his neglect with holidays and family outings. However, by the start of the 1950s it was clear that United had unearthed several outstanding schoolboy prospects and Jimmy was rubbing his hands in anticipation of what they could achieve.

As has already been mentioned, Jackie Blachflower was among the first 'Busby Babes', along with Dennis Viollet, Mark Jones, David Pegg, Geoff Bent, Albert Scanlon, John Doherty and Jeff Whitefoot.

However, the second wave was even more promising, as it included the likes of Duncan Edwards, Bobby Charlton, Wilf McGuinness, Ronnie Cope and Eddie Colman.

A typical Jimmy Murphy day would see him rise early, make the fire, a cup of tea for himself and his wife and breakfast for the children before saying his goodbyes. He caught the train into the city centre and then went on to either Old Trafford or the Cliff training ground. Everyone knew Jimmy for his cheery disposition and friendly manner.

Once at work, he would attend to the details in hand, open his mail and read match reports and scouting information. Murphy and his assistants were all moral men to the bone. Games and training were the topic, as they drank their cups of tea. Ideas and theories would be planned and discussed. Individual coaching sessions would be decided on and set out. Once the players were in their training togs, Jimmy and his assistants would be out on the pitch working with the lads. Tom Curry, known as 'Tosher' to everyone, was the first-team trainer. He had been with Newcastle United for a number of years before joining United in 1934. He was a dedicated man. Bill Inglis, who had played for Raith Rovers, was his assistant. On arriving at the ground, they would don their white coats - they looked like a pair of ice-cream vendors. The players would rib them mercilessly but it never bothered them in the slightest.

Arthur Powell, another loyal servant, was in charge of the groundstaff lads and would set out their duties. There was a great deal of laughing and joking and mickey taking. The players, young and old, would play tricks on Murphy and the other coaches, but there was not the slightest hint of any sort of backbiting or jealousy from any of the training staff. Busby would certainly not tolerate it under any circumstances and both he and Murphy fostered a close family atmosphere. You will not find any record of dismissals of any staff at Old Trafford from the moment Busby took control.

Ever since he joined Manchester United, Jimmy Murphy had been associated with so many star players that some people seemed to think that he was like a conjuror capable of producing rabbits from a hat. The list of players he had groomed was endless but Jimmy would be the first to admit that there was nothing magical about it. In fact, it was a long and tedious job before both coach and player could fashion a footballer of distinction. An aptitude for hard work, good physical fitness and a devotion to the profession were some of the qualities required.

Despite the daily grind, Jimmy maintained that grooming was a fascinating task. "It was a great thrill to spot the spark of genius in a youngster and carefully cultivate it until he shines for all to see. It's fascinating to watch the development of youngsters. Some mature according to plan right from their early days at the club while others, who are equally promising, inexplicably fade and drop out of the game. A few reach their best so late and so slowly that you almost give up on them in despair. Nevertheless, there are the odd one or two footballers who are so obviously thoroughbreds that you can place your complete faith in them," remarked Jimmy.

John Peter Doherty

Murphy, perhaps remembering his own good fortune as a player, always stressed that every player needs a slice of luck. John Doherty joined United as an amateur in 1950. He had played for Manchester and Lancashire Schools. He turned professional in 1952. As a smooth, classy forward with a terrific shot, he had the poise of a thoroughbred and appeared in the Youth team with great success. He was another of the original Babes, making his first team debut in 1952, aged just 17. However, he picked up a niggling knee injury that plagued him throughout his career. He had a cartilage operation and at the time those operations were usually career-threatening. After his two years' National Service in the RAF, John returned in the 1955-56 season and appeared 16 times, enough to win a Championship medal.

By this time, the competition for places in United's first team was fierce, to say the least. John Doherty's knee kept playing up and at 22 he was transferred to Leicester City for a £6,500 fee. Eight months later he was given a free transfer. John had been heartbroken at leaving the Reds and ironically, on the day of the Munich disaster he was having further surgery on his wonky joint. After a brief spell as player-manager at Rugby Town he returned to Manchester and settled down to regular employment. His footballing career had finished at 23!

John is now on the former players' committee and can be found at Old Trafford at every home game. John speaks about Jimmy with reverence. As an example of Jimmy's particular coaching style he recalled a game he played at Blackpool for United Reserves against the Tangerines. The Reds were winning 8-0 when John quickly took a throw-in. A Blackpool player intercepted John's hurried throw and passed the ball downfield to his forwards who scored a goal. Nevertheless, United won the match 9-1. The next morning, John was lapping Old Trafford when he spotted a serious-looking, frosty-faced Jimmy Murphy walking towards him from the tunnel under the main stand. Without a smile, Murphy beckoned John to him. "I want you back here after lunch, m'lad," barked Jimmy. "You cost us a goal on Saturday." At 2pm precisely, Jimmy was waiting at Old Trafford with a ball at his feet. John was in his tracksuit and they went over the technique of the throw-in that Jimmy claimed had cost United a goal. Jimmy took throw-ins himself, then got John to do it, not once, but over and over again until his arms felt like heavy pieces of lead. "Perfection," said John, "that's what he was after. 'Do it right, son,' he urged me, 'do it simply.' He was tough, but he did it for our own good. He was a great man."

The lad with the Monroe wiggle

Eddie Colman was a Salford lad to the marrow. Born in November 1936, Eddie was the only child of Dick and Elizabeth, known as Liz or Lizzie to friends and neighbours. The Colmans lived in the tough, working-class Ordsall area of Salford which is situated quite near Salford

Docks. Eddie's father was quite a useful amateur player around the area. The family lived in a two-up, two-down on Archie Street, which was the original Coronation Street shown at the beginning of each episode of the popular television series. He attended Ordsall Council School and was a hyperactive youngster, always up to all sorts of mischief. He was football mad, although he liked playing cricket as well and represented both Salford and Lancashire Boys. Eddie played inside-forward for Salford Boys and later, Lancashire Boys. "I thought Salford Boys officials had only selected me because they were short and needed to make up the numbers," remarked Eddie a few years after leaving school.

As a schoolboy Eddie was popular with teachers, pupils and neighbours. He had a bubbly personality with a perpetual smile on his round, chubby, angelic face. Playing for Salford Boys against Stockport Boys at the Cliff, Matt Busby and Jimmy Murphy decided they would watch the game and spot any likely youngsters. Within a few minutes Matt turned to Jimmy and no words were necessary. They knew he was United material. "How he never got picked for England Schoolboys I'll never know," said Jimmy.

At 15, he stood just 5 feet 7 inches and never grew an inch taller, but packed into that diminutive frame was a heart as big as a giant and a football brain way beyond his tender years. Both Wolverhampton Wanderers and Bolton Wanderers were hoping to sign Eddie onto their staff. But while he was playing for Salford Boys, he hurt his back and as United's Old Trafford ground was only across the bridge from the Colman home, he went there for treatment. He liked the atmosphere of the place and after that, Bolton and Wolves were never in the hunt.

Eddie's cousin, Albert Valentine, a few years Eddie's senior but his best pal, believed that up to the age of 15, Eddie was a little villain, not in the criminal sense, but someone who could have been easily led into trouble. As it turned out, Eddie turned into a young gentleman with beautiful manners. He joined the Reds in 1952 as an amateur and made progress through the junior teams and eventually into United's Youth Cup side. When Joe Armstrong first set eyes on him in a game on a

Salford school pitch he told Murphy: "If he had a grass skirt on him, he could move like a hula-hula dancer, he's sensational."

It was obvious to everyone at Old Trafford that the boy Colman was another 'special'. He developed into a character and all the players and staff liked him immensely. He had 'street smarts' and referred to the senior players as Mr Rowley, Mr Pearson, Mr Aston and Mr Carey. The older players fell for this charm from Eddie. Everyone loved how the youngster could wind up Jimmy Murphy. He was Jimmy's ideal pupil. Small, with a brilliant football brain, bags of flair and loads of 'bottle'.

Big Duncan Edwards had joined the club at the same time as Eddie. They became close friends and looked like 'This and That', so different in size were they. Eddie often ribbed Duncan. "What a wonderful partnership these two were," remarked Murphy. "They complemented each other marvellously. The best wing-half, or to use the modern terminology, midfield pair seen for many years."

Eddie became the life and soul of the club and was popular with everyone. He was part of United's successful Youth team, where his deceptive body swerve and dazzling dribbling ability had the United fans mesmerised and calling him 'the player with the Marilyn Monroe wiggle'. However, despite the suggestion of effeminacy about Eddie's movement, he was as tough as they come. Called up for his two-year stint of National Service in the Army, he became the Catterick Camp ratcatcher, among other duties.

He made his first team debut against Bolton in 1955, aged 19, while still in the services. During the game he came face to face with the ferocious Nat Lofthouse. Eddie calmly rolled the ball back and forth, sold the old 'Lion of Vienna' a dummy and swivelled past him. "I couldn't believe it," recalled Nat, "he completely bamboozled me with his body swerve. Unbelievable!"

Jimmy Murphy said Colman was a creative genius and had the experience of a veteran. He also said it was only when you played with him that you could appreciate the wisdom he had acquired. "Eddie was a tremendous worker," added Jimmy. Like all great players, Eddie knew when to move into open spaces that demanded opponents mark him. He enjoyed every minute of playing football and possessed the ability to make things easier for his colleagues because he was a thinker. It was Jimmy's view that Eddie's creativeness made him a world-class footballer. As an attacking wing-half his ambition was to create openings. When he had the ball, Eddie knew what he wanted to do with it and how to change the play.

So what makes a Manchester United player?

Jimmy was often asked how he spotted a budding footballing star. He would assure the questioner that it was certainly no accident. He said that United had a first-class organisation working behind the scenes seven days a week to make certain that the most important games were covered and that United received a vast amount of information from fans, former players, schoolteachers and 'amateur scouts.' They also received letters tipping them off about certain prospective players. Jimmy emphasised that he always looked for skill in any player he was interested in. He and Matt Busby could spot a player within ten minutes of watching him.

"I can tell a player with talent straight away," said Jimmy, adding that he might have to have a second or third observational check to see if the lad was the right type to bring to Old Trafford. The system Murphy built at Old Trafford during the 1950s and which was the foundation of everything that followed later, was the envy of managers and clubs throughout Great Britain. So what made a Manchester United player? Jimmy said ability and determination to become a professional footballer first and foremost. Secondly, he must listen to the advice doled out by Busby, himself and the United coaches, and thirdly, and this was most important, he must want to play for Manchester United and have club spirit at heart. Jimmy had shown several boys the door, lads who were potentially good players, but who by their attitude and behaviour at the club were not up to these high standards. Every club official could reel off the names of youngsters who didn't live up to their potential for one reason or another. Bad luck, a bad injury or the lad's own temperament were usually among the many reasons cited.

As if to illustrate the high demands made by United's coaching staff during this period, Oldham manager Billy Wootton tells the story of a player Matt Busby was interested in. "We arranged to meet at the White City greyhound track near Old Trafford," Billy recalled. "When I got there, Matt was with Johnny Carey, Henry Cockburn and one or two other players. We got talking about the possibility of Ray Addington joining United. Being honest, and having a great deal of respect for Matt, I thought it only right and proper that I tell him of my misgivings concerning Addington.

"'Matt,' I said, 'he's scored a lot of goals, but his stamina is very suspect, it really is.' I told him that I'd tried everything to rectify the problem but with no solution. In fact, I had to devise a team plan which suited the player. On hearing this, a frown came over Matt's face - he had been having a bad night, six of his fancied greyhounds had lost. Then Carey piped up and asked me: 'He can't work?' - meaning running up and down the field. 'No, not really,' I replied. 'Oh, in that case we don't want him,' said Carey. That was the end of that," Billy concluded, adding tellingly, "I later sold Addington to Manchester City for £10,000.

"In all my meetings, socially or on football matters with Matt, I never once saw Jimmy Murphy, not once! They never drank together. Jimmy was in his element working with the players at Old Trafford or the Cliff. He was always coaching. Matt was the figurehead alright, always gracious and charming with a warm smile but it was Murphy who put in the long hours helping the youngsters. Without him they would have been lost."

*

During the early 1950s Jimmy often mentioned a player named Alick Jeffrey. Never heard of him? Well, but for a twist of fate, Alick could have been the most famous British footballer ever.

Alick, like Duncan Edwards, was one of the most thrilling and sought-after youngsters of the 1950s. Many good judges have stated that Jeffrey would have been sensational if only life had treated him more kindly. Jimmy reckoned that the young Doncaster lad was destined to be the English Pele. According to Jimmy, Jeffrey had the lot: strength, ball control, physique, a football brain way beyond his years, pace and a powerful shot. "He was like a dominating presence in the forward line, just as Duncan Edwards was at half-back," remarked Jimmy.

Alick was born in the Yorkshire village of Rawmarsh near Rotherham in 1939. The lad's unique footballing skills saved him from joining his father down the pit as a miner. Instead, he played for England schoolboys and Jimmy and Matt thought he was set to join their football academy at Old Trafford, when it was discovered that he had signed for Doncaster Rovers. They were, of course, bitterly disappointed but kept tabs on his progress.

Young Jeffrey went on to make his first team debut for Doncaster Rovers, then in the Second Division, when he was just 15 years and 229 days old. He signed professional forms in 1956 and quickly added to his England schoolboy caps when he was selected for the England youth and amateur teams, aged just 16. Playing in an FA Cup tie he scored two beautiful goals which sent Aston Villa out of the cup. In later years Murphy's friend, Irish international Peter Doherty, who was his manager at Doncaster, said that Jeffrey would have been even better than George Best. "I have no doubt in my mind that Alick would have been the greatest goalscorer that England has ever seen. He could hit the ball over 30 yards harder than many players do over ten."

A dedicated trainer, Alick was always willing to listen and improve his game. He became known as the greatest footballing talent, the next wonder boy after Duncan Edwards. The great Newcastle and England centre-forward Jackie Millburn described him as the greatest young player he had ever set eyes on. "Alick will become a genius," added Stanley Matthews. Matt Busby and Jimmy were still keen to add him to their squad.

In October 1956, after Alick had scored 15 goals in just 17 matches in only his second season, Matt started transfer talks with Doncaster. He and Murphy envisaged Jeffrey playing alongside the other Busby Babes to rapturous applause and acclaim. Jeffrey spent a week training at Old Trafford and loved every minute of it. "I will come and sign you," Matt told him, adding, "you'll be a Manchester United player soon." However, before the transfer was finalised, Jeffrey was selected for England in an under-23 match against France at Ashton Gate, Bristol, on October 17th. It was his second cap for the under-23s - and his last. On this cold, wet, miserable winter's night, Alick broke his leg in two places. It was a terrible injury and his career looked over. The FA paid out compensation in full. The lad was heartbroken, and in 1957 Alick started singing in a trio along with his father and his former team-mate Charlie Williams, a tough-tackling centre-half, on the nightclub circuit. Charlie, of course, went on to fame and became a household name in the 1970s on *The Comedians*, the highly successful television series.

A couple of years later Alick attempted a comeback. He couldn't rejoin Doncaster because the FA demanded he would have to pay back the insurance money. So he played for Skegness Town, but fate saw him break his other leg. In 1961, fed up, he emigrated to Australia where he played for two years before coming back home in 1963. In December that year, he re-signed for Doncaster Rovers after the insurance compensation was settled. He played in 191 games, scoring 95 goals and everything seemed to be looking up for Alick when more heartache hit him. In 1966, he was involved in a car accident in which the driver, club captain John Nicholson, was killed. Alick was in a coma and laid up for a few months before he ever played again at Doncaster's Belle Vue ground.

Still, so impressive was he that Don Revie, then manager of Leeds, considered making a bid for him. However, for various reasons, Revie dropped the idea and Jeffrey joined Lincoln City in 1969, after a dispute with the then Doncaster boss Lawrie McMenemy. After playing just 22 times for his new club and scoring only three goals, Maurice Setters, Doncaster's new manager, asked him to give it another try at Doncaster, to which he readily agreed. By this time, Alick was in his early thirties and all the past injury problems seemed to catch up with him. He soon retired from football and bought a pub.

Over the intervening years people have often discussed Jeffrey and the salutory lesson of his rollercoaster career. "Alick Jeffrey would have been one of the biggest stars in football but for that first injury," said Nobby Stiles. In 1969, his former manager Peter Doherty remarked: "What a tragedy it was for Alick, his club and football when he broke his leg at Bristol." Jimmy Murphy always believed that Jeffrey would have been phenomenal playing with the Busby Babes during the 1950s but added: "You can have all the talent in the world, but you still need a huge slice of old-fashioned luck." For all his setbacks, injuries and bad luck, Alick was never bitter about what fate dealt him. He was often asked about the time he almost joined Manchester United and whether he regretted it? He said it would have been a dream come true for him but added: "Breaking my leg for England Under-23s might have saved my life. The injury certainly destroyed my potential and transfer to United, but I'd most probably have been on that plane in Munich, so I have to be grateful."

The Greatest!

Jimmy reckoned Duncan Edwards was the greatest player he ever brought through at United. The two loved and respected each other. "Any manager lucky enough to have big Dunc had half a team," Murphy was fond of saying. Matt Busby agreed: "Duncan Edwards was the best signing Manchester United ever made."

In 1952, the English First Division was falling over itself to sign the most promising footballer the British Isles has ever produced. As a youth Duncan was like a giant. Standing 5 feet 11 inches and weighing a mighty 13 stone 7 pounds, Edwards had the chest of a blacksmith striker, legs like young oak trees and a neck like Mike Tyson. And he got even stronger and better as he got older. "Duncan trained with exceptional enthusiasm," said Murphy. "The added incentive was that he was pleasing Jimmy," added Albert Scanlon.

If you could imagine the perfect footballer for your dream team, it would have been big Duncan. He truly was a colossus and no cause was lost with him on your side. Over the years, there have been many comparisons made to Duncan. Terry Venables, Kevin Beattie of Ipswich Town, former Manchester United captain Bryan Robson and more recently Liverpool's Stephen Gerrard have all been compared to the Dudley giant. But with respect to these players, they couldn't hold a candle to Duncan Edwards.

Robson stood out, in his generation, as captain of United and England, as a defender and for his midfield drive and tenacity. Gerrard may well do the same for Liverpool and England over the coming years. However, Duncan was far better in all these areas. He compares more than favourably to both players' records. He was capped 18 times for England before he was 21 - that in itself speaks volumes for his all-round creativity and brilliance. Many of the players mentioned could possibly have played in several different positions on the field but I doubt they could have played at centre-half, centre-forward or inside-forward with the class and authority Duncan showed throughout his brief career.

That Duncan joined United is put down to the kind of quirky fate which inevitably makes a good story. In 1952, Busby was eager to sign a promising England Schoolboy international inside-forward named Alec Farrall who lived in Hoylake. As fate would have it, Busby's close friend Joe Mercer lived in the same area as young Farrall. Matt asked his pal what the possibilities were of him getting the lad. Genial Joe had been coaching the England schoolboy team at this time and Matt obviously knew that Joe would know the capabilities of the player better than anyone else. Mercer explained that Farrall had set his heart on joining Everton. Busby, though disappointed, promptly dismissed the player from his thoughts. The canny Mercer then added: "Matt, there is a much better kid than Farrall and he's only 14." Matt listened intently. "He's the best of the present bunch of schoolboy internationals. This lad is potentially brilliant. He will make a world-beater if I'm any judge of talent," said Mercer in the colourful, enthusiastic way he had when talking about his favourite subjects, football and players. Busby asked for his name. "Duncan Edwards," replied Joe. That was the only recommendation the United manager needed. He immediately set out to watch this youngster himself and alerted Jimmy Murphy, Bert Whalley and Joe Armstrong. Over the coming weeks they all watched the youngster. Even Reg Priest, United's Midlands scout, was told to pursue the lad.

After several United officials had watched Duncan several times, Busby asked Jimmy what he really thought of the lad? "He can't fail to make it," responded Murphy. "I think he's a budding genius, we must move mountains to make sure we sign him." The only stumbling block was that both of them knew that he practically lived on the doorstep of United's fiercest rivals of that period - Wolverhampton Wanderers! They also knew that Wolves manager Stan Cullis had been charting Duncan's every move. This caused the pair a great deal of concern. However, it was in United's favour that they had taken over the 'glamour club' tag from Arsenal, as a result of the swashbuckling 1948 Cup-winning team - all the neutrals followed United.

Then again, it wasn't just United and Wolves who were anxious to obtain young Edwards' signature - the entire English First Division were after him. However, Busby and Murphy fretted for nothing because Duncan quickly let it be known that he wanted to join United. He told family and friends he admired their style of play. However, unlike today when kids of ten and eleven are being snatched by clubs, in those days no club dare approach a boy until he left school.

Sure enough, once Duncan reached 15, hordes of prospective managers converged on the Edwards' doorstep. It was a known fact that in those days many clubs were only too willing to offer payments as a signing-on fee. Times were hard and nobody begrudged the players' families payment for their talented and much sought-after sons. Busby phoned Murphy and told him to get things in motion regarding his immediate signature. The United supremo knew the competition was likely to be fierce and dirty but he was determined he would match his rivals word for word. However he made it clear that he had no intention of giving Duncan anything other than the promise that if he went to Old Trafford he would get the finest coaching and the opportunity of becoming the worldbeater Joe Mercer had forecast he would be.

As soon as Matt met Duncan and his parents in the living room of their little house in Dudley, he became his usual diplomatic self. Using all his charm, he convinced the Edwards that Old Trafford was the place for their son to be. His quiet manner and dignity left a huge impression on Duncan's mother and father. However, there was no need for Matt to 'sell' United to the lad; his battle was won when Duncan said: "Manchester United are the greatest club in the world. I'd give anything to play for your team, Mr Busby."

However, it was left to Murphy and Bert Whalley to settle the deal. A couple of weeks later, Reg Priest phoned Jimmy Murphy and urged him to get down to Dudley as quickly as possible. It seemed that other leading clubs were making overtures to Duncan and his parents to join their club. Bolton Wanderers were trying to get Duncan to change his mind and join them, because his cousin, Dennis Stephens, was already on their books. As a result, Jimmy and Bert set off for the Midlands in the early hours of the morning. Both were tired, but if they wanted the prodigy they needed to sign and seal the deal. Their car pulled up outside Duncan's house at 3.30am. Bert knocked the family up. After a lot of talking with Mr and Mrs Edwards, Jimmy said he needed to speak to Duncan. Shortly afterwards, Duncan walked down the stairs in his pyjamas and told them he had already told Matt Busby that Manchester United were the only club he wanted to join. He signed for the Reds there and then. "What a signing!" Murphy said later. "In travelling expenses and meals Duncan must have cost us in the region of £100!"

Duncan arrived in Manchester along with Gordon Clayton, his England schoolboy colleague. They were put in digs with about half a dozen other youngsters who had joined United. He played in several positions for United when the need arose but his favourite position was wing-half or left-half in the number 6 shirt.

On Easter Monday 1953, Duncan reported at Old Trafford for his duties as a groundstaff worker as usual. A few minutes later Matt Busby walked into the dressing room where the ground staff changed, walked over to Duncan smiled and told him: "Go and get your football boots, son, you're playing for the first team against Cardiff City." Although he was pleased with the news, Duncan took it calmly and asked Busby for permission to phone his parents, then ran to Ma Watson's - the best landlady anyone could wish for, said Duncan. His mother and father made plans to travel up to Old Trafford.

"His mother and me are as excited as a couple of kids," remarked Edwards senior, adding, "Duncan is the calmest member of the family. He won't let United down - he's used to playing in front of big crowds when he played for England Schoolboys." Even the older, more experienced players like Johnny Carey, John Aston, Jack Rowley and Stan Pearson proclaimed big Duncan's virtues and it is very unusual for older players to praise younger up-and-coming players who could conceivably take their places in the first team. Duncan was the fifth teenager to make his League debut for United that season - Johnny Scott, Eddie Lewis, David Pegg and John Doherty were the others on their way to soccer fame.

In one of his early games for the senior side, United played Manchester City, who were playing their deep-lying centre-forward tactics, or the 'Revie Plan' as it became known. Don Revie, who became better known as manager of Leeds United and England, was City's architect in making this plan work. There was no doubt that Revie was a 'thinker' and he often spoke about playing against Duncan when the lad first got into the senior team.

"I remember when Duncan first played against Manchester City. He had a habit of taking the ball upfield into our penalty area. At the time, we were playing our deep-lying game and we used to use Duncan's early immaturity as a means of starting our attacks," Revie recalled. "Roy

Paul, our captain, a very experienced player, used to let Duncan bring the ball up to our penalty box and we would bring our defence back into the box. When young Edwards tried to pass the ball to a colleague or attempt a shot from 20 yards or so, our packed defence would benefit by receiving the ball and swiftly switch it to the gap behind him. However, after Murphy cottoned on to what Edwards was doing wrong he told him to give a short ball to his team-mates in front of him while they were in the clear. Edwards had everything a great player could be expected to possess. He was immaculately built and had a wonderful temperament. Duncan Edwards became a magnificent footballer and it was Jimmy Murphy who helped mould him into the world-class player he became."

At 17, Duncan appeared in the England 'B' and Under-23 teams, and in 1955, at just eighteen, he became the youngest player to be capped for England when he shared in a 7-2 victory over Scotland. At 19, he won his first First Division Championship medal and at 20 he played in the 1957 FA Cup Final against Aston Villa at Wembley. It was little wonder then, that both Matt Busby and Jimmy Murphy were extremely confident that in Duncan Edwards, they had the lynchpin of a team for years to come.

Indeed it was Edwards' enthusiasm that seemed to lift United from the very good to the great. When he ran out on the field home or away, he would be like a young puppy, jumping up high, heading an imaginary ball and doing little exercises as the other players were shooting in at Ray Wood. Today, they talk about midfielders having an 'engine'. Well this lad Edwards was a half-back line on his own. He was a dynamic player in any position and lived for football morning, noon and night.

In the 1956-57 season Duncan played in 94 games for England, Manchester United and the Army, with whom he was serving his two-year National Service. Amazingly, in his 95th game, for England in Czechoslovakia, he scored twice with ferocious cannonball shots and was voted Man of the Match.

Bobby Charlton, a little younger than Duncan, was in the same

Army team as his Old Trafford club-mate. "I will never forget one Army cup-tie when we were trailing 2-4. Duncan and I moved up into the forward line and changed the score to 7-4 in our favour! Duncan scored four times in a ten-minute spell and, for one of the goals - and I am not exaggerating - he hit the ball so hard that the goalkeeper started to dive, flinched, and then deliberately got out of the way of the ball. English football has and will produce other talented players, perhaps another genius. But there will only ever be one Duncan Edwards."

The game of football and Manchester United were Duncan's only passions. No matter what team he played for, be it United's 'A' team, Youths, reserves or first team, he would treat it as if he was playing in the World Cup Final, so enthusiastic was he. He was like a tornado, up helping the forwards trying to score with his rocket shots, then in the next instant he would be back in his own half, tackling ferociously, winning the ball and starting another attacking move. He was also one of the most loyal people you could wish for.

Jimmy Murphy coached Duncan from the moment he arrived at Old Trafford. It wasn't unusual to see the two of them out on the pitch in hail, rain or snow practising techniques, free kicks, taking corners, heading, tackling and shooting. Murphy would go through every little detail bit by bit and Duncan was an eager pupil. He would poke fun in a light-hearted way at his mentor. When Jimmy was coaching some youngsters, Duncan would ask if he could join in and help. He became, even at this young age, one of the world's outstanding half-backs, and earned the accolades and the jealous glances of coaches throughout the continent. He really was a human tornado: he loved to attack, but because he played in a successful United team he was well covered, and the power and drive he produced time after time brought him vital goals. Nevertheless, he never forgot that his first job was to put the brakes on the opposition forwards. Duncan, the mobile powerhouse, was a wing-half who proved the accuracy of the old maxim that to have a top-class player in the half-back line was half the secret of a team's success.

Other United youngsters, such as Wilf McGuinness, a left-half like Edwards, said that he looked up to his powerfully-built team-mate. "When I joined United, straight from school, I had captained Manchester Boys and England Schoolboys," said Wilf. "Of course, I had heard and seen Duncan play for United's Youth team but when I joined the club and saw him close-up in training, wow, I looked at my physique in the mirror in the changing room and had a sly look over at Dunc and I thought: 'How on earth am I going to dislodge him from the left-half position, or even compete with him?' What a fantastic player, oh my God, he was in a class of his own, something very special, very special indeed. He could do the lot. Jimmy Murphy worked hard with all of us but he had a unique relationship with Duncan."

"There was no star distinction among the Busby Babes," Bobby Charlton adds. "However, right from the start, we all recognised Duncan was outstanding in our all-conquering Youth side. We used to get double figures every week without fail, and none of us were surprised when Duncan got a regular place in the first team at only seventeen."

*

Jimmy was reminiscing one day about the time he first became manager of the Welsh national team in 1957. He used to tell this amusing story whenever Duncan's name cropped up. Wales were playing England and while the Welsh team were getting changed, Jimmy started his usual meticulous preparation. He explained the tactics and went through every little aspect of the England team. Starting from the goalkeeper, through the full-backs, wing-halves, wingers, inside-forwards and centre-forward, Jimmy pointed out to each individual Welshman the strengths and weaknesses of his English opponent. Who to watch out for, which England players didn't like being closely marked, the danger men and so on. Finally Murphy reached a final crescendo: "Right lads! Let's get out there and show these English players how the Welsh Dragons can perform."

As the team stood up and made their way into the tunnel for their march onto the pitch, little Reg Davies piped up. The classy Newcastle inside-forward had sat uncomfortably through Jimmy's team talk, waiting patiently for his opponent's name to be mentioned.

He asked Jimmy if he could have a quite word with him. Jimmy was agitated and eager to get to his seat in the dugout and hurriedly asked Reg what he wanted. Reg, jogging lightly on the balls of his feet, was a sight to behold. He had matchstick-thin legs and bony knees, a sallow, anaemic-looking face and weighed in at about nine stones soaking wet through. Eventually, in a strong Welsh accent, Reg ventured: "Well now Jimmy, you have mentioned every other player's opponent, but you've not mentioned mine. Why not?" Jimmy could never stop himself smiling when recalling the story. He looked at Reg, put his arm around his shoulder and said in a soft tone: "Duncan Edwards is marking you today, son. Now there's a big crowd out there and the St John's Ambulance men and the First Aid team are going to be busy enough attending to the crowd, so I don't want you getting hurt. So just keep out of his effing way." Reg looking hurt but replied: "Oh, alright Jimmy. Whatever you say" and ran out.

What is clear is that Duncan loved Murphy. The young giant loved the way Jimmy described teams and individual players. But he was not averse to pulling his mentor's leg on occasion. Four months before the Munich tragedy, Jimmy and Duncan found themselves in opposition. Duncan was playing for England against Jimmy's Welsh team. In the week leading up to the match Duncan kept ribbing Jimmy about how England were going to annihilate the Welsh. Murphy's pride wouldn't let his young protégé get away with having a 'go' at his team and the banter was coming thick and fast leading up to the game. Jimmy knew Duncan was joking and he took it all in good heart. However, on the actual day of the match at Ninian Park, England were cruising to a 4-1 victory and Jimmy's voice could be heard loud and clear imploring the Welsh team to get stuck in and shouting other instructions, but it was all in vain. Duncan had been a powerhouse for England, breaking up the Welsh attacks, then delivering accurate pin-point passes to the

England forwards before breaking forward himself and joining them upfield. The Welsh team didn't know how to contain him - he was having a 'blinder' and was as near perfection as one could hope to witness.

Towards the end of the game, England were coasting it and Duncan rushed to take a throw-in not far from the Welsh dugout where Jimmy sat red-faced, bellowing instructions. As Duncan bent down to pick up the ball for the throw in, Jimmy was out of the Welsh dugout screeching at his players. Duncan smiled broadly at Murphy and commiserated: "You're not having much luck today Jimmy, are you?" Murphy was beside himself and as Duncan got ready to throw the ball, Jimmy shouted loudly: "You just wait till you report back to Old Trafford, son, I'll be telling you about everything you've been doing wrong in this match." The rest of the Welsh officials in the dugout with Murphy and the crowd who could hear his remarks were in hysterics as Murphy attempted to chastise Edwards, who had hardly putting a foot wrong all afternoon. It was a simple 'wind-up' by a young player who would be hailed as a huge superstar in today's highly-publicised soccer business.

Duncan's bike

One cold February morning in 1958, Duncan Edwards was pedalling furiously towards the Cliff training ground. His big frame was hunched low over his new racing bicycle as a fan, also riding a bike, glanced across and shouted:"Hey, Duncan, are we going to beat Arsenal on Saturday?" Duncan took one hand off the handle and smiled an acknowledgement: "Of course we are." The midfield colossus started pedalling a bit faster as he was slightly late for training.

Tom Curry and Bill Inglis, wearing their long white coats, were perished as Duncan rode through the big wooden gates and came to a halt before dismounting half-apologetically. "What's up then, Duncan? Walking not good enough for you?" said Currie whimsically. "It's my new bike. It's all right - the Boss gave me permission," replied Edwards.

Bill Inglis examined the bike and sniffed: "It'll be a Rolls-Royce and chauffeur next. What's the game coming to?" Duncan started laughing. "Not on twenty quid a week, it won't." Duncan was told to hurry up and get changed.

Out on the pitch, Jimmy Murphy was in his element, track-suited, taking part in a five-a-side. Duncan watched in amusement as Jimmy impishly got close to Eddie Colman on three separate occasions and niggled him with a shove, and an ankle tap, before finally making an over-the-ball tackle. Eddie's temper finally snapped and he brought down Murphy. Jimmy glanced up at him coolly. "Thanks Eddie. It took you forty minutes to do that. Why so long?" Eddie helped his coach to his feet and apologised profusely. "Don't apologise, son, always play it hard," said Murphy. Later, in the changing room, Eddie towelled himself after a shower as Duncan sat half-dressed on a bench, laughing at the incident he had just witnessed between 'Tapper' Murphy and Colman.

David Pegg

Born in Highfield, Doncaster, on the 20th September 1935, David Pegg played for Doncaster and Yorkshire Schoolboys. He went on to appear five times for England Schoolboys during the 1950-51 season, making his debut for the international schoolboys alongside future club-mate Duncan Edwards. David was a natural left-footed player who joined United straight from school. Despite an obvious talent for the game, David's mother Jessie was extremely concerned when her son left school. The lad himself was a Doncaster Rovers follower but United were among several First Division clubs eager to sign him. United had been trailing him for months as Whalley, Murphy and later Busby followed genial Joe Armstrong's recommendation. Eventually, Matt called to visit David and his family and Jessie was so impressed by Busby's calm, reassuring nature and exceedingly good manners that from the moment he spoke to her, it was no contest as far as other clubs were concerned.

David signed for United for £10 and he was soon starring in United's junior teams and later the FA Youth Cup team. Jimmy and Bert Whalley groomed him for stardom. He, Tommy Taylor, Bobby Charlton, Wilf McGuinness and Eddie Colman were close friends and knocked about with each other. Pegg was one of the first United players to own his own car, a Vauxhall Victor, and he often spoke about the time when he played for England Schoolboys at the famous Wembley Stadium.

"I have had some wonderful moments in my short career," he said, shortly after making his United first team debut. "To play for England boys was a rare thing, but to face Wales at the most famous stadium in the country was absolutely incredible. I can recall that time as if it was only a week ago. Given the day off school, I travelled down to London to meet the rest of the boys and officials. After booking into the hotel, and this was a treat in itself to a youngster like me, we were whisked off to another glamorous location - Highbury. I had read in the football magazines about Arsenal and the traditions of this club were something I knew about long before that first visit to train for the following day's match. We beat Wales 3-0 Jimmy Murphy always screws his face up when I remind him of this occasion, which is quite often. Behind me in the England team was a big, chunky lad, who already looked man-sized. His name was Duncan Edwards! Little did we know then that only a few years later we would be together in a championship team with Manchester United." Edwards would appear with David in every representative game he was selected for both as a junior and as a senior.

"What a great help it has been to get the service from this outstanding half-back," David continued. "I couldn't be happier playing for the Red Devils. My biggest problem was leaving home for the first time at fifteen; still, the time passed quickly. I was an apprentice joiner for my first two years and only trained on Tuesday and Thursday evenings."

Jimmy, as with all the talented kids at United, would spend hours on drills with David Pegg, working particularly on his delivery of accurate centres for his colleagues. David had fancied himself as an inside-forward at school. However, when he reached United, he was turned into a speedy and majestic outside-left. Long before George Best came on the scene, David was a pin-up favourite with the girls. This good-looking, immaculately groomed youth, a young Victor Mature look-alike some said, was swamped with female fanmail.

"After a spell in the third team and some great coaching from Jimmy Murphy, I was selected to play for the reserves in 1951," Pegg continued. "This was a wonderful opportunity and a huge step up the ladder. About a year later, I signed as a professional, another milestone. December 5th 1952 was the date. It was a Friday and the teamsheet seemed longer than usual coming down from Matt Busby's office. When it was pinned on the noticeboard in the dressing room, I hurried over to look. I felt disappointed - my name wasn't on the reserve team sheet - but in a split second as I noticed this, I saw I was selected for the first team. Also making his debut was another 17-year-old, inside-right Johnny Doherty, and we must have brought the team good luck."

David's inside-forward partner was the legendary Stan Pearson. Before the team went out on the field, Stan gave his young partner words of wisdom and encouragement and, as David admitted, the passing and advice doled out to him throughout the match was invaluable. "Stan was a lovely, quiet person and he taught me a tremendous amount. So too did Johnny Aston, the former England full-back. Jimmy Murphy was also pleased as punch for me and he influenced me a great deal."

David was never a great goalscorer but when he scored his first goal for the first team, after about 12 weeks, the other players never stopped pulling his leg. It happened at Sunderland. The ball went over to his left wing and, first time, he sliced it back into the middle. Someone got in the way and the ball bounced back as David was rushing in. He slammed the ball, it ricocheted off one player's leg, then another, before bouncing into the back of the net. Johnny Aston and Henry Cockburn

Jimmy Murphy's reputation as a footballer at Ton Petre school in the Welsh Valleys **(above)** led to schoolboy caps for Wales.
Jimmy made his debut **(right)** against England in 1922

A terrier-like player, Murphy made his way into professional
football with first Cardiff and later West Bromwich Albion.
He went on to win 22 caps for Wales at wing-half, in the line-up
(above - bottom row, 2nd from left) v. Ireland 1935.
Jimmy later starred in the Victory internationals for Wales
(below - bottom row with the ball at his feet)

Above: Jimmy was active in Africa during World War II and later as a PE instructor in Bari, Italy. It was following one of his infamous football talks that Matt Busby recruited him. **Below:** Jimmy shows former England Test cricketer Bill Bowes around a ruined Old Trafford in 1946. It would take another three years until United could play home games there.

Above: The team that made United famous.
Back Row: Delaney, Warner, Pearson, Crompton, Rowley, Lynn,
Chilton, Murphy (asst. manager). **Front Row:** Morris, Anderson, Carey,
Aston, Cockburn, Mitten.
Below: Matt and Jimmy take in a refurbished Old Trafford

Jimmy's coaching team
With right-hand man Bert Whalley.
(left) and with little Joe Armstrong and Bert Whalley
(below)

The camaraderie and spirit built by these four men under Busby were crucial to the development of old and young players alike.

The Ideal Right-hand man:

Jimmy's influence quickly grew as a succession of youth products were promoted to first team action. The result - the 1955/56 League Championship is shown below in a souvenir signed team picture.

Regards & good wishes
Jimmy Murphy

Good Wishes
Matt Busby

Manchester United League Champions
—— 1955 —— 1956 ——

United's first taste of Europe

Jimmy, Matt and Tom Curry with the United kids (Edwards, Whelan and McGuinness among them) before they take-off for Switzerland for the International Youth Tournament 1954 which they went onto win. This was the first taste of foreign travel for a United team that would become synonymous with Europe.

Manchester United Youth Team 1956
Back Row (left to right) Bert Whalley (coach), John Queenan, Bobby English, Tony Hawksworth, Reg Holland, Peter Jones, Wilf McGuinness, Jimmy Murphy (manager)
Front Row: Terry Beckett, Mark Pearson, Alex Dawson, Bobby Charlton, Dennis Fidler

Above: Jimmy with Duncan Edwards, Liam Whelan **(centre)** and Dennis Vlollet **(back to camera)** during training at the Cliff
Below: An informal pre-season line-up 1957.

took the mickey out of him unmercifully about his scoring 'prowess'.

Pegg was in and out of the first team until the 1955-56 season when he became more established. What a season that was for him! United, with the youngest team in the League, won the title playing exciting, scintillating football. "There were occasions," remarked David, "when the whole team dovetailed together into an amazing combination. The title was finally clinched in a hard game with our nearest rivals Blackpool. We looked set for an easy win, but failed to put our chances away, then we fell a goal behind. Then we got a penalty, and I didn't envy Johnny Berry as he ran up to take it. However, he scored, and we got back on top before big Tommy Taylor clinched the vital two points."

In the same season, David was chosen for England's Under-23 team against Scotland when Frank Blunstone dropped out. Blunstone, incidentally, would later become a coach at Old Trafford. He was partnered by the brilliant Fulham inside-forward Johnny Haynes and the opposing full-back was a really good one, Alex Parker of Falkirk, who eventually joined Everton. Soon afterwards, David was selected for the England 'B' team - he felt really confident when club-mates Duncan Edwards and Tommy Taylor were also selected and England triumphed 4-1. "There's a wonderful spirit at United," he said shortly before flying off to Belgrade on the ill-fated journey from which he never returned. "We have so many youngsters around that there is always a happy atmosphere and our treatment from manager Matt Busby, Jimmy Murphy and Bert Whalley keeps it that way."

Cannonball Bobby

Bobby Charlton was one of the most sought-after schoolboy players in the history of the game. A true thoroughbred of the highest calibre, Bobby was touted as a star at schoolboy level but he soon got rid of such notions when he arrived at Old Trafford. "There was no room for bigheads at the club, everybody was treated equally," said Bobby many years later. "Matt Busby, Jimmy Murphy and the rest of the staff treated everyone with respect and as part of the club, however, heaven help anyone who tried it on." Speaking about his arrival at Old Trafford, Bobby said that when a schoolboy international joined a big club he was inclined to think he knew it all - but they didn't know anything, really. "Jimmy Murphy and Bert Whalley helped me over that phase," said Bobby. "Jimmy was a hard taskmaster but a wonderful coach. He definitely made us all better players." Hour after hour, Jimmy would spend time with Bobby out on the training ground. Murphy saw greatness in the young, fair-haired, quietly-spoken lad from the North East but he knew he had to bring out the class and commitment from Bobby before the youngster could advance to a higher level.

Bobby is the first to praise Jimmy Murphy because he learned how to become a professional footballer under Jimmy's tutelage. During practice matches or five-a-sides, Jimmy would pull Bobby to one side to explain what the lad should be doing. For example, Bobby had a habit of sending long, spectacular passes from one side of the pitch to the other. They looked brilliant when executed the way Bobby could do it but Murphy would go to great lengths to tell Charlton that if the pass was intercepted by the opposition, it would put his own team under pressure. "Play the ball shorter first, son," Murphy would say. He would often stand in the centre circle and kick the ball to the four corner flags and Bobby would be like a greyhound out of the traps chasing after it. This would go on for what seemed like hours with Bobby feeling absolutely exhausted. "It helped me later in my career," admitted Bobby.

On other occasions, Jimmy and Bobby would run up and down the field, just passing the ball backwards and forwards to each other without any opposition. Simple things you wouldn't think were vital at the time but Jimmy would emphasise their importance. Other sessions would have Bobby practising shooting drills. "Accuracy, aim to hit the target, son," Jimmy would bellow. He would go through these individual coaching sessions time and time again until young Charlton was sweating profusely. Repetition was Murphy's answer but as Bobby admits, as a youngster the technique didn't always go down well. "I used to think, 'he has taught me this before, he doesn't need to tell me again'." But Jimmy would tell him again and again. It was very important. "You have got to learn to do it instinctively, whether you think it's right or not," he would reply.

One day, Bobby felt that Jimmy was going out of his way to goad him. Unable to hold his temper, Bobby shouted: "Why are you constantly having a go at me? I can't seem to do anything right." Murphy looked at his protégé and smiled, he knew he had got through to him. They carried on with the session and when they had finished he put his arm around Bobby's shoulder, like a father wanting to tell a son he had pleased him. "Bobby, son, there are a lot of talented lads here, some will make it but a lot of them won't. Bert, Matt and me believe you can become a great player, that's why we all spend so much time with you. So listen and learn."

Many years later, while talking about England's wonderful World Cup triumph, Bobby recalled his performance against Mexico in the opening round. The England team had been criticised for their lack of goals, but Bobby ended all the moaning and groaning by digging back into his memory bank and scoring two blockbusters. Both were brilliantly taken. For the first, Bobby was put through but was still some distance from goal. "As I was making my run and getting ready to shoot, I remembered what Jimmy used to tell me in our coaching sessions. 'Make sure you hit the target, Bobby son,' and I did. Sir Matt never talked about himself as the manager, it was always him and Jimmy. There were always the two. They bounced ideas off each other. We had Sir Matt and Jimmy. Jimmy was the coach. Sir Matt was the motivator, a great manager. Jimmy loved working with the lads. He was happier doing this. Both were special, and I hold them in high esteem."

Wilf McGuinness

Jimmy Murphy was essentially a man's man. The youngsters at Old

Trafford thought the world of him, but not because he was easy with them, far from it. Jimmy asked them tough questions from the very beginning and based on the answers he received, he decided the degree of attention the boy would get. If his judgement was ever wrong, then he was man enough to tell a story against himself. One such story concerned Wilf McGuinness.

Wilf joined Manchester United on the same day as Bobby Charlton and the two became close friends. They had played together in the England Schoolboys team which Wilf had captained. Today, when people see 'Uncle Fester' scurrying around Old Trafford with his bald head and ready smile they could never realise what a good-looking, handsome fellow he was as a teenager and young man. Never mind George Best, the girls used to swoon when they saw Wilf. He was a dapper dresser and had a bubbly personality. Born in the tough district of Collyhurst, the McGuinness family later left for Blackley where McGuinness attended Mount Carmel School. Wilf and his father were big Manchester City supporters.

Jimmy had watched McGuinness several times playing for Manchester, Lancashire and England Schoolboys, and wasn't over impressed or anxious to sign him. McGuinness's style of running didn't appeal to Jimmy. He didn't like the way the lad addressed or kicked the ball. However, the fact that Wilf was a Manchester boy swung the day in his favour and United eventually signed him. One day while training, Jimmy pulled Wilf away from the other kids, pointed out his faults in no uncertain terms and made him stand in front of a brick wall and learn how to kick in the correct manner to improve his weaker right foot. "Keep doing that for a bit, my lad," ordered Jimmy, "and I'll come back and see how you're progressing."

Wilf wanted to please Murphy and show how dedicated he was, so he did as he was told. Alternating between his right and his left foot, Wilf practised kicking and trapping the ball rhythmically against the wall. As the minutes ticked by, poor old Wilf was soon sweating, beads of perspiration pouring down his face. Some of the other players had finished their training and were heading for the bus stop on their way home. "Come on, Wilf, leave that now," they shouted. Wilf refused. He didn't want to offend Jimmy by stopping before he had been told. He also didn't know whether Jimmy was trying him out to see if he would take the easy option and stop. So he diligently carried on with the exercise.

By now, Wilf was drenched in sweat but still he kicked that ball. Every part of his body was aching and he was virtually exhausted but he stuck to his task. It had been more than an hour since Jimmy had told Wilf to kick the ball against the wall. The wall hadn't weakened in any respect but the same couldn't be said for an exhausted McGuinness. In truth, Jimmy had forgotten all about the youngster and when he returned to the spot, he found Wilf battling away, perspiration dripping from him and steam rising from his body, still hammering that ball. That marked a change in Jimmy's attitude. From that day on, he was pro-McGuinness. He took the lad more and more under his wing; made him skipper of the youth side and in secret sessions, taught him gamesmanship.

Wilf made his first team debut against Wolverhampton Wanderers on October 8th 1955 at Old Trafford. A couple of hours before the game, Jimmy pulled Wilf to one side. "Wilf, son," said Jimmy in that enthusiastic manner of his, "you're playing against Peter Broadbent today, now I want you to mark him tightly. This man wants to pinch money from your dear old mother's purse." Wilf didn't quite understand what Jimmy meant until Murphy later explained that the Wolves player would be doing his damnedest to stop Wilf earning a win bonus and his mother would be short when he paid her his weekly wage. Jimmy continued by telling the impressionable youngster how Broadbent would try and do things to stop him playing well and break his concentration. By the time Murphy had finished, he had painted a picture in Wilf's head of the Wolves player as an ogre - so much so that Wilf couldn't wait to get at him.

"Peter Broadbent was a lovely, mild-mannered bloke," recalled Wilf.

"I learned all this years afterwards, but at that time I had him down as a snide, a thief." During the kickabout before the game Peter, on hearing it was Wilf's first team debut, walked over to him and held out his hand to wish the youngster the best of luck. The experienced Wolves player received the shock of his life. "I told him to 'eff off' and called him a 'thieving bastard'. The look on his face was of complete shock and horror. Jimmy didn't mean it of course, it was just his idea of a pep talk. After we'd won 3-2, Jimmy was telling me how well I'd played and how I had coped with a very gifted, experienced player in Broadbent. 'Your dear old mother will be proud of you,' he said, beaming."

It was Jimmy Murphy who turned Wilf into a player - he taught him the rudiments of being a professional. During the summer, when most clubs were quiet, Jimmy would take the ferry over to Ireland with three or four players and train them along with United's Irish scouts. Wilf McGuinness and Duncan Edwards accompanied him on a couple of occasions.

"Both Matt and Jimmy, especially Jimmy, loved to experiment by putting players in different positions," Wilf recalled. "I recently saw a wonderful documentary about the famous Dutch club Ajax. It was a fascinating insight into how they develop players while the players were young. The Ajax coaches made them play in various positions. For example, a centre-forward would be made to play as a full-back or centre-half and vice-versa. A midfield player would be moved up front into a striker's role or out on the wing, while a full-back would be used in other positions. These were great ideas, because it makes players aware of how team-mates in other positions have to adapt in their particular position, besides improving their skill level.

"But let me tell you, United were doing this in the 1950s. Matt and Jimmy were far-sighted individuals about football and players. Jimmy had the wonderful gift of making you feel important and making you feel that you were a special kind of player. It made you feel good to be coached by him. His team talks were something else - he would be on his feet, fists clenched, snarling like a bulldog, and his language could be brutal at times, but he energised us, he made us feel like giants."

Terry Beckett

Terry Beckett joined Manchester United in July 1954, having played for Manchester Boys and England Schoolboys. Terry came from the increasingly successful soccer academy in Collyhurst, St Patrick's School - Lawrence Cassidy, Nobby Stiles and Brian Kidd were all St Pat's old boys. The first person to greet him at United was Albert Scanlon. Terry was a clever, neat inside-forward and quickly earned a place in United's FA Youth Cup team playing alongside Bobby Charlton, Duncan Edwards, David Pegg and Alex Dawson. Murphy converted him into a winger, playing either on the right or the left.

"Jimmy could be quite abrasive at times," Terry recalled "He wasn't malicious in any respect but it could be daunting to young players. We used to have a lot of practice matches. Jimmy Murphy would join in these games - he thought I needed toughing up so he would play opposite me. Even though he must have been in his early 40s he could still tackle hard. A few times he would shoulder-charge me over the line and Lol Cassidy would shout: 'Easy does it Jimmy, you're going to hurt him.' I realised what Jimmy was doing, letting me know how hard the game was. He didn't mind if I got stuck into him, in fact he would encourage me to do it. Other times he would watch from the touchline and shout instructions. When we finished and were walking back to the changing room he would put his arm round my shoulder and say: 'Don't take it literally what I say, you can play, that's why you're here.'

"I liked him a great deal, he and Bert Whalley worked hard with us kids. Jimmy's tough coaching must have done me good because I got into the famous youth team and you have to have ability to get to that level. I later became friendly with Alex Dawson and Mark Pearson. I used to take them to a barber's shop on Rochdale Road in Collyhurst. It was known as 'Harry the Barbers'. Harry was a Jew, a great character. He had these young Jewish kids working with him and they were famous for hair styling: DA cuts, bops, crew-cuts, anything you fancied. Mark and Alex liked getting their hair cut at Harry's."

Terry turned professional with United but in 1957 decided to leave the club for reasons he didn't wish to make public. Jimmy, Bert Whalley and Joe Armstrong turned up at the Beckett family home pleading with him to return to Old Trafford. "I joined Manchester City," recalled Terry. "Colin Barlow, another St Pat's old boy, was also there along with Alan Kirkham. I knew Colin of course, although he was a couple of years older than me. He had just finished his National Service. Those two made it into City's first team. I had to do my National Service and I was posted overseas. I played for my army team and did quite well."

However, Terry's career came to a sudden halt when a serious back ailment forced him to quit top-class football. "I was upset, of course I was," said Terry. "I would read in the newspapers about certain players getting into City's or United's first teams and I knew I was as good as them. In time you get over it. At least I played in United's brilliant Busby Babes Youth team and I played alongside players who became United legends. Players like big Duncan - what an incredible player, he had everything. Shay Brennan, the Perry Como of football, so relaxed was he on the field. Wilf McGuinness, a wonderful whole-hearted competitor and little Eddie Colman, one of the most indescribable wing-halves I have ever seen. Then there was the extraordinary and incomparable Bobby Charlton. Bobby played inside-forward and on the wing, he was a true thoroughbred." Whenever Terry bumped into Jimmy Murphy they would have a laugh and joke with each other. Today, Terry is one of United's scouts and is still connected with the club.

An unbeatable record

Between the inception of the FA Youth Cup and the Munich air disaster, Manchester United's Youth team were almost invincible. If testimony were needed for all the hours Murphy and his team put in on the training pitch, then this was it. Murphy's daring, open, attacking style drew large crowds to Old Trafford. The Youth team's attendances outstripped most First Division clubs.

If the FA Youth Cup provides a barometer of the health of a football club, then there is little doubt that in this period Murphy appeared to have the best talent under the best supervision. United won the Cup in 1953, 1954 and 1955, with a team that many First Division clubs would have happily fielded. However, with the graduation of Duncan Edwards, Liam Whelan and Eddie Colman among others to the first team, a new generation emerged. Among these were Bobby Charlton, Albert Scanlon, Mark Pearson and Alex Dawson - of which more later.

United's FA Youth Cup team began their fourth defence of the trophy against Preston at Deepdale on October 31st 1955. Murphy gave Alex Dawson his Youth team debut following a tremendous hat-trick the previous week against a strong Blackburn side. Preston had taken the lead after just nine minutes of play when Alex, running on to a beautifully placed through ball, was brought down by Preston's goalkeeper. Up stepped cannonball Charlton who nearly broke the net with the power of his penalty shot. But Alex wasn't finished - he scored another two before half-time, sending the Reds in 3-1 up. After the interval, Charlton grabbed a couple more, earning a well-deserved hat-trick but importantly, Dawson had also made his mark.

The Reds drew a strong Sunderland team next and despite atrocious weather, a crowd of 22,500 saw a thrilling game at Old Trafford. The previous week, Alex had scored the only goal as United's 'B' team beat Lancashire rivals Burnley 1-0, the Lancashire club's first defeat of the season. After Charlton had put the Reds in front with a neat header from a free kick, the same player sent Dawson away with a superb inch-perfect, defence-splitting pass, and Alex finished clinically to make it 2-0. Dawson grabbed his second just before half-time when he burst through the Wearsiders' defence and blasted home. In the second half, Dawson and Bob English each hit the post before Mark Pearson steered the ball past Routledge, the visitors' keeper. United ran out worthy winners 4-0, but it had been an excellent game.

For the fourth round tie at Old Trafford on January 28th 1956, United played Sunderland's rivals Newcastle United in front of 26,282 spectators. United attacked from the opening minute, Dawson only denied by swift goalkeeping. However, the young Reds were rampant, with wing-halves English and McGuinness winning the ball and feeding Beckett, Charlton and Pearson. So it came as a shock when the visitors took the lead through Spears. United charged back as the Geordie goalkeeper, Wilson, was kept busy, saving shots and headers, mainly from Dawson. After nineteen minutes Beckett sent a free kick straight onto Bobby Charlton's head and the United kids were level. Inspired by the crowd and Jimmy Murphy's instructions, they bombarded the Newcastle goal. After 30 minutes Beckett scored from a cross by Charlton. Just before half-time Dennis Fidler made it 3-1.

On the resumption, a Newcastle defender punched out a goal-bound shot and Charlton converted the penalty. Although the Geordies fought back, they were inundated by an avalanche of brilliant football from the young Reds. The icing on the cake was a Beckett cross from the right converted with a majestic header from Dawson - the fans were comparing young Alex with Tommy Taylor. With one from McGuinness and another from Dawson, United won the game easily, but both teams received a standing ovation from the crowd. Jimmy Murphy and Bert Whalley congratulated their players on a truly magnificent performance.

As Alf Clarke wrote in the following Monday's *Manchester Evening News*: "It was difficult to appreciate that the football served up when United Youths played Newcastle United Youths came from kids of fifteen years old. The crowd, which was a record for this competition, were on tiptoes with excitement. I have seldom seen such brilliance from mere teenagers. I have, of course, become accustomed to great displays from United's youngsters over the years, they have been the outstanding Youth team season after season since the end of the war. Is there a club in the country better equipped than United for the future? I doubt it. As one Newcastle director said to me after the match: 'You have a great side, but I regret that Bobby Charlton slipped through our fingers, because we had been keeping tabs on him from when he was only eleven years of age'."

In the fifth round, United drew a home tie against Bexley Heath and Welling. Who? Well, Bexley Heath was a nursery club of Charlton Athletic, then a formidable First Division team. The Kent side had a very good record, having reached the quarter-finals for the second time. United had played them two years previously, winning 2-1 after the Southerners had missed a penalty.

Bexley were coached by Charlie Vaughan, a former England Amateur International and Charlton centre-forward, and they were thirsting for revenge. The match took place at Old Trafford on St Patrick's Day 1956. The week before, Dawson had sharpened his goalscoring skills by grabbing a hat-trick against Stockport County 'B' team. Another large crowd, 23,850, filled Old Trafford and within ten minutes, the Reds were 3-0 in front. Fidler and two Bobby Charlton blockbusters had given the Reds the ideal start. These early setbacks disheartened the Kent side and by half-time United led 6-0, with further goals from Pearson, Charlton and Dawson. Within fifteen minutes of the second half, however, Bexley had scored, then United surged forward again and in a five-minute spell of breathtaking action, they added three more goals through Charlton, Dawson and Beckett. After 80 minutes, Alex Dawson scored goal number ten for the young Reds, completing his hat-trick before Bobby Charlton scored number eleven - a real Charlton special. With his back to goal, Bobby turned right round and met a centre from the right wing while he was still airborne and thundered it into the roof of the net. The crowd gasped and joined the Bexley goalkeeper in applauding such breath-taking skill.

Jimmy and Bert Whalley were bubbling with delight, although they didn't let the youngsters see their happiness. The hours spent on the training field were paying dividends. Not only had they a young forward of Bobby Charlton's calibre who seemed to be blossoming into an inside-forward of immense talent, they also had a ready-made goal poacher in young Dawson.

For the two-legged semi-final, United were drawn with deadly Lancashire rivals, Bolton Wanderers. Bolton were a strong, solid team that included goalkeeper Joe Dean, a Manchester lad United wanted to sign, and forwards Brian Birch and Neville Bannister - all three had first team experience. In the event, United won their two semi-final ties against Bolton and the two-legged final against Chesterfield. United had maintained their unbeaten record in the FA Youth Cup and the new generation had their first taste of glory.

The Lawman commeth

In November 1956, United's Youth team were drawn away to Huddersfield in round two of the FA Youth Cup. Jimmy Murphy and Bert Whalley travelled with the young players on the coach from Old Trafford. Matt Busby would follow later by car. It was a raw day, but there were quite a lot of supporters present as the referee blew his whistle to start the game. United were first to attack but the home defence held solid and slowly but surely Huddersfield came more into the game. Their inside right was giving the United defenders a torrid time. His blonde head would be back in defence clearing the ball one minute, then be terrorising David Gaskell, United's goalkeeper, the next. After 25 minutes, United's defenders were at sixes and sevens due to the wispy inside-right's persistence, forcing them into mistakes, and within minutes he had scored. A couple of minutes later, his inside-left partner McHale had also scored. Huddersfield 2 United 0!

Jimmy Murphy was shouting instructions for his wing-halves to get a grip of the little blonde bombshell. "What's his name?" shouted Jimmy to the opposition dugout. "Denis Law," came the reply. Urged on by Murphy and Whalley, the United youngsters started to play neat, attractive football. The young Law was chasing up and down the field, hunting for the ball - it was like a magnet at his feet. Then, from 25 yards, Bobby English sent a power-packed shot sizzling in the

Huddersfield net and the teams went in with the Yorkshire club leading 2-1 at half-time.

In the United dressing room Murphy was agitatedly counselling each individual, pointing out their mistakes and explaining how to eradicate them. Bert Whalley was encouraging the lads, while Matt Busby simply told his youngsters to listen to Jimmy's and Bert's instructions. Just before the players left the dressing room for the second half, Murphy clenched his fists and in no uncertain terms told the team exactly what was expected from them. After that, the lads couldn't wait for the referee to blow his whistle. They were inspired, none more so than Alex Dawson. Straight from the kick-off, United took the game by the scruff of the neck and attacked Huddersfield non-stop. It was only a matter of time before they scored the equaliser. From a corner kick taken by Kenny Morgans, Dawson flew into the 18-yard box and the ball was in the net. 2-2! A few minutes later, big Alex took a corner and Morgans headed a good goal. Young Law was still battling for the ball and causing mischief for United's defence. When a free kick was awarded to United, Murphy was out of the dugout imploring his lads to move into Huddersfield's box and attack the ball. Bobby English floated in a free kick and Dawson, moving like an express train, dived at the ball, sending it hurtling into the Huddersfield net. From two goals down, United led 4-2.

Both teams never let up - it was a cracking match full of good football, exciting goalmouth incidents, powerful shooting, ferocious tackling and enthusiasm. Law was still in the thick of the action for Town and Dawson was causing havoc every time he chased the ball into the Huddersfield area. The game finished with United comfortable victors in the end, although Law had given them plenty to think about. Busby was suitably impressed with Denis Law and it was because of his all-action performance in this game that United's manager offered Andy Beatie, the Huddersfield manager, £10,000 for Law's signature. The Huddersfield boss declined the offer and it was to be many years before Law eventually joined United.

In their third round tie against Sunderland Youths played at Old Trafford, United ran out 3-1 winners. The Sunderland team came to Manchester with a glowing reputation from the north-east. Nobby Lawton laid on chances galore for his team-mates but they were scorned. Within 20 minutes, the young Reds should have sealed the game on chances created Lawton alone. The young Newton Heath forward put his team in front but 15 minutes later Godbold got the equaliser. But 'Mr Goals' Dawson sealed United's victory with a brace. In the 66th minute, Hunter floated a high centre into Sunderland's penalty area, the defenders jumped for it but Dawson soared even higher and nodded it into the net. Then on 85 minutes, he got his second with a powerful drive that nearly lifted the nets out.

United drew Everton, another highly fancied team, in the next round. The first game ended a 2-2 draw at Goodison Park. "Dawson - A Name to Remember," wrote Ian Hargreaves in the *Liverpool Echo*. "The small crowd who watched Everton share four goals came away certain of two things. That there is plenty of up-and-coming talent in the Everton cupboard, and in 16-year-old Alex Dawson, United have an international centre-forward in the making. The brawny son of a Scottish trawler skipper, Dawson already seems destined for the highest honours. Speed, anticipation and shooting power are all there and but for the fine work of Everton's O'Shaughnessy and Johnson, he would have scored more than two goals. A regular member of Manchester United's Central League side, his record speaks for itself, and providing he keeps clear of injury, I can see nothing to stop him rising to the very top."

Mark Pearson aided Alex skillfully and the two wingers, Kenny Morgans and Reg Hunter, delivered accurate crosses for Dawson. Everton took the lead through Ashworth, but after 55 minutes, United got a corner and Morgans placed it perfectly for Dawson to score with a glorious header. Another Liverpool reporter wrote: "Dawson's unbelievable header was of the real Billy Dean variety." That was some tribute to give young Dawson, to be compared to the legendary 'Dixie'

Dean.

In the replay, there were no arguments about the victors. Nobby Lawton got the opener when he dispossessed an Everton player in the penalty area and drove a crisp shot into the net. Within four minutes Everton equalised, but a few seconds later Pearson scored a cracker with a left-footed drive. Alex Dawson got the Reds' third when he side-footed the ball into the net while he and Reg Hunter added further goals to make the final score 5-2 for United.

In the fifth round, United drew a home tie against Blackburn Rovers. Pearson glanced a header forward for Dawson to go racing through the middle and drive an unstoppable shot into the net and English got number two. Blackburn played nifty football and looked dangerous but in the second half, Morgans made another goal for Dawson and Lawton got the fourth before Morgans and Hunter completed a 6-0 rout of Rovers.

The first leg of the semi-final against Southampton was staged at The Dell on April 4th 1957. In front of 19,320 spectators, United beat Southampton 5-2. However, it was a great deal tougher than the final scoreline suggests. After a few seconds the Saints missed a penalty before taking the lead only to gift the Reds an equaliser with an own goal. It was a cracking game, end to end with bags of excitement. Just before half-time, Bobby English put the Manchester lads ahead. Pearson, Dawson and Hunter added further goals - Dawson and captain Ken Morgans the pick of the United lads. In the second leg at Old Trafford, United were shocked down to their toe-nails when they were beaten 3-2, their first-ever defeat in the competition. United were very unlucky - they played some breathtaking football and Alex had a shot and two headers hit the woodwork with the Southampton goalkeeper well beaten. Nobby Lawton also hit the bar with a header but Dawson put United into the lead with a tap-in. However, Southampton went into a 3-1 lead with the 17,000 crowd hysterical. Dawson made it 3-2 when he scored late in the second half to make it 7-5 to United on aggregate. It was a first class game to watch.

In the first leg of the FA Youth Cup Final at Upton Park, on the May 2nd 1957, the United kids won 3-2. United were pegged back by the London side until Dawson scored in the 38th minute, then, in three glorious minutes in the second half, the United youngsters struck twice with the score 1-1. Nobby Lawton got United's second after Cartwright had equalised for the Hammers, then Hunter got the third before Georgie Fenn scored from the spot for the Cockneys. Jimmy Murphy wasn't too happy with his lads and told them he expected a vast improvement in the second leg at Old Trafford.

On Wednesday May 8th 1957, in the return leg at Old Trafford, Alex Dawson started off meaning business. He harassed and shoulder-charged Goymer, the West Ham goalkeeper, and tackled the Hammers' defenders trying to retrieve the ball. The Cockney lads were worried by Dawson's immense strength. Reg Hunter scored first for the Reds after 30 minutes play, Mark Pearson scored United's second after a mistake by the worried goalkeeper, before Pearson again scored the third. Alex was in his element, his shots and headers fizzing inches wide or being blocked by West Ham's defenders. Then in the 63rd minute he got his reward for harassing the defence, converting a simple chance. It was all Dawson again after his goal. He was out-jumping everybody - rasping headers were bouncing off the woodwork and posts. He got his second goal in the 70th minute then he went all out to get his hat-trick as United ran out 5-0 winners (8-2 on aggregate) and clinched the FA Youth Cup for the fifth successive time since its inception.

At the start of the 1957-58 season, Alex Dawson and Mark Pearson were preparing for their third FA Youth Cup campaign. Jimmy Murphy brought in Nobby Lawton to play in Alex's position. The youth team appeared to have the world at their feet as they cruised into the fifth round following an 8-0 hammering of Newcastle United at Old Trafford - Dawson (4), Pearson(3) and Johnny Giles among the goals. However, this game was the last Youth team appearance for both Alex and Mark. Four weeks later, the club was pitched into turmoil as the plane bringing the first team players and officials, plus a posse of newspaper journalists, crashed at Munich. The two teenagers would be needed for first team duty.

A Glorious Legacy

*"Matt and I were like a couple of teenagers
jumping up and punching the air with delight."*
JIMMY MURPHY

In seasons 1953-54 and 1954-55, United finished fourth and fifth in the League, completing a transformation of the first team from the remnants of the great '48 side to the youngsters Murphy was bringing through. The team were beginning to gell at the highest level and a season later the young Manchester United team won the First Division Championship. Jimmy's 'little seeds' had indeed flowered and the Busby Babes had arrived.

Newspaper reporters, older football fans and critics couldn't believe that this team of youngsters would be able to hold their own with seasoned, hardened professional players, but they did. Tommy Taylor, the man Jimmy had pursued from the first moment he saw him play, was the leading goalscorer with 25 goals from 33 games while the shadowy Dennis Viollet scored 20 in 34 matches, maintaining his tally of the previous season. The coaching staff at Old Trafford were, to put it simply, 'made up' because they had won the prestigious Championship with only three players who had cost the club a fee.

Goalkeeper Ray Wood had joined the club in 1949 as an 18-year-old for a small fee; Johnny Berry, a powerful, compact and fast raiding right winger had signed from Birmingham in 1952 season; and, of course, there was Tommy Taylor, who went on to become a cult figure. "This is only the start," Jimmy told close friends. "We have youngsters coming through who will challenge for every position. Our 'little seeds' have finally blossomed."

The following season saw the Red Devils going for the treble of League Championship, FA Cup and the prestigious and highly acclaimed European Cup. History shows that domestically they won the Championship again and reached Wembley in the FA Cup Final, losing 2-1 to Aston Villa. "I am absolutely certain that they would have won the double but that unfortunate incident between Ray Wood and Villa's Peter McParland," said Jimmy. They also reached the semi-final of the European Cup losing to the all-conquering Real Madrid.

Real Madrid were the best team in the world and won the European trophy for the following five years. Nevertheless, the European Cup has become part and parcel of Manchester United's history.

United's first game in the tournament against Belgian champions Royal Sporting Club of Anderlecht took place in Brussels on 12th September 1957. United had defied the Football League by taking part in this competition, mainly because Busby and Murphy wanted to broaden the club's horizons but also because of the extra revenue it would bring in through the turnstiles. In the fifties, English football had become something of a laughing stock after the brilliant Hungarians had thrashed England twice by big scores. The critics said we were behind the times and the Continentals had overtaken us on the football field. As far as Busby and Murphy were concerned, the European Cup was another opportunity to make United into the best club in the world.

Those European nights were proud occasions. It was an 'us against them' situation, where United fans were patriotic without vicious remarks, acts of violence or bad manners. It was indeed like the wonderful 'Voyage of Sinbad!' Readers must understand that working-class supporters could barely afford a week's holiday in Blackpool or Morecambe, let alone Rhyl and hardly anyone holidayed in Spain or other foreign destinations. So playing against these top continental teams was like a holiday for all of us. It took us out of our dreary lives and working conditions.

"When we won the title in the 1955-56 by a whopping eleven points from Blackpool, the average age of our lads was 23," said Jimmy when reflecting on those early adventures in Europe in the 1950s. "Don't forget, these lads were the forerunners for English teams in Europe. Manchester United were on a crusade and we had a wonderful spirit of adventure and the boys played brilliantly. Our team formation was superb. Those two Athletico Bilbao games were as good and as exciting as I've ever seen. Spain was snowbound when we arrived and on the day of the game the weather got even worse. But our boys showed true grit and character. At half-time we were 3-0 down and the pitch was like a cow field, the mud was that thick and clinging. We made it 3-2 after some terrific football. Then Bilbao went into a 5-2 lead. Most other teams playing in these conditions miles away from home would have been content to see out the game but we had brought our boys up to never surrender, and Billy Whelan scored a dream goal. If a Brazilian had scored it he would have been acclaimed a world-beater."

It was indeed a once-in-a-lifetime goal. With barely five minutes left, Billy moved over the mud like a hovercraft, beating five big tough defenders on a marvellous dribble before belting the ball into the net from the edge of the box. A truly great goal by a truly great player. "In the return at Maine Road, we needed to score three clear goals before we could go through to the semi-final. Could we do it? Well apart from our own fans, I seriously doubt many other people thought we could. We had this wonderful young team though who never knew when they were beaten and besides that, we had a centre-forward called Tommy Taylor!

"What a partnership he and the whipcord Dennis Viollet had, it was unbelievable. At times people often thought Dennis had just got up from a sick-bed, so thin and pale was he. But what a clever player. The crowd that night, over 70,000, helped the lads through. The encouragement they gave made us all proud to be associated with Manchester. They roared, sang, rang bells and clapped. Dennis scored what looked like two perfectly good goals but for some reason or other the referee disallowed them. It was 1-0, a goal scored by Dennis Viollet that counted. Pulses were beating faster and faster as the second half started. As Matt and I sat on the bench near the dugout we were twitching, then in the 70th minute, for the umpteenth time, Tommy turned Jesus Garay inside out and blasted a snorter of a goal. Remember, Garay was one of the best centre-halves on the continent. Matt and I were like a couple of teenagers jumping up and punching the air with delight. Five minutes to the final whistle and we were level on aggregate. Could we do it? Could we pull off a sensational victory? Well that man Taylor tore down the wing, beat Garay again and was setting himself up for a shot at goal when he spotted Johnny Berry in a better position and laid the ball off for him to score and send us through at our first attempt into the semi-final. The moral to this story is that although Tommy was a devastating finisher himself and nobody would have blamed him for shooting for goal, he laid into the path of little Berry for him to score. The next morning's newspaper headlines read: 'The Greatest Victory In Soccer History' in the *Daily Express*. Yes, those European nights were certainly occasions to remember."

The first leg of the European Cup semi-final was held in Madrid in front of 135,000 spectators, and United lost 3-1. Besides being an exceptionally talented side, Real Madrid were not behind the door when it came to handing out the rough stuff. Tommy Taylor took a terrible pounding but never gave up. The rough stuff surprised the many English journalists who travelled to Spain. The young Red Devils faced an extremely experienced team with several world-class players such as Alfredo Di Stefano, one of the greatest to ever grace a football field - this man had the lot. Raymond Kopa was a fantastic French international; Francisco Gento, the classy direct flying left-winger, was another world class forward; at the back they had Marquitos, a dreadnought defender who took no prisoners; while Rial was also in the world-class bracket.

Nevertheless, these young United lads never knew when they were beaten and they believed that they could pull a two-goal deficit back at home. In the second leg, played this time at Old Trafford under the newly-installed floodlights that had cost £40,000, the match drew over 65,000. The fans didn't like the way the Spanish masters meted out the rough stuff again and it soured a great occasion. Both Jimmy and United captain Roger Byrne were of the opinion that the United team had attacked far too much in an effort to pull back the two-goal deficit. The final score was 2-2, Tommy Taylor and Bobby Charlton getting a goal apiece.

Bill Foulkes remembers that game: "Madrid deserved to go through to the final but they couldn't handle Tommy Taylor. He frightened them with his power in the air, they were pulling him down whenever he went up for a ball, and I mean tugging him down. The referee allowed them to get away with these methods. But we were a young side and would have got better with experience." The truth was that the Real Madrid team were the 'crème de la crème'. Jimmy always maintained that it was inexperience that beat the young Babes but like Matt, he was firmly convinced that eventually United would conquer foreign opposition and become champions of Europe.

Murphy: Manager of Wales

At the start of 1957, the Welsh national team manager Wally Barnes relinquished his position when he joined the BBC as a commentator. The Welsh FA asked Jimmy if he would take the job on. They had watched with interest the success he was having at Manchester United alongside Matt Busby. Jimmy was proud and honoured. Although he was now a dyed-in-the-wool Mancunian and his family had settled in Manchester, he was still a patriotic Welshman. Jimmy knew that the Welsh FA were notorious 'skinflints' and always looked after themselves first before thinking about the players. He was also aware that few envied his task, because Wales were the 'whipping boys' of the home countries.

Since 1952, when Wales had shared the honours in the Home Championships with England, their record in a dismal 22 matches had seen them win only three - they had drawn or lost on 19 occasions. It was a mammoth task, but there was no man better suited to breathe new life and pride back into the team. Jimmy's task was made much harder because great Welsh stalwarts like Alf Sherwood, Ron Burgess and one of Jimmy's favourite players, Manchester City's dynamic wing-half and captain Roy Paul, were coming to the end of their international careers. He discussed the Welsh FA's request with Matt and he decided he would accept the job as their permanent manager, the first-ever such position in the history of Welsh football. Shortly afterwards, the Scottish FA approached Matt Busby with a similar request - to become their team manager.

In those days a selection committee would pick the national team. However, although only taking the positions on a part-time basis, both Jimmy and Matt insisted that they must be involved in the selection of the team.

"The Welsh FA committee was made up of what has been described as 'the butcher, the baker and the candlestick maker.' The same could be said of the various international committees of England, Ireland and Scotland as well. They were a pious, self-righteous and puritanical body of people," Colin Webster remarked many years later. "Some of the committee's antics resembled 'Fawlty Towers'. It was ridiculous, I don't know how Jimmy put up with it." As an example of how things worked, just before the 1958 World Cup, Wales flew behind the Iron Curtain for two vital World Cup qualifying games with East Germany and Czechoslovakia. As the Welsh team flew from London there were only 12 players but an incredible, unbelievable 10 selectors on the plane. At times there were more selectors travelling to matches than players. Some of the antics are laughable now but they certainly weren't in the 1950s.

In this period, Wales could boast world-class players of the calibre of brilliant Arsenal goalkeeper Jack Kelsey, Tottenham's mercurial left-winger Cliff Jones, 'Gentle Giant' John Charles and Swansea Town's gifted Ivor Allchurch. Other stalwarts included captain Dave Bowen of Arsenal, Mel Charles, brother of John, Mel Hopkins and Terry Medwin, to name but a few. Getting them all together however, would be something else.

Jimmy would often attend meetings at the Welsh FA's offices in Wrexham and would at times sit there absolutely flabbergasted at the goings on. The selectors wanted to pick the team but Murphy wouldn't stand for that. However, they respected him enough that following a long debate they usually agreed to Jimmy's demands. But the players idolised him - he was one of the lads. He would have a pint of ale with them and a cigarette and then get on the piano and play it beautifully.

When Murphy accepted the Welsh job in 1957, United were being described as 'The Team of the Century' and Jimmy was full of vigour and enthusiasm, so he wouldn't tolerate any interference from a sanctimonious selection committee. In the event, the job almost certainly saved his life, as the Welsh embarked on the most successful period in their history.

Munich

"He had brought these players through the system right from 15 and now they were gone. His lifetime's work gone and it was down to him and him alone to keep the club functioning. Just think of that for a moment. How would you feel?"
HARRY GREGG

Jimmy Murphy proved his love and loyalty to both Matt Busby and Manchester United in the aftermath of the 1958 Munich disaster. Jimmy would have been seated next to Matt Busby on the ill-fated trip from Belgrade had he not been returning from Cardiff where his Welsh team had played a World Cup play-off against Israel.

Murphy had been a little worried about Busby, knowing that the United boss had, only a few days earlier, undergone an operation on his legs. Jimmy wondered if his friend would be strong enough for the journey. Jimmy told Matt that with the Red Star game being so important he should travel to Belgrade. Busby wouldn't hear of it and told Jimmy to attend to his duties with the Welsh team and everything would be fine in Yugoslavia. Murphy usually sat next to Busby on the aircraft and always had the room next to Matt's at the hotel when the team were away. But Bert Whalley would take Murphy's place on the trip.

It's history now that United won through to the next round of the tournament - what is less well-known is the outcome of the World Cup play-off in Cardiff. There was drama when Israel's goalkeeper and captain, Yaco Chodoroff, injured his shoulder, had his nose broken, and played on with concussion. After the game he was taken to hospital. However, the Welshmen did not score until ten minutes from the final whistle: Ivor Allchurch and Cliff Jones scored the goals that took Wales to their first World Cup Finals - an incredible acheivement in itself by Murphy.

The following day, Thursday, was freezing cold and Manchester was shivering under grey clouds and snow as Murphy left his train at London Road (now Piccadilly) Station. Jimmy immediately jumped into a taxi and headed for Old Trafford. The last few days had been hectic for the club and Jimmy was thinking of the game United had three days later against top-of-the-table Wolves. He had work to do before he could go home. He wanted to check that everyone was fit and have everything ready for when Matt and the players returned. He leapt out of the taxi and, like a whippet, rushed upstairs to his office, completely oblivious to everyone. He had no idea of what had happened on the runway at Munich until Alma George, Matt Busby's secretary, shouted for him to stop. It was quite obvious to Alma that Jimmy didn't know anything about the tragedy that had taken place less than a couple of hours earlier. She explained what had happened. His face was frozen. He couldn't comprehend what was being said to him. He eventually walked toward his office like a zombie.

Tragically and dramatically, fate had stepped into Jimmy's life. He was 47 and this volatile and voluble Welshman now found himself virtually manager of Manchester United. In Jimmy's hands rested the immediate destiny of this great club. It would be Jimmy Murphy who would have to take the first steps on the long, hard, uphill struggle to regain glory for the 'Red Devils'. Once the news sunk in about the air crash, Murphy was shaking and sobbing uncontrollably as he sat at his desk. It was a living nightmare. He picked up his telephone and rang the newspapers, the police and the BBC for information. He just didn't know what to do in this situation.

Slowly the news of the tragedy trickled through to him. When he heard that Roger Byrne, Tommy Taylor, David Pegg, Billy Whelan, Geoff Bent, Eddie Colman and Mark Jones had perished, he sobbed and sobbed. When news came through that the club secretary, Walter Crickmer, was also dead he was stunned even further. Then, like a bombshell, he was told his closest friends Bert Whalley and Tom Curry were dead, and Matt Busby was fighting for his life. It became too much for him.

He was living through a nightmare and wanted to wake up. The scene in that little office could not be described. It was desolation! Murphy's whole world was collapsing around him. Those players and club officials were like close family to Jimmy. It was 4am when he left Old Trafford for home but he couldn't sleep and ended up drinking a bottle of whisky as his mind wandered back and forth to the first time he had set eyes on those young men now no longer with us. He laughed and smiled spasmodically.

His thoughts then drifted to Matt Busby: how they had opposed each other in their playing days and how Matt had offered him the job with United. Bert Whalley: a lovely, quiet saint of a man who after injuring an eye thought his career and relationship with the club he loved had ended. Murphy and Busby decided they needed a man of Bert's honesty and integrity to help the kids become United players of the future. Bert and Jimmy had worked hand in hand. Tom Curry: a patient and scrupulously honest person who was like a father confessor to the players. Walter Crickmer: diligent, hard-working and as straight as an arrow, Walter could laugh and joke with the best of them. But what about Duncan Edwards? They threw away the mould when Duncan was born, Jimmy was fond of saying to anyone discussing the wing-half. Jimmy lapsed into a deep sleep with his head on the kitchen table, recalling in his mind's eye the wonderful days and nights he had spent coaching the young giant.

The following day Jimmy flew out to Munich with Matt Busby's wife Jean, daughter Sheena and son Sandy, and the wives and relations of the injured. As he walked into that Munich hospital he looked around and it became another nightmare for him, seeing those brilliant young athletes lying in their beds, broken. Poor Duncan Edwards, as ill as he was, kept asking about his treasured watch. The watch in question had been presented to him by the officials of Real Madrid after United's matches against them the previous season - it was his pride and joy.

When Sister Solemnis was administering to him he told her his watch had gone from his wrist. "Somebody's thieved my watch," he told her. "Be calm. Please. There was no watch on your hand when you were brought in," she tried to assure him. But Duncan was adamant. "I must have it back. Please find it for me." The Sister told him she would do her best and she would also ask the helpers to search for it again. Jimmy went to Duncan Edwards' bedside, trembling with emotion. Sister Solemnis spoke to Jimmy in broken English, telling him that Duncan had been asking for his watch. A watch found by the rescue people had just been handed to her. She handed Jimmy the broken watch. Jimmy confirmed that it belonged to Duncan. The watch was mangled and would have been impossible to repair. However, he carefully strapped it back onto Duncan's wrist.

Duncan seemed aware and momentarily opened his eyes. "Hello, Jimmy, what time's the kick-off on Saturday?" said the pain-wracked youngster. Jimmy forced a smile and answered. "Usual time, Dunc,.three o'clock." "I'll get stuck in, Jimmy," said Duncan. Jimmy gently told him he had confidence he would. Duncan lapsed into unconsciousness and Jimmy leaned over him anxiously. "You've got your watch back, Duncan," he whispered quietly. Jimmy straightened up. There were tears streaming down his cheeks.

He looked around and stared at his stricken friends. Later, having composed himself, he put his head inside Matt Busby's oxygen tent.

Matt, having regained consciousness, recognised Jimmy. They grabbed hold of each other's hands and cried. It was a very emotional and touching scene.

Frank Taylor, a prominent journalist, was also badly injured. He was the last of the survivors to leave the Munich hospital and he said that Jimmy Murphy called at his bedside and had a long chat with him. "Jimmy was normally one of the most cheerful and talkative men in football. He sat silently brooding, the heartache locked inside him. He was upset that his close pal Bert Whalley had died. How he kept his composure in the hospital I'll just never know. I don't think people realise just what a momentous job of work Jimmy did after Munich by keeping United afloat. Think about it for a moment: the club could have been in dire straits with hardly any experienced players to call upon. But with just two new signings and Harry Gregg, Bill Foulkes and later Bobby Charlton, he took them to Wembley. That takes some doing, he inspired those players to play way above themselves. He was a wonderfully loyal and honest clubman beside being the coach for most of those dead and injured United players. I felt deeply for him, his life's work wiped out."

Later that night in the Regina Hotel in Munich, Harry Gregg and Bill Foulkes, along with a doctor, pressed a button in the elevator to take them to the floor where their rooms were situated. Gregg's eyes watched the levels monitor as the lift descended. It opened and Foulkes and the doctor entered the lift, but Gregg told them he would go up the stairs to his room. So he walked up three flights of stairs. At the top Harry heard a deep sobbing noise, and as he turned, he saw Jimmy Murphy, sitting on the stairs, sobbing his heart out. Harry hesitated, then decided to leave Jimmy to his own thoughts and turned away, unnoticed.

"Jimmy Murphy did a remarkable job for Manchester United after Munich," said Harry. "When you think about what he did for the club at this period it takes some believing, it really does. He, like us, was heartbroken. He had brought these players through the system right from the beginning at fifteen and now they were gone. His lifetime's work gone and it was down to him and him alone to keep the club functioning. Just think of that for a moment. How would you feel? It must have been terrible for dear old Jimmy. He tried to keep us buoyant but many times I saw him break down sobbing. He was a special kind of human being."

The nightmare continued once Jimmy was back in Manchester. Let nobody be under any illusions - it was a monumental job to keep United afloat. Funerals had to be attended and a barrage of inquires answered at Old Trafford. He was struggling with grief, thinking about those players and their families and all the hard work on the Cliff training ground that had been destroyed within a few seconds. Despite all these sombre thoughts, he knew he had to field a team against Sheffield Wednesday in the fifth round of the FA Cup.

"We got a postponement," announced a disconsolate Murphy to the press. But the day came nearer and nearer, he pulled a piece of paper from his drawer and as he jotted down a list of the players he had available and saw what was left, tears streamed down his cheeks. He was alone in his office. He found it a struggle to think straight let alone clearly. He knew he needed an experienced inside-forward and then a wing-half. He made enquiries for many, many players. Most of the ones he wanted were either not available or the fees were much too high. But he was lucky when Paddy McGrath, a friend of his and Matt Busby's, helped him sign Blackpool inside-forward Ernie Taylor. He eventually signed his wing-half in Stan Crowther, the Aston Villa player, who incidentally played against United in that infamous 1957 FA Cup Final. He registered Crowther an hour or so before the Sheffield Wednesday game. Stan should have been cup-tied, having already played in the FA Cup that season for Aston Villa, but because of United's plight the FA allowed him to play.

Jimmy had also tried to sign two players he knew well from his involvement with the Welsh team. They were both Welsh internationals who played for Swansea. Mel Charles, brother of the more famous John

Charles, was one. However, Jimmy was told he was not available, and when he enquired about a young flying left winger named Cliff Jones, who he had been monitoring for both Wales and United, and who he rated highly, Swansea asked for a £35,000 fee.

Paddy McGrath, Matt Busby's best friend, was born and bred in Collyhurst. A former professional fighter from the same stable as Jackie Brown, Paddy always said that there was no disputing that Jimmy Murphy was a wonderful coach and motivator but added: "Jimmy never liked the transfer and negotiating side of management, and dealing with money." Anyhow, the deal was quashed and Tottenham moved in and snapped up Jones. Cliff turned out to be a world-class player. Bobby Mitchell, the Newcastle winger, Colin Grainger, Billy Elliott, Jim Iley and Brian Pilkington were other players under consideration - however none were signed.

*

"What happens to Manchester United now?" asked sports journalist Arthur Walmsley a few days after the crash. "Can they ever regain the greatness of the last decade?" Mr Walmsley went on to say that although his heart said they could and very soon, his head preached caution that the road back was going to be long and hard. "The United team that was shattered at Munich was no miracle. It was the cream of a Soccer University whose members had graduated to greatness after years of study and careful coaching by Matt Busby and his staff. It was the end product of a belt system which had its beginnings in immature youth and its finality in near perfect football. It is this system which gives great hope for the future at Old Trafford. Gone is Bert Whalley, the devoted junior master of the United soccer school and the future of maestro manager Matt Busby is still uncertain. But there is still one brilliant man of football left to keep the belt system moving at Old Trafford and bring the shadow team of youngsters to the top.

"That man is Jimmy Murphy, the assistant manager, whose part in the build-up of the fabulous United set-up comes a close second to that of Busby himself. He will have to do three men's jobs - his own, Matt Busby's and Bert Whalley's - but he will not be working without material. Some of that material has already taken a firm and finalised shape." He then mentioned Freddie Goodwin and Wilf McGuinness as replacements for Eddie Colman and Duncan Edwards. "Both Wilf and Freddie would be automatic first team choices with any other club." In attack, Mr Walmsley said Jimmy Murphy could only rely on the genius of Bobby Charlton, of the once fabulous store of forward talent. "Tommy Taylor, David Pegg and Billy Whelan are dead, and the footballing futures of Albert Scanlon, Johnny Berry, Dennis Viollet and Kenny Morgans are in considerable doubt. The reconstruction of the forward line is going to be Jimmy Murphy's biggest task. Yet here again, he is by no means bankrupt of talent, even though that talent is still mostly immature. In 18-year-old giant Alex Dawson he has a centre-forward who has already been hailed as Scotland's future attack leader. Mark Pearson, 17-year-old inside-forward, is another close to first team standards. Murphy will keep United moving," said Mr Walmsley, "and Murphy, if he has to, is good enough to do it alone."

Stan Cullis, the manager of Wolves, United's greatest rivals in those days, told the press that in his opinion United used to have three good teams but now they only had one. "But make no mistake," said Cullis, "it will still be a good one. They are extremely well-drilled and they have basic ability. That drilling has been under Murphy's expert tuition. He has looked after the younger element all the time." Mr Cullis went on to say that Jimmy left Matt Busby free to concentrate on the first team. He said that the Busby-Murphy partnership was a happy and immensely successful one. "They have implicit faith in each other. That faith and determination to rebuild United will be the stronger for what has happened."

Journalist Len Noad, a close friend of Murphy, wrote in the *Weekly News*: "Jimmy Murphy, who can play a church organ with the depth of feeling and musicianship that comes so easily to the Welsh, will throw himself into the job of resurrecting United with all the fervour of his race. I only hope somebody is good enough to give me a transcript of Jimmy's first talk to the United staff. In that maiden speech as acting manager of Manchester United, will be revealed his true greatness. And in the midst of all this worry and despite the mental whirl in which he might find himself, there is something he will always remember to do. Write a weekly letter to his mother who still lives in the Welsh valleys."

John Charles telephoned Jimmy from his home in Italy and discussed United's plight and search for new players. John was Italy's leading goalscorer. "I only wish I could be in Manchester to help you," said the giant Welshman, "and believe me I am very sincere when I say that." Of course Jimmy would have loved to have had the services of Charles. However, the problem was that John still had twelve months left on his existing contract and he was hero-worshipped in Italy - the Italians would offer him riches galore to remain there. But taking everything into consideration, John would gladly have foregone all their offers and played for United. John told Jimmy that he would be over in England in the coming weeks and would be filling his national manager in on United's European Cup semi-final opponents, AC Milan. "I will do everything possible to help Jimmy and United when they come over to Italy. I have the highest regard for Jimmy as a manager and coach. Some of the things he has taught me in our training sessions with the Welsh team have improved me immensely. Also, he is a really wonderful motivator, the best!"

Jimmy told the press that the chairman, directors, the back-room staff and the players had responded magnificently. Jimmy could see something was about to take shape out of the chaos. His problem was to drill his makeshift team into a pattern of play. Jimmy knew a team's style had to be based on the players available and he knew in his heart that the team had too many weak positions and square pegs in round holes to play in the traditional Manchester United style, which he had been coaching for so many years. Fortunately the club was safe in the league table and Jimmy told the team that his aim was for them to concentrate on the cup.

Gradually a pattern emerged, with Ernie Taylor scheming and Freddie Goodwin up in support of him. All the time he had to juggle with his resources, pulling players out of the team when they were too tired, gambling on one man, then another. Before the first game after the disaster, the now famous fifth round FA Cup tie against Sheffield Wednesday, he inspired the team by reminding them of the players who had died so tragically and those still injured and finished by saying that, with the Old Trafford crowd behind them, they might just achieve a miracle.

The cup-tie was played out in an atmosphere of undiluted emotion. Crowds began arriving at the ground hours before the kick-off. Extra police had to be called in to help control the huge throng. Ticket touts, some of whom had travelled from London, were offering tickets at hugely inflated prices. One young fellow offered £1 for a 2-shilling popular-side ticket. The near 62,000 crowd were crying and laughing nervously and were visibly drained, but they created a wall of noise.

Murphy had taken his squad to Blackpool to get the players away from the mourning of a devastated Manchester. The team had trained on the beach outside the Norbrek Hydro, taken walks along the sand, breathing in the brisk fresh air in an attempt to prepare themselves for their return to Old Trafford. Not surprisingly, the youngsters were totally bemused by this atmosphere. With hindsight, deep down inside the tragedy affected them badly. They were now expected to rescue United's cause - a heavy burden for players so young.

The gates at Old Trafford were locked two hours before the kick-off that night. Before the referee blew his whistle to start the game, the spectators were already emotionally drained and many thousands were distraught - though they willed the team on to victory. Grown men and women were openly crying, even hard-nosed policemen were seen shedding a tear. If ever a game was won on sheer will power then this must surely have been it. Sheffield Wednesday were beaten 3-0 as the new United or 'Murphy's Marvels' as the newspapers christened them (a sobriquet not appreciated by Murphy or his team) converted the crowd's emotion into a stunning performance.

Every player gave a hundred percent, then dug down to their bootlaces and came up with a little extra. Also playing in United's hastily patched up team was Mark 'Pancho' Pearson - a terrier of an inside-forward who could make the ball talk, so clever and skillful was he.

Shay Brennan, at just 20, who had played table tennis most of the day because he thought he hadn't a chance of being selected, ended up the hero, scoring twice. Before Munich, Brennan was in United's third team. Bill Foulkes captained the team and Harry Gregg was in goal. In normal circumstances, these two players would never have been allowed on the field. After all, they had both been involved in the plane crash and must have been affected physically and mentally. But these were not normal circumstances, so both Harry and Bill led by example.

At the final whistle, a roar of sound hit the night air that could be heard for miles around. The fantastic Busby Babes, the incredible Red Devils of Manchester United, had risen again in the smoke, tears and cheers of Old Trafford. In the bath after the game, the bright-eyed boy, rejoicing in the name of Seamus (known as Shay to his club-mates) Brennan, was crying with emotion. This after a sensational first game in which he scored twice, to become the first hero of the new Babes. Up in the stands, a commentator was talking to Dennis Viollet, Kenny Morgans, Albert Scanlon and Ray Wood in the ward of their hospital in Munich.

Centre-forward Alex Dawson, recalling this historic night, the rebirth of Britain's most famous club said: "There was a minute's silence and all the team were aware of how important this match was going to be. Little Ernie Taylor was the master craftsman. He held us together, shouting instructions and encouraging us. After about fifteen minutes he nearly scored himself when his drive from about twenty yards hit the foot of the post. Afterwards, Jimmy told us that Roger Byrne, Mark Jones, Billy Whelan and the other lads who had died would have been proud of us. It was a night that will remain in my thoughts until I die. I'm just glad that we did the lads proud."

Bionic Bobby

After he was released from the Rechts der Isar hospital in Munich, Bobby Charlton returned home to Beatrice Terrace, Ashington. After a few days of him moping about, his mother Cissie made an appointment for him to see Dr McPherson, the family GP. After a long chat the doctor explained that he had been in the RAF during the war and seen many of his friends killed. He advised Bobby to get back to playing football as quickly as possible. After a couple more days Bobby phoned Old Trafford and told Jimmy Murphy he was coming back to Manchester. Jimmy was pleased - he needed Bobby desperately. As a precaution, Jimmy tried out Bobby in a hastily-arranged practice match behind closed doors at Old Trafford. Bobby said afterwards he felt stiff and slow, nevertheless Murphy told him he would be playing in the sixth round of the FA Cup against West Bromwich Albion, two games in which he returned to somewhere near his best form.

It can be argued that most of the players who survived the Munich crash were never the same force again afterwards. However, it must also be stated that two in particular went on to serve United brilliantly for a number of years after the disaster. Bobby Charlton was one, Bill Foulkes the other. Before Munich, Bobby was regarded as a United star of the future - his cannonball shooting being a speciality - but while he had gained a regular first team place at the expense of Billy Whelan, little attention had been paid to him in the reports of United games. But following the disaster, Bobby seemed to undergo a transformation, when in reality it was just that his game was now scrutinised in minute detail and highlighted by the newspapers. Nonetheless he seemed to mature almost overnight and was capped by England soon after - he went from strength to strength. His final record as a player with United and England needs little introduction or explanation - it is fair to call him England's greatest-ever footballer.

For both Bobby and Bill Foulkes, the Munich disaster was a watershed that unlike so many of their fellow survivors, they were able to overcome. Foulkes' career was transformed when he moved from his previous position at full-back to make the centre-half spot his own for the next decade. Like Bobby, Bill was a part of United's FA Cup, League Championship and European Cup winning sides, their presence a constant reminder of the vibrancy, optimism and tragedy of earlier times during the colourful mid-sixties.

Was this United's greatest ever performance?

On March 1st 1958, United travelled to the Hawthorns for a sixth round FA Cup tie against West Bromwich Albion. It's safe to say that United's followers thought this was one test their favourites wouldn't pass. West Brom were a cultured, classy team, packed with hardened professionals. Don Howe and Bobby Robson featured prominently, while the half-back line of Dudley, Kennedy and Barlow was one of the strongest and classiest in the division. Meanwhile, the potent strike force of Ronnie Allen and Derek Kevan posed a threat to the steadiest of defences. In the run-up to the game, West Brom manager Vic Buckingham told the press that while his team had sympathy with United's plight, they were determined to knock them out of the Cup. So in front of a bumper 58,250 crowd, a fascinating cup-tie got under way.

Immediately one player stood out like a giant. That man was pint-sized Ernie Taylor, standing a mere five feet high. Ernie played what was probably the greatest game of his long and illustrious football life. So big was United's heart that the highly-fancied West Bromwich were panicking and making mistakes. After about six minutes Ernie put the Reds in the lead, only for Allen to equalise a few minutes later. Then a minute before half-time, Taylor's fierce shot hit the bar and Alex Dawson dashed through at terrific speed to beat the goalkeeper to the ball and head home the rebound to put United ahead again. It was a magnificent piece of opportunism. This certainly wasn't a game for the faint hearted. The second half saw West Brom pile everything into attack. The last 20 minutes saw Harry Gregg achieving the impossible, diving full length, clutching shots from under the bar and fearlessly throwing himself at the feet of oncoming forwards. Meanwhile Bill Foulkes steadied his team under one of the fiercest onslaughts any defence could ever have faced. With four minutes left, Roy Horobin scrambled the equaliser, though many believed that Ronnie Cope had cleared the ball before it crossed the line. Only this lucky, late goal robbed the Reds of a well-merited victory.

"I'm not like Matt Busby," declared Jimmy after the game. "Matt can keep quiet when he's really upset. I cannot keep quiet when I see and hear the players, and now the supporters, made the victims of cheap criticisms." This was Jimmy's reply to the cynics who claimed that United were trading on the disaster. Jimmy was blazing about these accusations. "The Manchester United fans have shared our successes. They have been the proudest supporters in the country. Of course they stuck out their chests and boasted that they belonged to Manchester United. We had the good fortune to give them something to boast about." Several newspapers claimed that the United followers were hysterical and teams playing against United were put under unfair pressure. Jimmy was wild and said neither he nor the United fans expected special treatment from any source. "All we ask," said Jimmy, "is to be allowed to play our own way and try and get to Wembley. Our fans are fantastic, shouting us to Wembley."

The replay took place at Old Trafford the following Wednesday, March 5th and 60,560 fans packed into the stadium. Most people believed that United's best chance of winning had gone with the first game. They believed that classy West Brom would not allow the young United lads the opportunity of repeating the zeal and zest they had displayed the previous Saturday. United suffered a huge blow when Stan Crowther, their recent signing, was injured and failed a fitness test, so 20-year-old Bobby Harrop took his place in the team. There were an estimated 40,000 locked outside when the gates were closed at Old Trafford. Women screamed and were carried fainting from the crush outside, mounted police had to force their horses into the densest parts of the crowd to rescue people in danger of being crushed.

The United players were particularly upset about the death of Duncan Edwards who, despite fighting bravely, had finally succumbed to horrendous injuries. Jimmy Murphy was more upset than most but masked his heartbreak by geeing his team up for another assault on the cup.

In the event, Bobby Charlton had an absolutely brilliant game and from the chances he created, United should have taken an early lead. The crowd outside were receiving a commentary from the lucky fans inside the ground but it wasn't until the 89th minute, with normal time running out and extra time looming that Charlton, who had moved over to the right wing, set off on an heroic dribble - beating man after man. Then an explosion of noise hit the night air, shaking the windows of the surrounding houses. It was heard three miles away. It was ear-splitting, shattering. Bobby had crossed and Colin Webster had side-footed the ball over the line for the only goal of the match. Caps, hats and scarves were thrown into the air. Jubilant fans danced a jig with those nearest to them. The Busby Babes, Murphy's Mites, call them what you will, had achieved the apparently impossible again. The vision of FA Cup glory, so soon after such tragedy, shone brighter than ever before. Bobby Harrop played splendidly and fully justified Murphy's faith in him. But this was a magnificent team performance.

Three days later, United faced West Brom again, this time in the League and the bubble burst as United received a real walloping (4-0) from the Midlands team. However, nobody at Old Trafford was unduly surprised or worried by the result. As the *Empire News* said: "We're all expecting too much from 'Murphy Minnows'. Kids like Mark Pearson and Alex Dawson should not be expected to turn out in five high-pressure matches in 17 days without showing some sign of wear and tear. Jimmy Murphy's biggest problem is to retain for Cup duty the energy and enthusiasm of his magnificent bunch of fighters. At the same time, he must see these lads running themselves into the ground in the lost cause of the League championship. What a dilemma!" The newspaper was correct in its assessment, especially about the younger players.

The England Headmaster

Jimmy was still desperate for players to help with United's various teams. Kids out of the reserves and 'A' teams were being hurriedly promoted to help fulfil fixtures. Then, a couple of weeks after the crash, into Old Trafford walked Bob Hardisty, Derek Lewin and a diminutive little chap named Warren Bradley. These three gentlemen came from the famous amateur club Bishop Auckland, up in the North East. They had come in answer to Jimmy's SOS.

Warren stood a mere 5 feet 5 inches and was born in Hyde, a few miles from Old Trafford. He had served in the RAF and on his demob had become a schoolteacher in the North East. The intention of the three amateur players was to help out United's Central League team until such time as United felt able to use their own players. As a teenager, Warren had played for Bolton Wanderers on amateur forms. He was a speedy and courageous little right-winger and he impressed Jimmy so much that when his friends moved back to the North East, he stayed on at Old Trafford. He eventually made 66 first team appearances, scoring 21 goals. He was also capped by Sir Walter Winterbottom for the England team. Not bad going for an amateur who had just come to the club in an emergency. He did of course, turn part-time professional for United.

"I had never met Jimmy Murphy," said Warren, who stayed on at the club until 1962. "Of course I had heard of the good work he and Matt Busby had achieved over the years in developing the famous Busby Babes teams, and the players they nurtured were destined to dominate British football. Imagine my surprise when before my first game for the reserves, Jimmy came into the dressing room. The younger players, who had been brought up with the club, were in awe of him, they really were. Wilf McGuinness respected Jimmy enormously and said that he had made him and the other lads into the players they were and would become. There were no hystrionics from him and he didn't throw cups against the wall or anything like that. However, when he started his talk the dressing room, which is usually a noisy and boisterous place, fell silent. As he spoke he moved his hands about, walking around, looking straight at players. He was so enthusiastic and eager that his words came out like machine gun bullets. Nobody else spoke or interrupted him. He was so passionate and explicit about the game. He left little doubt about what he wanted the players to do and how he wanted them to perform on the field.

"His love and pride for Manchester United shone through and he expected anybody wearing the famous red shirt to feel just like him. Mind you, looking back on it now he must have been under enormous pressure to keep things ticking over at the club. The younger players told me he was like this every time they played. But they loved him. He had a magnetic influence over players.

"After the FA Cup Final against my old club Bolton Wanderers, Jimmy went on to do a magnificent job for Wales in the 1958 World Cup in Sweden. When the following season started, I was still teaching and playing in the reserves. Matt Busby returned and took over the reins again and Jimmy went back to helping the youngsters. I think he was happier helping to develop the youngsters and he never liked the publicity of management one little bit. Sir Matt was completely the opposite of Jimmy. He was quiet, courteous, sociable but very determined and firm. He had a knack of saying the right thing to you and making you believe that you were a good player. Both Matt and Jimmy were charismatic but in different ways. I was teaching and playing for United and it was difficult, but a wonderful experience and nobody at the club ever said to me that I wouldn't get selected for the first team if I didn't turn professional."

The Black Prince rides to the rescue

United were drawn against Second Division Fulham in the semi-final of the FA Cup, to be played at Villa Park. Just a few days before the match, Tom Finney said that, although it was a few short weeks ago that he first heard the numbing news of the Manchester United air disaster, "United have proved that real greatness means much more than a galaxy of star players. It means possessing a thing called Spirit. Believe me, I am not being sentimental when I say that I've stood back in proud bewilderment at the fantastic recovery made by these men at Old Trafford. Behind it all, of course, is this incredible man called Jimmy Murphy - a man who has been a rival of mine as a player, as the assistant manager of a rival Lancashire club, and as the manager of a rival national team. This for Jimmy must have been the most remorseless month ever spent by any man behind the scenes of modern sport. Yet it is still a quality greater than even Jimmy Murphy possesses which has prompted this miracle of Manchester. There would have been nothing but sympathy for them if they had announced: 'We just cannot see this season through.' It would have been a perfectly human reaction. But now, as they fight on, we see them for what they are; - a superhuman club."

Nevertheless, victory over Fulham would not be easy. They were one of the classiest teams in the Football League with some fine players. Johnny Haynes, their captain and inside-forward, was among the best players in Europe, if not the world and went on to captain England. Gibralta-born goalkeeper Tony Elio Macedo was reputed to be amongst the best keepers in Britain while the bearded Jimmy Hill was another brainy inside-forward who posed a danger to any team. Flying winger Tosh Chamberlain and robust centre-forward Arthur Stevens would threaten United's makeshift defence. Roy Dwight, George Cohen, Roy Bentley and Jim Langley also figured in a side that on paper were more than a match for Jimmy Murphy's patched-up team.

"I am one of Manchester United's greatest admirers," stated Johnny

Haynes in a daily newspaper. "However, Fulham are determined to hammer United. We know the majority of the country are willing United to win our semi-final, but I can assure you that every Fulham player will not be pulling any punches when we meet them because we want to get to Wembley ourselves."

In United's dressing room at Villa Park, Murphy went round each individual player talking to them and encouraging them to give of their best. "Remember boys," he shouted, "no game is ever lost until it's been won. Don't any of you forget it!"

As it happened, in front of 69,745 spectators, United and Fulham served up one of the most exciting and thrilling semi-finals ever seen. Bobby Charlton scored two beauties with his left foot. His goals were exquisite masterpieces of execution and improvisation. It was end-to-end action until referee Kingston blew the final whistle. In the final couple of minutes, Bobby almost scored the winner and his hat-trick when he drove in another blockbuster which hit the underside of the bar. The fans were hoarse and drained of emotion with the atmosphere of the occasion. The match ended all square at 2-2. The replay at Highbury caused a great deal of frustration and bitterness in Manchester. It appeared unfair that the Reds should have to travel to Fulham's doorstep for such an important game. There was also the United fans' expense and travel arrangements to take into consideration.

Despite all the fuss and commotion, the match was played at Highbury, on the afternoon of Wednesday March 26th 1958. It was one of the first matches to be televised live, which not only affected the size of the crowd but meant that many Mancunian businesses were deserted as dental appointments and funerals were made top priority by employees. In reality, the entire city was glued to their 12-inch black-and-white Bush television sets, while those who couldn't afford a telly crowded outside television shop windows to get a view of the game.

And what a game it was on that damp, dismal afternoon. 18-year-old Alex Dawson scored with a diving header after 15 minutes, only for Stevens to equalise eleven minutes later. Tony Macedo, Fulham's hero at Villa Park, who had received special permission from the RAF to play in this game, seemed out of sorts and worried by young Dawson's shoulder charges. In the event, Dawson scored a record-breaking hat-trick, as United thrillingly won through 5-3, with Shay Brennan and Bobby Charlton getting the other two goals. Jimmy thought the world of Alex and was always encouraging him. He was overjoyed at the result and ruffled Alex's hair in congratulating him at the end of the match.

As the players trooped from the mud-clinging pitch, the Fulham players congratulated United's depleted team. Bobby Charlton, however, looked distraught as, head bowed, he made his way to the dressing room with several Fulham players slapping him on the back. Alex Dawson was obviously exhilarated about his brilliant hat-trick, a record which he still holds to this day as the youngest and last player to score a hat-trick in an FA Cup semi-final. The United party quietly celebrated on their journey back home and there was some sense of fulfilment from the team, Jimmy Murphy and the other United officials.

Cup Fever

Like all the United players, Freddie Goodwin was inundated with requests for FA Cup Final tickets. Freddie had been a regular first team player since Munich and was thrilled and delighted when United finally reached Wembley. Another of the unsung heroes that helped rescue United during their darkest hour, Freddie, who stood 6 feet 2 inches, was a friendly affable person, with not a hint of conceit in him. He said that since arriving back home from Highbury after that remarkable semi-final victory he and his wife had managed only one night at home. "We just daren't stay at home," said Freddie, "we couldn't sit by the fireside, put on our slippers and watch television or relax. The fans wouldn't leave us in peace." He had only recently moved house and was surprised that fans had discovered his address.

From six o'clock onwards, his doorbell never stopped ringing with complete strangers asking if they could leave their names and addresses for a Cup Final ticket. He answered one call and found six youngsters standing there with money in their hands. He also received numerous letters seeking tickets. He got a letter from some friends of Eddie Colman begging his help in obtaining tickets. Cliff Gladwin, the Derbyshire fast bowler who Freddie had often played cricket against, told him that in past years he had always been playing cricket on Cup Final day, but in 1958, Derbyshire started their fixtures later than usual, and he'd just love to see the final. Alec Gaskell, who had spent three seasons at Old Trafford as a centre-forward before moving to Newcastle and later Southport, asked Freddie if he could supply him with a ticket.

One gentleman knocked on Freddie's door and his wife Sylvia answered it. The man said he was a coal merchant and offered a ton of coal for any kind of ticket - again it brought a "Sorry, it can't be done". Freddie took all the requests in his stride. Of course he couldn't supply everyone with a ticket and took the time to write, phone or explain personally that it was impossible. One letter he received was from a supporter he met at Roger Byrne's funeral. He wasn't asking for a ticket, he had the required number of tokens to get one from the club. However, he asked Freddie if he could arrange for him to meet all the team before they left for Wembley to shake the hands with each player and wish them the best of luck. "Just an afterthought," remarked Freddie, "I'm just thankful we weren't on the phone at home then!"

On April 14th a *Daily Sketch* report was headlined "This is a disgrace!" referring to news that four Manchester United players: Bill Foulkes, Harry Gregg, Bobby Charlton and Kenny Morgans had flatly refused a compensation offer of £500 made by British European Airways for their afternoon of terror at Munich. This was disgraceful, penny-pinching, and quite unrealistic compensation offer by BEA, who were required to pay up to £3,000. Bill Foulkes told the paper that as athletes they had to take the view that the accident could have an effect on their footballing futures. "Part of the plane gave me a crack on the head, and even now I get headaches," he explained. Bobby Charlton received a letter telling him he had been awarded £500 but like Foulkes and the others he refused it. Bobby said he had sought legal advice.

Even as they approached the Cup Final for the climax of the greatest story in football history, these players lived with the fear of delayed shock or a nervous reaction. These young men had to show an outward face of courage and normality, long after the nation's compassion had ebbed away. Yet who knew how deeply their terrible experiences would cut into their athletic lives? Not BEA's insurance expert.

A BEA spokesman said that the figures offered were assessed on what particular hardship had been suffered by each claimant: "It's conceivable one chap thinks he has suffered more than another." He added that the position was quite fluid and each claim was open to negotiation. BEA received admiration for their thorough and compassionate on-the-spot deeds at Munich but, said the paper, they had insulted the four players. BEA were told they couldn't measure the destruction of football's finest club team in terms of personal injuries alone. The paper appealed to BEA to make the broadest possible gesture. On a footnote, it was mentioned that BEA were negotiating separately with the more seriously injured survivors.

*

In the six weeks since Munich Murphy and Manchester United had performed miracles that no one dreamt possible. But now the one question on everyone's lips was: "Could they pull off the biggest miracle of all? Could they win the Cup Final?" Standing in their way were Bolton Wanderers, United's opponents on Wembley's green, gleaming turf on May 3rd. Bolton were a tough side, blending punch with craft, as well as being slick operators of a masterly offside trap. They were just the sort of team to throw Jimmy Murphy's makeshift Manchester eleven in this final Cup hurdle. Nat Lofthouse, Bolton's captain and England international, said his biggest fear was that United would be carried along by the same tremendous emotional surge he experienced when Bolton met Blackpool in 1953 in what has gone down in history as the 'Matthews Final'.

"It was fantastic," said Nat, "I shall never forget it. The 100,000 erupted in a great surge of feeling that swept us out of the Cup. Of course Matthews was a marvel but I have never known anything like the atmosphere that day when Stanley played his greatest game. And I think it may happen again when we play Manchester United." He went on to say that he had no doubt that the excited, ecstatic thousands of supporters, when they crammed into the great, grey bowl of Wembley, would give United the ovation of a lifetime.

After their final League game of that never-to-be-forgotten season, Jimmy took his squad away from Manchester to prepare them in his favourite location - the Norbreck Hydro Hotel in Blackpool. He was relieved the season was almost over, although he still had three Cup games left before a much-needed break for the summer could be taken. The FA Cup Final against Bolton was his first priority but United also had a two-legged European Cup semi-final against AC Milan to cope with.

Understandably Jimmy was worried. He knew the team had done remarkably well in reaching the FA Cup Final, but he was also aware they had achieved this feat without two genuine wingers. He had been aware of this problem when taking over Matt Busby's job after the crash. After all, he'd lost four wingers in one fell swoop, players who were internationals at either senior or junior level. This would be a huge problem for any First Division club especially as David Pegg, Johnny Berry, Kenny Morgans and Albert Scanlon were first teamers. It is true he had tried to sign a couple of wingers from other clubs but for one reason or another, he had not managed to complete a deal.

One night, after most of the hotel lights had been extinguished, Jimmy was sitting at a small table in the hotel with two young journalists, David Meek and Keith Dewhurst. The trio were enjoying a quiet drink when Jimmy, looking melancholy, told them that he and Bert Whalley were out every night coaching the boys who had been involved in the crash. "Or we would be watching juniors in games or persuading their parents to let their sons join us. Coming home late on trains," added

Jimmy, "Yes, every day and night we were working for United. Every night until maybe one night, I'd be at home unexpectedly and the wife, she'd say, 'Good grief! Who are you?'"

Taking a few sips of his drink, Jimmy continued. "We were ruthless, you know, and we had this dream. To do it perfectly. We'd win everything but with the proper elegance. We'd play the sweetest football. We'd have great players. Poetic. Eleven grown men chasing a ball. Very poetic. I'm nearly fifty, see. So's Matt. Can't ever do it again. Can we?"

David Meek said he thought coming back would be an awful strain on Matt Busby. "Aye," said a sad-faced Murphy, "don't you two go worrying him, either. The lads will try to act as normally as possible. They have an idea what he'll be going through." With that, Jimmy finished his drink and got to his feet. He smiled at the pair who had listened to him so intently. "You're good listeners, boys. I need that. Always have, I suppose. Bert Whalley was my pal. I really miss him."

He had been pondering his team selection for the FA Cup Final for a couple of weeks leading up to the big day. He had tried several permutations but whichever way he looked at the situation he knew he would have to play Bolton without two wingers. And he knew that the wide open spaces of Wembley were ideal for fast, clever wing men. Very few people knew it apart from his family, but after the Munich disaster Jimmy hardly ever had a full night's uninterrupted sleep. He found the events of that terrible tragedy too shocking to contemplate. He was disconsolate and truly heartbroken. He would come home late at night when his family had gone to bed and sit in his armchair, pour himself a glass of whisky and lose himself in his thoughts. Apart from his wife and children Manchester United was his only love and passion. It maybe clichéd, but it is nevertheless true to say that when those players died something in Jimmy Murphy died along with them.

Keith Dewhurst, a prominent journalist with the old *Manchester Evening Chronicle* which closed a few years after Munich, was close to Jimmy Murphy. On Wednesday April 23rd 1958 he wrote a rivetting article on him. "Manchester United's Jimmy Murphy is a short,

Munich

explosive character who hates crowds and publicity, and people who do not know him well think that he is hard and difficult to approach. When they know him a little better they think that he is a kind of spectacular joker. His team talks are epics of colourful language and wild gestures, far removed from the calm analysis of Matt Busby. His stock greeting of 'Hello, my old pal', equally effective for handling pressmen, players, genuine old pals, barmen, waiters and the people who pretend to be genuine old pals in the hope of scrounging tickets, has in fact become a joke among the team. Everyone is 'old palling' everyone else.

"The players may smile at Jimmy's jokes and mannerisms, but they know that these mask one of the shrewdest soccer brains of all time. When you really know Jimmy Murphy you know a man of deep feelings and sympathy which he does not choose to expose all the time for the world to knock around. You know a masterly talker and story teller. You know perhaps the best football coach Britain has ever seen. Murphy has the managerial flair, too. His handling of the Manchester United team since Munich has been superb. He has had only a handful of players, and some of those are not really up to first team standards. Yet look at the way he has used them. Look at the hunch that paid off when Shay Brennan hit two goals in the Sheffield Wednesday Cup-tie. Look at the dropping of Mark Pearson and the restoration of Brennan in the Highbury replay - another match-winning move. Look at the switching of Ken Morgans to the left wing, a move which has at least solved a desperate problem, and may yet win the cup. Look at Murphy, buffooning to keep the players' morale up, and yet all the time thinking, thinking, thinking. Staying up all night in London before the semi-final. Deciding on the Morgans switch when everyone thought he was asleep in the corner of the train compartment. I know what he will say to skipper Billy Foulkes before the Cup Final. I can only say the same to Jimmy: 'Best of Luck, My old Pal'."

Every neutral was hoping for a United victory. Matt Busby made a miraculous recovery and took his place at Wembley alongside the rest of the United staff. Jimmy and the players wanted him to lead them out at

129

Wembley, but Busby wouldn't hear of it and told Jimmy he must lead out the team. Besides, he was too ill and needed crutches to help him with his balance. He did hobble into the dressing room to wish the lads luck and he told the team to follow Jimmy's instructions. The United players wore a special badge on their shirts depicting a phoenix rising from the ashes. It was a fact that United had risen again. Just before the team walked out of the dressing room, Jimmy turned to them and said: "Lads, to get this far has been a miracle. I would just like to say to each and every one of you from the bottom of my heart a big thank you for all you have done. Win, lose, or draw, I am proud of each and every one of you."

There was no fairy-tale ending for Manchester United. Although nothing would ever erase the memory of the never-to-be-forgotten games, this patched up team played in an effort to reach Wembley, Bolton deserved their 2-0 victory, Nat Lofthouse scoring both goals. There was a great deal of discussion as to the legality of his second, when he charged both Harry Gregg and the ball into the net. It would never have been allowed today, but it counted in 1958. There was also another much-talked about incident involving Colin Webster and Bolton forward Denis Stevens. Webster clashed violently with the Bolton player - it was said he head-butted him - and both teams almost went at it hammer and tongs before the referee helped stop a riot.

Dennis Viollet returned for the final after playing in only one League game since Munich. He looked a ghost of his former razor-sharp self, although to be fair to Dennis, the whole United team failed to function. Although the United officials were upset and disappointed they congratulated Nat Lofthouse and the Bolton team on their victory and took the defeat like true sportsmen. In truth all the turmoil and heartbreak of the past few months seemed to catch up with the players. Jimmy believed that United never did themselves justice, he said that the team had taken far too much out of themselves, both mentally and physically in those heart-rending, hectic weeks after the disaster. Nevertheless, the team received a fantastic welcome when they arrived back in Manchester. Hundreds of thousands filled the route down to Manchester Town Hall.

*

The late Colin Webster always insisted that it was Jimmy Murphy who almost single-handedly dragged Manchester United to Wembley. "Murphy was our inspiration on that emotional and heartbreaking journey to Wembley in 1958," remembered Colin. "He was heartbroken, like we all were, about the lads that died and the people injured. Many times I would see him in the dressing room on his own sobbing his heart out. At that time the club was in turmoil. We players were under a tremendous amount of pressure from well intentioned but sorrowful and heartbroken supporters who were willing us to succeed for the people who had perished in Munich. It was the kind of situation that nobody is prepared for. I personally attended several funerals and it made me depressed and affected me inwardly a great deal afterwards. However, once Jimmy got us out on the pitch he would mask his own feelings and preach a sermon we all wanted to hear and in fairness to the team, especially the younger players, they all did everything he asked of them and more.

"Yes, of course this could have been the reason why a few of them never made it as regular first team players with Manchester United because, through the circumstances of the crash, these lads were pushed much too quickly into action for the first team and believe me it was hectic action and very physical in the games following Munich."

Colin said that Jimmy would devise plans for the makeshift United team in those important FA Cup games and that his team talks were heart-tugging speeches made with tears in his eyes and extravagant hand gestures. Jimmy almost begged them to win for their former team-mates. Colin, like a number of other older players and officials, firmly believed that Jimmy was never cut out to be a club manager. "He was happiest coaching the players, he hated the paperwork involved with management. He was in his element outside with the players, working on moves and suggesting different things and so on. He could inspire you to climb a mountain so convincing was he when talking. I was a little older than the other lads, I'm not talking about Ernie Taylor or Bill Foulkes and Harry Gregg, but kids like Shay Brennan, Mark Pearson and Alex Dawson. They had been groomed by Jimmy and hung on to his every word and went out and pulled that little bit extra out for him. We older players gave everything we had to give of course, but the youngsters didn't have the experience to relax a little. They were exceptionally good kids and their pedigree was sound."

Looking back on one of the most remarkable runs in the history of the FA Cup, it could be said that while the tie against Sheffield Wednesday was won on raw emotion, the 2-2 draw achieved at West Bromwich Albion could be called United's greatest-ever performance, when considering the circumstances, opposition and form of the team. The semi-final win against Fulham, moreover, was a triumph for Murphy's tactical system - the team played good, exciting football following Dawson's unnerving of Fulham's defence and goalkeeper.

"It was the most rewarding day of my life," Murphy would later recall. "It was a fitting tribute to the old team when I knew we had reached Wembley. Though defeat in the final against Bolton was a disappointment, I personally don't think it really mattered."

Murphy's World

"I am sad to say that Wales has never got anywhere near the achievements of 1958. How do we find another Jimmy Murphy? It's impossible!"
KEN JONES

As if leading United's recovery after Munich was not enough, Jimmy Murphy was not afforded a break - he was to lead Wales into their first and (up to now, only) World Cup Finals. With the most limited resources, the Welsh had lost only five of their previous 16 international matches. From being hopeless outsiders they reached the last eight in the 1958 World Cup, only losing to eventual World Champions Brazil by a solitary Pele goal. It was a truly fantastic and memorable achievement, and the success was down to one man: Jimmy Murphy! The players were behind him to a man. The squad had been selected in April 1958 and although every other nation selected 40 players from which to pick a final 22, the Welsh selectors, to keep costs down, only selected 18 players for Sweden with the remaining four staying at home on stand-by.

There were only seven or eight players certain to be in the squad and they were: goalkeeper Jack Kelsey, left-back Mel Hopkins, captain and left-half Dave Bowen, golden-haired inside-left Ivor Allchurch, flying left-winger Cliff Jones, right-winger Terry Medwin and, of course, Wales' greatest-ever footballer, centre-forward John Charles of Juventus. The other players selected included Mel Charles, younger brother of John, who could play centre-half or centre-forward, Stuart Williams, a full-back, Derrick Sullivan who could play either full-back or wing-half, wing-half Trevor Edwards, powerful inside-left Colin Baker, Ken Leek, reserve goalkeeper Ken Jones, inside-forward Roy Vernon, tenacious wing-half Vic Crowe and United's Colin Webster.

The selectors couldn't agree on the 18th player. It was a toss-up between Cardiff's experienced 29-year-old inside-forward, Ron Hewitt or 18-year-old Manchester United winger Kenny Morgans. There was no doubt in Jimmy Murphy's mind that the pre-Munich, Morgans would have been an absolute certainty to go to Sweden, but though Kenny had played a few reserve and the occasional first team game, he was still suffering the ill-effects of the crash. Murphy wanted to play him in the FA Cup Final but decided that young Kenny was neither physically or mentally able to play in such an important game. In the end, the selectors opted for Hewitt. Kenny had been told before United's crash that he would be going to Sweden if Wales qualified. Later he was told that he should take a year's complete rest but because of United's desperate situation, he had to help out and play. In reality he had lost his speed and was never the same wonderfully exciting player he was before the disaster. Jimmy was upset that the teenager wouldn't be going to Sweden but thought the long rest might do him good for the following season.

Jimmy's hands were tied over three further players. Trevor Ford, Ray Daniel and Derek Tapscott were three of Wales' greatest post-war footballers. These three would certainly have been in Jimmy's squad under normal circumstances, but the Welsh FA chairman, Milwyn Jenkins, told him that for a variety of reasons there was no chance whatsoever of any of them being selected.

Jimmy was a great admirer of Trevor Ford, an old-fashioned centre-forward who specialised in scoring goals and charging goalkeepers. Ford, a fiery, all-action type of player, was banned by the FA for three seasons, although he had been playing on the continent for PSV Eindhoven in Holland. The reason for the suspension was because he had written a book entitled *I Lead The Attack*, which was extremely controversial to say the least. In his book, Ford mentioned illegal payments made to him and other players by his former club Sunderland. Technically, Wales could still have selected him for the World Cup and he would have been a great asset, but the sanctimonious Welsh selection committee would not consider him under any circumstances. Ford couldn't understand all the fuss about his book, and claimed he was just telling the truth. He always believed he could have helped his country and cried when he was told he had no chance of playing for Wales again.

Ray Daniel was a brilliant defender, stamped class with a capital C. He wasn't selected, it was believed, because of a harmless incident in Czechoslovakia after Wales lost 2-0. Daniel was an outgoing person who spoke his mind, liked a laugh and a sing-song but during the defeat in Prague he had unluckily scored an own-goal. This wasn't held against him but it certainly didn't help his cause. On the team bus returning to the hotel after the game it was quiet and everyone was dejected when suddenly Ray started singing loudly. He was singing songs from the hit musical *Guys and Dolls*. Not surprisingly, Welsh FA secretary Herbert Powell took offence. Mr Powell, a prudish bachelor, was a religious man and a staunch member of the Church of Wales who was known to sing hymns while travelling with the team. He rose from his seat and walked to the back of the bus to where Daniel was sitting. He told the player to stop singing and a quiet conversation followed and whatever was said, Daniel's international career was finished. He never played for Wales again and aged 29, would have been a certainty for Jimmy's team.

Derek Tapscott was a goalscoring forward with Arsenal and another who would have been in Murphy's World Cup team in Sweden. Why wasn't he selected? After all, he was only 25. Well, according to Derek, it was because just before the World Cup he was approached by a prominent Welsh selector who asked him to leave Arsenal and join Cardiff City, promising him that if he joined Cardiff he would be in the squad for Sweden. He refused, and consequently wasn't selected. He would have been able to help Wales a great deal as he could play at centre-forward or inside-forward. In later years, Derek said he believed that had Wales selected him and Trevor Ford, their chances would have been all the greater. Ironically after the World Cup, in September 1958, he did sign for Cardiff agreeing to go back to Wales after his father became ill. He was capped twice soon afterwards.

The selection of 25-year-old Colin Webster raised a few eyebrows and was most certainly influenced by Murphy. Colin was a very misunderstood player. He wasn't a regular first team player at Old Trafford, although a very valuable squad member. He came under Murphy's wing because he played regularly for the Central League team. Jimmy knew him like the back of his hand. He knew Colin was a tough competitor and hardly ever intimidated by big, rough defenders. He wasn't very big at 5 feet 8 inches and weighing about 11 stones, he was a dour-looking man who always looked serious but had a wonderful sense of humour. Years later, I used to meet him on my trips to South Wales for boxing tournaments. I would get him a couple of tickets to watch the fights and afterwards we would go for a meal and have a drink. Colin always wore his Manchester United club blazer. It still fitted him perfectly and he was always proud to wear it. During his playing days, he was known as the 'Bad Boy of Welsh Football,' for reasons that will become clear later. He could handle himself, of that there is not the slightest doubt.

"The most money I earned was with Worcester City, where I got forty quid a week and a few extra quid for every goal I scored," he once told me. During his five years in Manchester he liked to drink in Frascati's on Oxford Road, a lively place with music and entertainment. Colin was often in the company of Tommy Taylor. "Jimmy and Matt thought I used to encourage Tommy to go drinking," he said laughing. "That was a joke. Tommy could drink me under the table any night of the week. I enjoyed my time with United. Jimmy was great to me. I was often under the cosh from him and I know that he didn't agree with many things I did but he never held a grudge." Colin said he wasn't one of the Welsh selectors' favourite people, and he knew he wasn't at all popular with them. "Yes, I wasn't one of their blue-eyed boys, I knew that. It was Jimmy who selected me for Wales, not them." He said he was banned from playing for Wales again because of an incident in a nightclub during the competition, of which more later.

On June 2nd 1958, the Welsh team finally boarded their aeroplane bound for Sweden. Jimmy sat with trainer Jack Jones and team doctor William Hughes. Milwyn Jenkins, the chairman of the Welsh FA, secretary Herbert Powell and his sister Violet sat together and eleven selectors, some accompanied by their wives, plus five Welsh FA councillors, sat at the front. All the players sat together at the back. What did Jimmy think about this? Well, as already stated, Jimmy was tired and heartbroken after the Munich tragedy, so he said very little but thought a great deal. Before Munich, there was no way he would have allowed all these officials to travel but he just smiled and got on with the job of helping his country achieve some pride and respectability on the world stage.

In truth, the Welsh squad, while they had a number of quality players of the calibre of Kelsey, Bowen, Jones and Allchurch, were short of truly top-quality players. Most of the squad plied their trade in the Second Division. Murphy also had the added worry of not knowing if John Charles would be given permission to play for his country by his club Juventus and the Italian Football Federation. Jimmy was annoyed that the Welsh FA had not flown to Italy and spoken to whoever was in charge of the John Charles situation and sorted it out. As a result, he was left wondering wheter or not his trump card would arrive in Sweden.

The planning for the Welsh team's World Cup campaign took some believing - it was truly farcical. Less than a week before flying to Sweden, they had assembled in London to train and prepare. One or two had forgotten their passports and training equipment. The official Welsh FA tracksuits didn't turn up so the squad had to use an assortment of hand-me-downs. The Welsh FA told Jimmy they had secured a beautiful training complex, with a ground and all the facilities at Finchley. For one reason or another, that fell through. Unbelievably, Jimmy was forced to train his team in Hyde Park. All the players complained that the preparations were abysmal.

Both England and Wales were staying at the Lancaster Court Hotel in London. A couple of days before the they left for Sweden, Jimmy had lunch with his friend Walter Winterbottom, the England team manager. During lunch, the England manager told Jimmy: "You and the Welsh selectors are very fortunate indeed." Jimmy looked puzzled and asked why. "Because," he said, "you have so few players to choose a side from. Look at the headaches we have. We've got too many players." Jimmy shot back at Walter: "Give me two of your headaches, Tom Finney and Bobby Charlton, and I will win the World Cup."

Afterwards Jimmy thought about what Walter had said to him replying: "How can anyone possibly have too many good players?" Jimmy was of the opinion that there had been a decline in the standards of English football at international level. He pointed out that despite having only three stars, Harry Gregg, Danny Blanchflower and Jimmy McIlroy, Northern Ireland had held England to a 3-3 draw in Belfast, and were a shade unlucky not to lose. Jimmy pointed out that of the Welsh team that was due to play Scotland in a few days time, "Six of my players are playing out of position. This, more than anything, proves the value of numbers in choosing a national team. If any team ever had too many players it was Manchester United before Munich and that was judged to be our great asset." He believed that England, with such a wealth of talent to chose from and such proud traditions, should be outstanding in European football. "A good England team is the symbol of the health and prosperity of the game throughout Britain. To complain that there are too many players to chose from is frankly obscuring the problem."

Jimmy couldn't wait to get his squad over to Sweden. The goings on of some players and officials took some believing: one player got onto the wrong plane and had to be taken off quickly. It was a miracle that he kept his temper. Nevertheless the team were based in the Grand Hotel in Soltsjobaden, a truly magnificent hotel on the Baltic Sea. The players paired up to share rooms and soon broke into their own groups. There was no rift as such between the players but it cannot be denied that not everything was rosy. Certain players palled up with each other while others kept their distance.

"It's true," admitted Colin Webster, "that there were separate cliques within the squad. This was something Jimmy would never have tolerated at Old Trafford. There was no falling out or anything like that, but a few of the lads were referred to as 'senior pros' and they liked to stick together." The selectors were also staying in the same hotel as the players. Powell was in charge and let everybody know he was. Truthfully these selectors knew little or nothing about football, and apart from big John Charles, they didn't even know their own players. All of them were religious people, so on the coach journey to the games they wouldn't allow smoking or swearing, and they sang hymns. It was all pretty shambolic to say the least. Despite the turmoil, Jimmy kept the players' spirits up, he was there to do a job and that was to get the best out of the men at his disposal and results once again proved what a great man he was in a crisis."

Jimmy could only remember one occasion during a lifetime in football when he attempted to predict the result of a match. It was when Wales played East Germany in Leipzig, during the World Cup qualifying rounds 18 months before the finals in Sweden. Before the Welsh team left their dressing room, Jimmy turned to face them and shouted: "I want you to remember boys, this effing lot were shooting at your families and bombing our houses a few years ago." Some people might have found Jimmy's remarks offensive. However, Jimmy didn't dislike the East Germans any more than he did any other nationalities, he was just winding his players up. Jimmy's team talks were always passionate.

There is another little story about Jimmy's pep talks. Wales were playing England at Ninian Park, Cardiff. "See that load of effing prima donnas in the other dressing room, they've come down here with their little white shorts pulled up around their arses just to take the piss out of you, so get out there and give them something to remember you by." The Welsh lads took him at his word and tore into the English team, taking no prisoners. Jimmy still wasn't happy when he met his team in the dressing room at half-time. "Come on Jimmy," said one of the Welsh team, "we're giving them plenty of stick." Jimmy looked at him scornfully. "Giving them some effing stick, are we?" said Jimmy. "Well, you tell me why they keep effing getting up!"

In 1957, Cliff Jones scored a hat-trick in a 4-1 Welsh win over Northern Ireland. He recalled: "Obviously we were all excited and feeling on top of the world. The banter was flowing while we were having our bath after the game and the dressing room was full of Welsh newspaper reporters, Welsh FA officials and goodness knows who else. As I stepped out of the bath Jimmy came over to me. 'Turn around boyo,' he said. 'I always said when a Welsh player scored a hat-trick while I was in charge of the team I would kiss his arse.' And he kissed mine amidst a chorus of giggles and shouting.

"Jimmy was a great character. You must have heard the story about when Wales played England in 1957 and Jimmy, when giving his team talk went through the England team one by one and what he wanted us to do against our individual marker or vice versa, yet he never mentioned anything to little Reg Davies. I remember Reg asking Jimmy: 'What do I do if Edwards comes through with the ball?' Well the sequel to that was Jimmy looked at him without any trace of emotion on his face and said calmly. 'Get out of his effing way quick, Reg son.'

"But after the game Reg sought Duncan out and they swapped shirts. That was Duncan's last game for England. In later life Reg went to Australia. A couple of years ago he came back to this country on a visit and brought big Duncan's England jersey with him. I asked him what he was going to do with it because he could have made a tidy sum of money selling it to memorabilia collectors. 'Yes, I know I could have made a lot of money selling it, Cliffie,' he told me, 'but I took it to Manchester United, it belongs there.' The jersey is now in Manchester United's Museum for all to see."

Now getting back to the East Germans, they were a very poor side and Wales had scored early in the game. Jimmy, sitting on the bench near the Welsh team dugout, turned to Jack Jones, the little Welsh trainer, and told him: "Jack, we'll get six today." In fact, shamefully, Wales were beaten 2-1. They did, however, get another chance when they were drawn out of the hat to play Israel, with the winner to go to Sweden following the refusal of any Arab countries to play the Jewish state.

When Jimmy finally got to Sweden it was with mixed feelings. On paper Wales had no chance at all. Welsh playing resources were always limited and they had only 15 or 16 players to choose from. Their one really great player was John Charles, known throughout football as the 'Gentle Giant'. The Welsh team had been in Sweden for four days before they knew for certain that the Italian Football Association would allow Charles to join up with his Welsh team-mates. A country like Wales could not afford, as England could, to try and build an ideal team and patiently experiment with players. They had to make plans to suit the few players at their disposal. "I was mentally very tired after the strain of the Munich air disaster," remarked Jimmy. "Our FA Cup run took a great deal out of me as well. It wasn't until we actually arrived in Sweden that I decided what tactics to use."

There is always something new to learn about football. The experience of Wales' qualifying matches against East Germany, Czechoslovakia and Israel, and being part of Manchester United when they played foreign teams in the European Cup, proved invaluable to Jimmy's planning for Wales' World Cup assault.

For days he pondered the problem of how Wales, with such limited resources, could make any impression in world-class company. Then

Jimmy remembered his own playing days and the Arsenal defence as it was during its great era of the late 1930s. Time after time, the West Brom players had moved the ball up to the edge of the Arsenal penalty area but when they looked for someone to pass to, all they could see were Arsenal's red and white shirts. It was impossible to shoot for goal because there were more red and white shirts in the way. There was no way through. This, Jimmy decided, was the perfect answer to the Continental style of play. He realised that the Continentals were all great ball-players, and when they attacked, the wing-halves came through with the ball. This, he reasoned, was the great danger against foreign opposition: when the wing-halves came forward hoping to draw you with their brilliant ballplay and short passing. "Time after time I have seen British teams lured and defeated like this," he said. "The obvious lesson is to refuse to be drawn. It is very difficult to score when there are six, seven or eight defenders in the penalty box, and it doesn't matter how close to goal they come with their close-passing movements if they cannot see a target to shoot at."

So Jimmy decided that Wales would adopt a retreating defensive system, falling back to cover when the opposition had the ball but all moving up in the foreign style when Wales were on the attack. He didn't have much time to drill his players but they responded wonderfully well, and the results spoke for themselves. In fact, he always believed that with a fit John Charles, they would have beaten Brazil and reached the semi-final of the World Cup.

Wales played Hungary in their first game, a team Murphy rated the best Wales had played during the previous 30 years. Wales drew 1-1 in one of the best games of the competition and their morale soared.

Their next game against Mexico saw another 1-1 draw. However, there was an unsavoury incident during this match involving Colin Webster which infuriated the Welsh committee. Wales were expected to thrash Mexico but were frustrated by their inability to break them down. Webster went into a challenge with defender Gutierrez in front of a large contingent of Mexican fans. Gutierrez went down and looked badly hurt. Webster claimed it was a 50-50 challenge, but so irate and incensed were the Mexicans that some ran on the field towards Colin. In fairness to Webster, he didn't received a caution from the referee, Mr Lemesic of Yugoslavia, but every time the Welsh team touched the ball they were booed and jeered. To make matters worse, there was some trouble between the Welsh reserves and the Mexican fans sitting in the stands. The Welsh officials sat there scowling at Webster and afterwards Jimmy ripped into Colin for his over-zealous tackling and his approach to the game - dropping him for the following match against hosts Sweden. Still, Wales had only themselves to blame for not winning decisively.

"Looking back, I'm glad in a way that we didn't win this game," said Jimmy, "because we learned more from our replay against Hungary than from any of the other matches." He admitted that the Mexicans had surprised him. They were fit and fast and lacked only a good experienced schemer and a good finisher. He said the only difference between France, who finished third, and Mexico who were soon eliminated, was that France had Raymond Kopa and Just Fontaine.

Wales had a third draw, 0-0, with Sweden and qualified for a play-off against Hungary. Murphy had learned from their first game against the Hungarians. He'd spotted that they used longer passes than most continental teams and so instructed the Welsh defenders that they need not resort to retreating defensive tactics. In fact they played Hungary in the normal British open style and were more adventurous. Again the change of tactics paid off for the Welsh and despite going a goal down, they fought back to win 2-1 - a marvellous achievement for Wales. Murphy was obviously delighted. "For us Welshmen to take our little country to the last eight of the world's soccer powers is a great, great moment," he said triumphantly.

John Charles came in for particular close attention in this game and it was the injuries he sustained here that prevented his appearance in the quarter-final against Brazil and forced him to miss the first two months of the Italian League season. "The second match was a very tough game and the Hungarians were taking no prisoners," said Charles. "When we went a goal in front, Jimmy and Jack Jones, our trainer, were dancing a jig on the touchline - it was so funny. I was kicked unmercifully and received no protection from the referee whatsoever. They were really going over the top, Jimmy was furious and several times he ran towards the pitch shouting at the referee and linesmen to do something about the violence that was taking place on the field of play.

"After another violent tackle on Ron Hewitt, which put him out of the game, Jimmy was on the touchline remonstrating with the officials. Sipos, the burly tough-as-nails Hungarian defender, was eventually sent off. In the last few minutes, we nearly lost it and Jimmy was running up and down the line beseeching the referee to blow his whistle to end the game. We won 2-1 and it was our finest hour. In the dressing room after the game, Jimmy was unusually quiet, going around shaking hands with all the players and thanking them. It should have been us thanking him."

Following their unexpected victory, a party was quickly organised by the joyful Welsh selectors in the Copacabana Club, which was situated underneath the Grand Hotel. It was a plush, luxurious setting and everyone was told to wear collar and tie. Jimmy recalled the night as a lovely relaxing time. Colin Webster and a few of the players decided that before going to the party they would go into Stockholm for a few drinks. Jimmy sat with the Welsh officials and told his players to have a few drinks and enjoy themselves but to act sensibly. John Charles, his brother Mel, Ivor Allchurch and Cliff Jones and a few of the other players who hadn't gone into the city, enjoyed the entertainment. The Welsh party were in a joyful mood and the selectors and their wives seemed deliriously happy.

Jimmy, who was enjoying a few drinks himself, suddenly got to his feet and sang 'Land of Hope and Glory', with pride and passion to deafening applause. Just after midnight, Jimmy and the other officials retired to their rooms. About an hour or so later, Colin Webster, Ken Jones, Kenny Leek and a couple of other players arrived in the club. One

Above: Jimmy, Matt and Bert Whalley with United's prolific post-war trophy haul.

The Invincibles?

Manchester United were the first British team to take on the great Real Madrid side of the late fifties. Among United's staff there were few doubts that, despite this defeat in 1957, they would one day beat their illustrious opponents. Here Foulkes and Ray Wood watch Rial score Real's opener in the Bernebeu.

Left: Munich survivor Bill Foulkes inspects the damage in the aftermath of a crash that devastated Murphy and Busby's well-laid plans. Alongside the fatalities almost all on board never recovered their full form and fitness. Bill himself went on to play a significant role in the club's revival in the sixties.

Right: Jimmy visits survivor Dennis Viollet in hospital. Despite Dennis's remarkable recovery he eventually died, in 1999, as an indirect result of head injuries sustained in the crash.

Right: Meanwhile Jimmy and Harry Gregg leave a beseiged Old Trafford, February 1958.
With most of his first team either dead or seriously injured, his boss Busby not expected to survive and a third of the season still to play, the task facing Murphy was of Himalayan proportions.

Left:
The scale of United's problems after Munich are summarised by the fact that the entire playing and coaching staff fit in this picture.

Right: Fortunately United had the ideal man for a crisis in Jimmy Murphy. Here he gees up a recovered Bobby Charlton and new signing Ernie Taylor.

Bionic Bobby

Bobby Charlton made a remarkable recovery after the Munich air disaster. So much so that he missed United's two legged European Cup semi-final against AC Milan while on international duty for England. Here Jimmy and Bobby ponder United's reserve options at Old Trafford, March 1958.

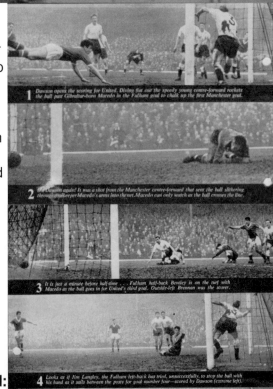

1 Dawson opens the scoring for United. Diving flat out the speedy young centre-forward rockets the ball past Gibraltar-born Macedo in the Fulham goal to chalk up the first Manchester goal.

2 It's Dawson again! It was a shot from the Manchester centre-forward that sent the ball slithering through goalkeeper Macedo's arms into the net. Macedo can only watch as the ball crosses the line.

3 It is just a minute before half-time . . . Fulham half-back Bentley is on the turf with Macedo as the ball goes in for United's third goal. Outside-left Brennan was the scorer.

4 Looks as if Jim Langley, the Fulham left-back has tried, unsuccessfully, to stop the ball with his hand as it sails between the posts for goal number four—scored by Dawson (extreme left).

5 We've done it! Dawson throws his hands in the air jubilantly as the ball from a shot by Charlton rolls inside the post with Macedo so far out of position he can only look on.

Right: Wembley Bound:

Alex Dawson's hat-trick in the semi-final replay against Fulham took United to Wembley for the second year in succession.

Jimmy and captain
Bill Foulkes walk out
at Wembley to meet
Bolton Wanderers
before an emotional
1958 FA Cup Final

Above: Jimmy greets HRH the Duke of Edinburgh before the match.

Right: Despite being twice read the last rites, Matt Busby made a remarkable recovery and took his place on the Wembley bench. Nevertheless United still lost the final 2-0

National Pride

Remarkably, following 3 months in the toughest hot seat in football, Murphy spent his summer not relaxing but coaching Wales in the World Cup in Sweden.

Unfortunately Jimmy's committment was not matched by the Welsh selectors who forced their players to train in Hyde Park before their departure for Scandinavia

Above: Welsh captain Dave Bowen and Jimmy meet Swedish captain and AC Milan star Nils Liedholm before a warm-up match in Gustavsberg

Below: The Welsh squad pose by the team coach complete with selectors and wives onboard

of them went onto the stage, grabbed the microphone and tried to sing a Welsh song but he was drunk and the club security men removed him. It was very embarrassing to say the least. John Charles and the other players who had been in the club all night felt embarrassed and uneasy with the antics of their colleagues. The other guests were disgusted and annoyed at the players' antics. Then, all of a sudden, all eyes turned to Colin Webster who was being frog-marched out of the club by security staff. It was later revealed that he had head-butted a waiter named Verner Felt following a misunderstanding about a girl - the waiter lost three teeth in the affray and the club manager wanted to call the police and file an assault charge against the United player.

John Charles calmed troubled waters the next morning but the Welsh officials and Jimmy were besieged by Felt and the Copacabana Club's management. The Welsh officials wanted to keep the incident quiet so they paid him some money while John Charles had a whip round with every squad member donating a few quid each, and even Jimmy chipped in. Nevertheless, Murphy was raging about Webster's act of stupidity and gave him a real ear-bashing, and wanted to send him home. Welsh FA Secretary Herbert Powell agreed, but it was pointed out to him that if the newspapers found out, they would have a field day and sensationalise the incident, giving innocent players a bad name. It was also realised that they were suffering injuries and playing Brazil in a matter of hours, so Colin was reprieved for the time being.

He played against Brazil only because John Charles was injured and Wales had nobody else to put into the forward line. However, after that incident, he never played for Wales again and a couple of months after coming home from Sweden he was quickly transferred from Old Trafford to Swansea City.

In the dressing room before Wales went out to play, Jimmy sat his team down, got their undivided attention and said: "Lads, I am disappointed in these Brazilians. They are over-rated and if we get stuck into them we can get a result." He then gave a run-down of their best players. "Even their so-called great players, who have been praised to the high heavens, have grave weaknesses. Nilton Santos is supposed to be the best left-back in the world. Rubbish! You, Terry Medwin, will pulverise him. Their right-winger, Garrincha, is bandy and too selfish and as for that young inside-left, what's his name? Pele, he's got nothing but speed and a shot. The only decent player they've got is Didi, and he's not as good as Ivor Allchurch or Tom Finney."

The Welsh players, far from looking glum, now felt confident as Jimmy outlined his tactical plan. Wales used their retreating defensive plan and the classy Brazilians played right into their hands. They used five passes where four would have done and four where three would have done. The Welsh defenders always had time to fall back and cover. Even when their master schemer Didi had the ball on the edge of the Welsh penalty box, he had to play it square to the wings. And he was a master of the through pass.

During that game in Gothenburg, John Charles was injured and sat on the bench beside Jimmy. As the game progressed, the Welsh wingers were crossing the ball into the Brazilian box repeatedly. The Brazilian centre-half, Bellini, was heading these balls away, but not cleanly. Too many were catching the top of his head. Jimmy believed that John Charles would have soared above the Brazilian and scored. Every time a centre came over, Charles was rising from his seat and heading it in his mind. John put his hands to his head and turned to Jimmy and said: "Oh Jimmy, look at those centres coming across." Murphy nodded.- he knew that had Charles been in the team, he would most certainly have got on the end of those crossed balls.

Wales lost 1-0, Pele scoring in the 68th minute. Under the circumstances, this was a remarkable result, especially as Brazil went on to become World Champions. Jimmy knew that if only he had been able to call on Ford, Tapscott or Daniel they could have done even better. Jimmy said that Brazil never looked like scoring against Wales and the goal they did get was a scrappy one that came off a Welsh defender's boot. But the magnificent performance of the Welsh in Sweden endeared them to everyone.

Throughout their matches, Jimmy had been changing the forward line, juggling his resources to get more thrust. He mentioned a number of players in his team who he believed were outstanding in all the games. According to Jimmy, goalkeeper Jack Kelsey was the best keeper in the World Cup competition. He also said he had not seen a better right full-back than Stuart Williams nor a finer centre-half than Mel Charles. And he praised inside-forward Ivor Allchurch. Jimmy also stated that the Welsh captain, left-half Dave Bowen, was a great inspiration to the Welsh players. Not only did he play well in every game, he also captained the side superbly and was always urging on and instructing his team-mates.

"And what of John Charles?" asked Jimmy. "The plain fact was that John was a disappointment for me and to himself." Jimmy went on to explain that Charles was not as good as he could or should have been, because in his estimation, Charles had lost speed in that crucial burst over the last 15 yards before shooting. His view was that it was perhaps the way the Italians trained. Jimmy said that the Italian training schedules were obviously different from ours in England and John had to play to instructions to suit the Juventus style of play. "I have had several chats with John about it and given him my advice for what it is worth. I think we shall soon see the return of the great John Charles." Jimmy also pointed out that in Charles's last two seasons in England before signing for Juventus, he had scored 42 and 39 goals for mid-table Leeds United. "If we'd had that John Charles with us in Sweden, we would have had a great chance against Brazil," added Jimmy.

On several occasions after the World Cup, Jimmy reflected on the Welsh team's performance in Sweden. He would smile when talking about the Welsh officials and selectors. He would wince when discussing certain incidents on and off the field. He laughed when thinking about Jack Kelsey, like Jimmy a chain-smoker, and how they cadged cigarettes off each other, and the way certain players sneaked a few drinks into their rooms thinking he didn't know what they were up to.

"Most of our players thought we would be on our way back home within a week," remarked Jimmy. "I'm sure the selectors thought the same and that was why they picked the best hotel in Sweden as our base." Murphy knew that many of the players thought the arrangements were very badly organised.

"None of the players blamed Jimmy," Cliff Jones recalls. "For a World Cup we needed preparation. We also didn't know whether John Charles was going to play or not. Because of his Old Trafford commitments, Jimmy wasn't able to run the rule over our opponents. The committee should have organised something or somebody to help him, but they didn't. Jimmy was fantastic, and despite all the upheaval and the heartbreak he must have been going through about the Munich crash, he kept us buoyant and made us believe in ourselves. Everybody connected with our World Cup team had nothing but praise for the way he motivated us and got us organised.

"Any player who has never listened to Jimmy has certainly missed one of soccer's great experiences. He was the complete opposite to the everyday manager or coach that players met with their own club teams. We had Bill Nicholson at Spurs, a great manager, but very serious about everything. Jimmy was unbelievably passionate, he really was. But he had this wonderful gift of making everyone, not only players, but officials as well, feel relaxed and part of a unique set-up."

In later years, Colin Webster declared: "Jimmy did a job that no other manager or coach could possibly have done with the players at his disposal. I'm not saying this out of favouritism either, because it was me who Jimmy rollicked more than anyone. I know he was instrumental in me leaving Old Trafford, but I have nothing but good to say about the man."

Welsh journalists John Lloyd and Ken Jones also have nothing but praise when discussing Jimmy's part in Wales' World Cup glory. "We must appreciate that it was ridiculous to compare South American footballers, for example, with those produced in the British Isles," said John Lloyd. "They play a completely different style of game because of the conditions under which they stage their matches. Even the Continentals in Group Three of the World Cup in Sweden played a different style of game to our lads. Wales met Hungary twice and drew 1-1 and beat them 2-1 in a play-off. Of course, they were not the great team they were when they beat England twice but they were still a force to be reckoned with. The Hungarians were cynical and ruthless in the two matches and dear John Charles was fouled constantly throughout the games.

"In the play-off, some of their tackling on John was disgraceful. Jimmy was never one to demonstrate towards the referee and linesmen but during these games he was running out of the dugout and appealing to the match officials. It was comical in that second game. With seconds to go, Hungary nearly equalised and Jimmy kept sipping whisky out of a little flask in his pocket. He flew out of the dugout again and was running up and down the touchline shouting at the Russian referee to blow the final whistle. Sadly, John Charles was that badly injured he took no further part in the competition. Consider for a moment what Jimmy did with limited resources on the playing front. He was a great, great coach and motivator - the best."

Top sportswriter Ken Jones concurs: "Wales have had very little to crow about over the past forty years or so but that 1958 World Cup in Sweden will always be remembered by Welsh fans and neutrals everywhere. Jimmy Murphy got those players to play their hearts out for their country. I have to admit that many of the South American and Continental players outshone us as individuals, but through sheer willpower, hard graft and perseverance, the Welsh team battled them on equal terms. It was all down to Jimmy. He was one of the great thinkers of the game, yet he taught his players simply.

"He built a Manchester United-like club spirit within the Welsh squad, despite the officials. There is no argument that the greatest 90 minutes of Welsh footballing history was the play-off victory over Hungary, quickly followed by the Brazil game. Murphy was the architect of this. The players idolised him and wouldn't hear a word against him.

You know why? Because he treated them honestly, fairly and with respect and they also knew that he was with them on the field of play in spirit. He worked tirelessly on the training pitch and gave speeches in his team talks that would have gladdened the hearts of those old Welsh academics and preachers. I am sad to say that Wales has never got anywhere near the achievements of 1958. How do we find another Jimmy Murphy? It's impossible!"

A Wanted Man

A few days after the game with Brazil, Jimmy received a telephone call from one of the top Brazilian officials. In broken English, the official congratulated Jimmy and his team for putting on an unforgettable performance. He then surprised the Welsh manager by asking him if he fancied going to Brazil to coach their players. You wouldn't have to ask most coaches twice for them to accept an offer like that but Jimmy hesitated, pleasantly surprised by the Brazilian approach.

The official, thinking Jimmy was holding out until he heard what the salary would be, apologised for not mentioning it. "If you join us your salary would be £30,000 a year!" Jimmy was flabbergasted! Thirty thousand pounds to coach the most naturally gifted players in the world. That was some compliment for the Welshman to ponder. However, it was no contest. Matt Busby and Manchester United meant more to him than all the money in the world. He thanked him, but declined the offer.

Jimmy's loyalty was unquestioned. Arsenal had also approached him about becoming their manager. It happened just before the World Cup began. Sir Bracewell Smith, chairman of Arsenal, put out feelers to find out if Jimmy would be interested in the job. This was the only offer of many Jimmy received over the years that made him think seriously. However, after a short deliberation, he politely turned it down. "There were several English clubs who offered me the opportunity of becoming their manager, more than a dozen First Division clubs alone, but the

Arsenal offer was the only one that I thought seriously about. I hesitated, they had this tradition and aura about them. However, after hesitating momentarily, I turned them down."

On another occasion John Charles pulled Jimmy to one side and told him Juventus were looking for a manager. Jimmy looked surprised. "Jimmy, it's worth £20,000 a year, are you interested? Because I've been asked to find out if you are. They would like you to manage and coach their club." Jimmy was touched that John was trying to put a well-paid job his way. He thanked him but told him he wasn't interested. "Apart from anything else John, I can't speak Italian." Jimmy felt honoured they should even know Jimmy Murphy, let alone want him as their manager. How can one place a figure on loyalty? He couldn't leave Manchester United, still rebuilding after Munich.

"My heart was at Old Trafford," Murphy once said. "I wanted to help Matt pick up the pieces and start all over again. Just like we did in 1946." One thing should be made crystal clear - all these other clubs were willing to pay Jimmy a great deal more than he was earning at Old Trafford. And with a wife and six children to support, nobody would have blamed him if he had accepted these offers. However, he was happiest working with the players and he wasn't really interested in being stuck in an office wheeling and dealing. He wanted to develop and improve youngsters and make them into world-class players for his beloved Manchester United.

*

Once back on British soil, England manager Walter Winterbottom came in for severe criticism. Jimmy said that the reconstruction of the England team would be an outstanding feature in the forthcoming home international tournament. "Ideally," said Jimmy, "international team-building should be a four-year plan -that is from World Cup to World Cup. In practice, England are the only home country at present in a position to do this." He spoke in defence of Winterbottom and said that Walter did try to build a team for the World Cup and was having considerable success. Jimmy also pointed out that his plans were wrecked by the Munich air crash, which was almost as serious for England as it was for Manchester United.

"England could have won the World Cup with Roger Byrne, Duncan Edwards and Tommy Taylor," said Jimmy. "Byrne, Edwards and Taylor - three great players and mainstays of the England team. I honestly don't think I have ever seen a better full-back than Roger Byrne. Duncan Edwards was the man of power with the ideal temperament who could often pull victory from apparent defeat. So much of the forward line's effectiveness depended on Tommy Taylor constantly roaming and pulling defences out of shape. Their deaths meant new players had to be tried. Whoever comes into a team has to be part of a pattern and it takes a long time for a pattern to develop. It is unfair to expect new players to immediately slip into a rhythm or create a new one of their own. For England and Walter Winterbottom, the problem of 1958 will be to try and create a new rhythm." Jimmy went on to say that it was a remarkable tribute to Manchester United that three of the five British Isles team managers were United men - Matt Busby, Walter Winterbottom and himself.

The Recovery Continues

On Tuesday September 30th 1958, on Jimmy's recommendation, Matt Busby announced that Johnny Aston was to join Manchester United to help look after the youngsters. But there was more to it than that. Eventually Johnny, the man capped 17 times for England, would take over the coaching job left vacant since the death of Bert Whalley in the Munich disaster. Aston joined United, his only club, from junior football. He came as a forward just before the war, but then after he was demobbed in 1946, he was tried at wing-half and later full-back where he settled down to win an FA Cup medal in 1948. Shortly afterwards, he became very ill with TB and a testimonial was arranged at Old Trafford which brought him a £4,285 cash reward.

Following this good news came more sad news. Jackie Blanchflower had eventually lost his battle to play professional football. After the horrific injuries sustained at Munich, Jackie had hoped he could get his full fitness back. "I have to face up to things," said a disconsolate Blanchflower. "Since the crash, I have been secretly hoping that I would be able to play but I shall never be fit enough to play football again. I don't know what I shall do by way of finding another job, but I have got over the first hurdle and it cannot be soccer."

Jimmy was sad at hearing the news about Jackie. "He was amongst the first intake of youngsters to arrive at Old Trafford," said Jimmy. "He was a lovely, quiet lad. He came to us as an inside-forward but although he was a lovely footballer with beautiful skills and control, he was slightly short of pace for a forward. We tried him in several positions and he eventually settled as a centre-half. He was a cultured pivot and eventually played for Northern Ireland. He battled with Mark Jones for the centre-half position in our first team. Mark was the complete opposite in the position to Jackie. Mark, built like a heavyweight boxer, was all power and no nonsense in his play, clearing his lines as quickly as possible, while Jackie would bring the ball under control and look to play the ball out of defence. Two wonderful players, so sad."

In October 1958, there were strong rumours flying around football that Leeds United wanted Jimmy as their new manager. The speculation persisted for a few days. Jimmy told the press he knew nothing about the Leeds offer. "I have heard nothing at all from the Leeds chairman Mr Bolton or anyone connected with Leeds United," said Jimmy. Leeds had been without a manager since the sacking of Raich Carter several months before. Jimmy emphasised once again his views on the subject of his leaving Busby and United. "There's no chance of that happening. My family and I love it here in Manchester. We are settled and I still have a huge job to complete here at Old Trafford," he told reporters.

However, the speculation persisted. The fact was that Jimmy had been offered six jobs over the previous few months and he had politely turned each one down. In late November 1959, the *Liverpool Echo* speculated as to who the new manager of Second Division Liverpool would be. Although Phil Taylor was still officially in charge, it was common knowledge that he was feeling the strain and was about to resign before he was pushed.

There were big changes taking shape in professional football and the manager's position was in the vanguard of these. The old brigade of managers wearing suits, shirt and tie and who were hardly ever seen in a tracksuit were slowly being phased out. It was no secret that Tom Williams, the Liverpool chairman, was a great admirer of what Matt Busby and Jimmy Murphy had achieved at Old Trafford. These two had pointed the way when they joined United after the war. The Anfield club advertised for a manager and although very few applied, Mr Williams wanted Jimmy Murphy. Jimmy heard the rumours but he was loyal to the core, he had no intention of moving to Liverpool or anywhere else for that matter. Of course he was highly regarded by the top clubs but his life and passion was for Manchester United. In the event, Liverpool went for an up-and-coming Scot called Bill Shankly, who was similar in method and passion to Jimmy.

It's Temperament that Makes or Breaks!

In October 1958, eight months after the Munich disaster, Jimmy and Matt Busby were in opposition as managers of Wales and Scotland. Jimmy was on record as saying that if Matt Busby was put in charge of the Scottish national team there might have been a few eyebrows raised over his team selection. And so in his first game back as Scottish manager Busby gave 18-year-old Denis Law his first international cap - the Huddersfield youngster was one of the stars of a 3-0 victory over the Welsh. Jimmy had been an admirer of this fiery-tempered but outstanding inside-forward ever since Denis played against United in a Youth Cup tie a couple of years earlier.

The result was a huge disappointment for Jimmy. He wanted the loyal Welsh supporters in Cardiff to see for themselves the great improvement that had taken the Welsh team so far in the World Cup. "Unfortunately we really flopped," said a bewildered Murphy. "The most upsetting thing about the game was our lack of fire and enthusiasm."

Once back at Old Trafford after the international match, Jimmy was holding a discussion with Jack Crompton, Joe Armstrong and a few of the United staff. He said the difference between football at club and international level was both obvious and subtle. He pointed out the number of players who were outstanding for their club yet failed so miserably at international level and in many cases could not even produce their week-to-week club form.

"One of the vital factors that makes or breaks a player in the end is having the right temperament," he told them with a great deal of emphasis. He explained that a player needed complete self-control and coolness to make an impression and produce his best form at such a high level of skill and experience. "Now and again, players have luck and flatter to deceive; but time always shows whether a man has got what it takes to stay at the top with the best," he said. He mentioned Billy Wright, Nat Lofthouse and Mel Charles as classic examples of men with this quality of temperament. "Young Law will, I believe, prove another," added Jimmy, then, full of enthusiasm about the subject under discussion he continued, "he looks for the ball and goes into action right from the start of a game. But above all he has an air of confidence and ease which stamps him as a player thoroughly at home in the highest class, and in my humble opinion he is one of the greats of the future." With this kind of ringing endorsement it was scarcely a shock that Busby and Murphy should move heaven and earth to bring Law to United.

The Forgotten Heroes of Munich

"Jimmy and Matt Busby rarely ever put young players into the team if we were struggling. However, after the crash it was a different story... it must have been hard to play your best in that patched up team, but Mark, Alex and Shay did."
NOBBY LAWTON

One aspect of the Munich air disaster that is often overlooked is the effect it had on the youngsters at the club. The careers of the final intake of United kids before the disaster were effectively sacrificed in the wake of Munich. The likes of Mark Pearson, Alex Dawson, Bobby Harrop and Shay Brennan were forced into action before they were really ready. Not for them the smooth conveyor belt through United's system to the top, rather the harsh reality that, far from learning their apprenticeships behind master craftsmen like Duncan Edwards, Roger Byrne and Tommy Taylor, they were now expected to perform miracles under the spotlight of the media and a mourning, expectant Manchester.

The Real 'Pancho'

In the 1950s Mark Pearson, nicknamed 'Pancho' because of his Edwardian hairstyle and sideburns, was potentially one of the best inside forwards on United's books. Standing a mere 5 feet 6 inches tall and weighing just 10 stones, Mark was solidly built and was also one of the hardest and toughest competitors in football. He appeared to be another Murphy star in the making.

Born in Ridgewood, a small village near Sheffield, Mark made his name playing for North East Derbyshire and England schoolboys, for whom he appeared four times in 1955. He later won an England Youth cap. He was a clever dribbler with a good shot in either foot and was one of the best schemers of that period. He looked an absolute cert to make the big time. Although very quiet and unassuming off the field, Mark had a volatile temper on it and this caused him a great deal of trouble. As Bobby Charlton says: "Mark really was a quiet lad, if he were sitting in a room with you, you wouldn't know he was there. Like many others, however, Mark didn't like being treated roughly, and when that happened his reaction was to flare up and retaliate."

For all that, Mark was Jimmy Murphy's kind of player and an incident in a practice match at the Cliff against the reserves highlighted the volatility of this gifted inside-forward. Matt Busby was watching the action and Jimmy was playing, alternating between the two teams. Pearson was in the reserve team and both sides were going at it hammer and tongs, trying to impress the boss. Jimmy was going in hard at Mark and after taking quite a few knocks, Pancho decided to do something about the situation. It all happened in a flash.

Suddenly and violently Jimmy was flattened, the impact knocking him off the pitch into a barrier on the far side from where Busby stood. Jimmy looked to be seriously hurt. Matt Busby was angry. The game was immediately stopped as everyone gathered around the Welshman. Mark looked like he was going to be hauled over the coals, but Jimmy suddenly got to his feet, shook himself down, smiled at Mark and told him that was what he wanted to see more of from him. This was typical of 'Spud' Murphy.

Pearson loved Jimmy and responded to his coaching. Both Matt and Jimmy never tired of telling reporters of the terrier-like inside-forward they had on their books who they felt certain was to become a world-beater. Pearson eventually made his first team debut in the first game after Munich against Sheffield Wednesday and, following that emotional night, Mark went on to play 80 first team games in the red shirt.

However, Pearson quickly gained a reputation as a player with a very short temper. A reputation not helped by his performance a few weeks after the Wednesday cup-tie. March 9th 1958 was Manchester United's black Saturday. It was the day battle raged at Turf Moor, Burnley. United lost 3-0 and there was a great deal of rough play. Mark was ordered off following a clash with Les Shannon and there were taunts aplenty. United had travelled to Turf Moor a week before facing Fulham in the FA Cup semi-final and as so often can be the case, the hero of today can be something else tomorrow. That was how the Burnley supporters, or a considerable number of them, regarded Pearson when he was ordered off the field half an hour into the game. Instead of taking the short cut across the pitch to the dressing room Mark did a circuit toward the touchline and was subjected to deafening abuse.

It had been a cracking game for the first half-hour and United had played superbly but Shackleton, the Burnley centre-forward, had frequently challenged Harry Gregg, United's goalkeeper. Shoulder charging was allowed in this period but after another challenge, Gregg and Shackleton became involved in an altercation. Harry fell and the two players rolled over in the mud. The referee, Mr Oxley, spoke harshly to the United player. A minute later he had words with Burnley outside-right Newlands, following a foul on Ian Greaves. Quite rightly, the referee was trying to cut out the bad feeling which had crept into the game. Shortly afterwards, Stan Crowther was warned by the referee who gave Burnley a free kick from which they hit the post.

Mr Oxley ordered the kick to be retaken and as the ball was placed there was a collision in which Burnley's Shannon fell to the ground and all of a sudden Pearson was sent off. All hell broke loose. Shortly afterwards, Shannon picked the ball up near the United dugout to take a throw-in and something was said which caused the referee to speak to someone in the United dugout of Jimmy Murphy, Jack Crompton and Ernie Taylor, who was injured and not playing.

As a result, the following day's headlines shouted louder than normal: "Burnley Protest! United Reported For After-Match Incidents." There were similar reports in most of the papers and this particular game was talked of and written about for weeks afterwards. In the 1950s, Burnley were a top First Division club with great potential, they later went on to win the First Division championship in the early 1960s and played in the European Cup before their later decline.

Keith Dewhirst, writing for the *Manchester Evening Chronicle* asked: "Why was Mark Pearson made a scapegoat?" After checking his own observations with the players he had no hesitation in blaming the referee Mr Oxley: "There can be no doubt that before the uproar, Greaves and Crowther were tackling a little harder than was necessary, or that Burnley's Shackleton was bustling and shoving too much. None of this looked likely to cause serious trouble. However, it was a decision by the referee that started all the trouble. As I saw it, Gregg went up for a high ball. Shackleton challenged. Gregg went down and claimed he was pushed, and as the ball rolled loose he impeded Shackleton. When he got up, Gregg and he were arguing. Both men were well inside the penalty area. Now this was either a foul on Gregg (I think it was) or a penalty. It could not possibly warrant a free kick to Burnley outside the penalty area, but this was what Oxley gave.

"Both teams were furious at this decision. Both teams started to clog without mercy. Battle raged. Newlands and Crowther were booked. Twice the captains, Bill Foulkes and Jimmy Adamson, went to the referee to try and quieten the players down. Each time Oxley ignored them and restarted play before the two captains had time to pacify their men. Then came the Mark Pearson incident. Hitherto Pearson had taken no part in the fighting. He had dropped back to help his defence and tackled Shannon. What followed would be farcical if it were not so serious. Shannon coolly whipped the ball away from Pearson who missed it altogether. Another United player crashed into Shannon, fouling him. Shannon, evidently thinking it was Pearson, turned on Mark with his fists raised. Mark raised his own fists and was immediately sent off. Pearson was an innocent bystander! If a player has a bad game I must say so but there is no reason why a referee should be treated differently. Mr Oxley had a very bad day at Burnley."

David Meek of the *Manchester Evening News* said that United's new team had not played together long enough to click into gear with only ten men against Burnley, particularly with key schemer Ernie Taylor missing. "Before Pearson was sent off, the Reds played attractive football and honours were even. But after the marching orders issued to young Mark they hadn't a chance. Should Pearson have been sent off? Referee Oxley, after cautioning players on both sides in a sudden five-minute spell of bad-tempered incidents, was bound to be severe with the next offender he spotted. Was this just bad luck for United? It happened to be Pearson, who up to the incident had played a blameless game. Like all the incidents in the game, it was six of one and half a dozen of the other."

This still left Burnley's out-spoken and forthright chairman 'Master Butcher' Bob Lord's claims unanswered. He made two points. Firstly that Manchester United players had performed 'like Teddy Boys' and secondly that they did so because they did not like being beaten. The second argument was childish, and smacked of sour grapes from Mr Lord. A couple of days later, Burnley complained to the Football League about incidents they alleged took place after the match. It was understood that a United official stormed into the Burnley dressing room after the game and had to be restrained. Then two Burnley directors endeavoured to get in touch with a certain United official, in an attempt to calm troubled waters and bring a reconciliation but claimed they were met with a disgusting gesture and were told the person they wished to speak to was much too busy. Later the refreshments the Burnley club sent into the United dressing room were sent back untouched.

Lord later denied he had used the expression 'Teddy Boys' to describe the Manchester United players' behaviour at Burnley, although the press were adamant he used those words. Mr Lord said someone else said it and it had been pinned on him. He said he knew who said it, but he wasn't going to tell. He told the press:"We are not concerning ourselves with the match itself. It's the after-match incidents which we are chiefly concerned about as a club. These were very unfortunate incidents, I can tell you, and it's no good Manchester United saying nobody is going to ride roughshod over them when it's turning out to be just the opposite. We are as sympathetic as anyone over the Munich disaster, just as we were for the unfortunate people in the Bolton disaster, but there is a limit to everything, though United don't seem to think so. We take exception to derogatory remarks about myself as chairman of the club. I am determined that this matter shall be cleared up and cleared up satisfactorily and to ensure that, I'm prepared to shout for fair play from the house tops." This row raged for weeks. Leading up to the semi-final, Jimmy asked Mark Pearson to shave his sideburns off. The headlines in several newspapers became "Murphy Kills United 'Teddy Boy' Taunt" after pictures of Mark before and after having his sideburns removed.

Nevertheless Pancho was in trouble again in September of the same year while appearing for the reserves against Liverpool reserves at Old Trafford. He had his name taken by the referee. At the end of the game against Liverpool Mark was very upset and asked Jimmy Murphy, "Was I in the wrong?" Jimmy draped his arm around Mark's shoulder. "If so, I'm very sorry," said the very upset youngster. Murphy told him that in his opinion, he had been harshly treated.

"What happens to Pearson now?" the newspapers were asking. "What steps would Busby take with this go-getting inside-forward?" Matt had a heart-to-heart talk with Mark after he had had a brush with the referee in the season's opening game. Instead of giving him a rollicking, Busby gave Mark a pep-talk because Matt was convinced Pearson was in the clear - Jimmy Murphy's report did not blame Mark in any way. He believed that the lad was being victimised. Busby told Mark to carry on playing just as he had been. "He is by nature a strong, aggressive player and a very good one." Busby went on to say that Pearson would be an asset to United for many years to come. "I feel there is a little victimisation in this and it's a case of 'give a dog a bad name'," he said. He told reporters that previously he had had no hesitation in carpeting Pearson, however on this occasion he would receive nothing but sympathy.

What did Mark himself feel about the way his career was moving? Well for a start the 'dirty player' tag was getting on his nerves: "I dread every game. The 'Teddy Boy' smear has branded me a sinner. Referees and players have started gunning for me and taken the thrill out of the game I love. I haven't enjoyed a match all season, in fact I'm so down in the dumps that after the referee took my name against Liverpool reserves I walked off the pitch and sat on the trainers' bench. Jimmy Murphy made me see sense, but I don't want to continue playing.

"I fear for my future," said Mark dejectedly. "Football is my living and I know that Manchester United will not tolerate dirty players. The Boss, Mr Busby, had me in his office a week ago to tell me that I must try harder to keep my temper. Three times this season I have been in trouble. Every game, I go out on the field determined to behave myself. I try to play a clean game, but truthfully I feel that I am a marked man. Players are after me and so are referees. I am getting kicked off my feet, but as soon as I retaliate the referee cautions me.

"I'm only 18 and inexperienced, I'm easy meat and cannot fool the referees like the older, vastly more experienced professionals. It all dates back to the game against Burnley when I was sent off. United were described as playing like 'a lot of Teddy Boys,' and as I was the only one sent off everyone seems to have assumed I was the worst offender. So now I carry the can. I admit I lost my temper but so did a lot more players and I was certainly no worse than the player I got mixed up with. Now word seems to have got round. In one game a club switched one of their old-timers to mark me because he was known for dishing it out, which he did!"

Mark said that he felt he was being unfairly penalised by referees for fair tackles because his name was Mark Pearson. In one game he became so annoyed he kicked the ball into the stand and the referee booked him, and that was his first offence of the game. "I play a hard game. That's the way I've been trained but I don't think I'm a dirty player. In junior football I wasn't continually in trouble, in fact I was the captain of my school football team. I also captained Derby Boys, played four times for England Schoolboys and also for the England Youth side and I was never accused of being a dirty player. Then came the 'Teddy Boy' smear and I can't seem to shake off my bad name. This is the kind of atmosphere which I have to play in nowadays."

While playing against one team, a big, tough defender walked over to Mark and told him: "Just wait until the return game, I'll kill you." Matt Busby told Mark to take it and appeal to the referee if necessary, but that he must not take the law into his own hands. "I suppose I shall just have to try to grin and bear it, but I wish referees would just give me a chance. I have quietened my game down, but it's not doing my football any good. I have started to hang back, frightened to go into a tackle in case the referee pulls me up. All I want to do is lose my bad boy reputation, though how I'm going to do this is worrying me a great deal."

In October 1958, 'Pancho' was ordered off again, and the warning signs were flashing against his continuation with Manchester United. However, Mark developed into a wonderfully skillful player but injuries, mainly to his ankle, held back his progress. He had some brilliant games after Munich and took part in some notable victories. One that stands out in particular was against the great Tottenham Double-winning side in January 1961. The young, rebuilt United team took on the mighty

Spurs on a Monday night. With goalkeeper Harry Gregg injured and up in the forward line replacing rampant centre-forward Alex Dawson, United beat the all-conquering Londoners 2-0, Mark netting one of the goals.

He was in and out of the team until he left in October 1963, to join Sheffield Wednesday for £22,500. He played a total of 80 first team games, scoring 14 goals. There are many theories as to just why such a brilliant prospect failed to make it with United. Many believe he was another youngster who was pitched into the first team too soon after Munich, some say it was his temperament, others that he was injury prone. He felt bitter at the way he was let go and never seemed to catch his early promise. He left Sheffield for Fulham in 1965 before joining Halifax Town in 1968. He retired from the game in 1972.

Nobby Lawton

Norbert 'Nobby' Lawton was born in 1940 in Newton Heath, a breeding ground for many United recruits over the years. He attended Christ the King School and later St Gregory's where one of his school friends was Philip Murphy, one of Jimmy's sons. He was a stylish inside-forward for Manchester and Lancashire Boys when he was spotted by United in 1955, becoming an amateur until he signed professional forms in 1958. Young Lawton was a member of the 1955 Manchester Boys team that reached the final of the English Schools Shield, but disappointingly lost 4-3 to Swansea Schoolboys over two legs. Bert Lister and Roy Cheetham, two lads who joined Manchester City, were in the same side.

When Nobby Lawton first joined the Reds, he trained every Tuesday and Thursday night, coming under the watchful eyes of Murphy and Whalley. "When I first joined the club there was a wealth of great players, all potentially brilliant. And when I looked at first team players like Tommy Taylor, Duncan Edwards, Eddie Colman and Roger Byrne I had nothing but admiration for them," said Nobby. "They were undoubtedly great players in every respect and great people into the bargain. The thing that struck me about Old Trafford though was this family atmosphere. I can't describe it really but there were no 'big heads' if you know what I mean. Everybody from the first team players to the likes of newcomers such as myself were treated with friendliness and respect."

Nobby played mostly for the 'A' and 'B' teams, and was making steady progress when he turned professional in 1958 shortly after the Munich disaster. Nobby had been a member of the successful United FA Youth Cup team and after Munich was looked on as one to watch for the future. "To give you some idea of what a warm, family club United were in the fifties," said Nobby, "I remember playing in the first leg of the FA Youth Cup Final at West Ham in 1957. We won 3-2 but instead of going straight back to Manchester we were taken to a posh hotel in London where our first team were staying prior to the FA Cup Final at Wembley a couple of days later. I was thrilled, staying in this hotel with the likes of Duncan, Roger, Eddie, Tommy and the rest. Everyone was so friendly. The parents of Tommy Taylor were also in the hotel as were Duncan Edwards' mother and father. They spoke to us as if they had known us since we were kids.

"Unfortunately we lost 2-1. At the reception in the hotel that night nobody was down in the dumps, everyone was confident that there would be plenty of cup finals in the future. It was a remarkable feeling to be part of the club. We were all made to feel important. It was the overall warmth and friendliness of Jimmy, Matt and the other officials with the families of the first team players going out of their way to make us feel part and parcel of the club.

"There was another incident that sticks in my mind and that was after Munich, in about 1960. I was playing for the reserves at Barnsley and as I was walking into the players' entrance I saw Tommy Taylor's mother and father waiting outside. I walked over to them and they welcomed me like a member of the family. They remembered me being in the hotel in 1957. It was sad, here I was going to play for United's second team and their son was dead. Jimmy came over and took them inside the ground. Lovely people and United were a special club in those days."

Nobby's progress was curtailed when he was taken seriously ill with pneumonia and was out of action for over a year, losing more than three stones during his illness. "After my illness I was given the all-clear to return to training by the specialist and I was as thin as a rake," recalled Nobby. "I can say it now all these years afterwards but the illness left me with an inferiority complex when I returned to Old Trafford, it really did. The other players made fun of me something awful. They weren't malicious with their remarks, it was just the usual banter between young footballers, but I was upset. I tried to hide my feelings but Jimmy Murphy saw how hurt I was. He was fantastic to me, he encouraged me at every opportunity. As most of the other players will tell you, Jimmy was a hard man to please, hard as nails but he had a tender, affectionate and lovely nature and could make you feel ten feet tall.

"I remember playing in the FA Youth Cup, it was the semi-final against Southampton down at their ground, and we were staying in a hotel about five minutes from the ground. A couple of hours before leaving for the match Jimmy called us into a room for his team-talk. Honestly, it was one of the most significant and heart-rending speeches I have ever heard from anyone. He was enchanting and marvellous. When he finished I was so confident of beating Southampton that I felt like getting my kit on and running down to the ground and playing them on my own. Like a lot of the other players, I don't think Jimmy ever quite received the praise he deserved for his part in making the club what it was and what it has become. He was always plotting and planning behind the scenes away from the limelight."

Nobby was a quiet, likeable lad, and his close friends at Old Trafford were Alex Dawson and Mark Pearson, who he used to pal about with in the close season. In the aftermath of Munich, Nobby is of the opinion that Alex and Mark played with a spirit fostered by Jimmy Murphy. "Thinking about it now, over forty years later, you can analyse the situation much better. Lads like Alex and Mark would never have played in the first team so quickly but for Munich. Alex had of course played in the first team before the crash but he will tell you himself that playing with United's pre-Munich team was uncomplicated, because those experienced world-class players made it easy for youngsters to be blooded in the first eleven. They looked after younger players. Jimmy and Matt Busby rarely ever put young players into the team if the team was struggling. They knew younger players should be introduced when a team is playing well and not under pressure. However, after the crash it must have been hard to play your best in that patched up team, but Mark, Alex and Shay Brennan did. That's why, when you take everything into consideration, Jimmy Murphy did an exceptional job keeping United going in this period. He was a great man!"

Nobby made his first team debut at inside-left, on April 9th 1960, away to Luton Town. The Reds won 3-2 with Alex Dawson bagging a brace and Warren Bradley scoring the other. He played in the following two games, a loss to West Ham and a victory over Blackburn. At the end of the season he was surprisingly chosen for Manchester United's 17-strong party to America and Canada. He had shown just how good he could be in his three senior games.

In season 1960-61 Nobby managed only a single appearance in a 1-1 draw with Newcastle. In 1961-62 he played four successive games at wing-half, his favourite position - in this period the team was being constantly changed as Busby and Murphy looked for the right team formation. Nobby came back into the first team for a run of 16 consecutive matches, notching 6 goals from his 20 games that season, including a hat-trick against Nottingham Forest, who United beat 6-3. He had been playing well and finding his rhythm when, on April 4th 1962, while playing against Leicester City at Filbert Street, he broke his leg in a 4-3 defeat.

"I did it in the first half," remembered Nobby, "I was carried back to the dressing-room and when the lads came in at half-time I told Jimmy (who was in charge, Matt being in hospital) that my leg felt better. Jack

Crompton, our trainer, filled the bath with cold water and told me to gently step in. Wow, I nearly hit the roof. The pain was unbearable. 'You've broken it,' said Jack. So I was taken to hospital in Leicester. They put heavy plaster on the leg and immobilised it. I was asked if I wanted to remain there overnight, but I told them I'd sooner go back to Manchester. The ambulance took me back to Filbert Street where the lads were getting changed. I was carried onto the team bus and laid across two seats. When the lads got on they were complaining because they couldn't play cards, it was all done in jest.

"However worse was to follow. Jimmy had forgotten that the team were booked into a city centre restaurant for a meal before heading back to Manchester. Of course I couldn't go into the hotel so Jimmy brought me out a tray of food and drink. As he went back into the restaurant he left the bus door open. I was in agony with my leg when all of a sudden, this drunken Leicester supporter decked out in his scarf and rattle came onto the bus. I couldn't get rid of him no matter what I tried. He told me how rubbish United and me were. The funny thing about this fellow was two years later, when I was playing at Wembley for Preston, I received a letter from the same guy asking if I could send him two Cup Final tickets. 'I was the person who kept you company on the coach after you broke your leg' he wrote.

"Eventually the team got on the bus and we headed back home. There was no direct motorway in those days and the journey home was horrendous for me as we went over every hump and bump on the road, I was in agony. Jimmy and Jack Crompton were debating where to take me. They both decided to drop me at St Joseph's, which was a private hospital run by Roman Catholic nuns. It was comical when I think about it now - the hospital was in darkness and locked when we arrived in the early hours of the morning and there was Jimmy and Jack throwing little pebbles at the windows trying to attract the nuns' attention. When this didn't work they took me in the coach to my home in Newton Heath. I was carried in and put on the settee. The following day Jimmy came to our house and seeing the pain etched on my face called an ambulance and had me taken to St Joseph's. The surgeon came in to see me and said he had seen the reports from the Leicester hospital. 'I'm sorry Mr Lawton,' he said, 'I will have to remove the plaster cast, it's much too tight. However, the bad news is that we haven't got the saw that cuts through the plaster, so we will have to do it the hard way and it will be painful. I'll give you a painkiller.' I spent four days in bed. Jimmy visited me regularly and told me everything would be fine, he was wonderful to me."

Nobby also played in the FA Cup semi-final against the classy Tottenham team at the end of March at Hillsborough. "We got walloped 3-1," recalled Nobby. "Let's be fair, Spurs had a great side then. We were kids, inexperienced, they were experienced masters and they taught us a lesson. We tried hard, we really did, but trying wasn't quite enough against those Spurs aristocrats. I felt dejected and coming back on the team bus Jimmy and Matt spoke to me and tried to boost my confidence, telling me it was a learning curve."

After recovering from his broken leg, Nobby made 12 first team appearances the following season before leaving the club he had grown up with as a lad. Denis Law and Paddy Crerand had joined in this period. Matt Busby decided to take the first team squad to Blackpool and they stayed at the Norbrek Hydro. One morning after training Matt Busby pulled Nobby to one side and told him that Jimmy Milne, the Preston manager, was inside the hotel and wanted to speak to him with a view to signing him. "It's up to you what you decide," Matt Busby told him. "You can go or stay. I'll leave it up to you."

Out of courtesy Nobby spoke to Mr Milne but he was far from impressed. After lunch, Nobby discussed Preston's offer with Harry Gregg and Noel Cantwell and a few other senior players. Their advice was if he didn't fancy moving then he should stay at Old Trafford until he received offers that suited him. However, a couple of days later, United secretary Les Olive told Nobby that Jim Milne was still keen to sign him. There had also been offers from other clubs, one of which was Charlton. Nobby didn't elaborate on the subject of the move but said:

"I listened to what Les Olive had to say and I knew where I stood with United. I walked away and signed for Preston and I never, ever went back to the club. I didn't even go back to collect my boots." He had played in 44 first team games, scoring six goals.

At Preston, he joined up with his pal Alex Dawson and because he was playing regular first team football, he became a midfield driving force. He was made captain of the club and his subtle skills earned him rave notices in grounds all over the country. He eventually played over 200 games for them, scoring 22 goals before he was sold to Brighton, where he and Alex Dawson teamed up once more, Nobby playing 112 games. He later had a spell with Lincoln City before he retired in 1972, after recurrent knee problems. He appeared in over 300 Leagues games for the clubs he served. Even today, he suffers with his knees.

Speaking of his departure from United, Nobby said: "I don't wish to sound conceited, but when I joined Preston, I found it easy. Having been with United from leaving school and being associated with fantastic players like the lads who died at Munich and all the characters at United afterwards, plus the coaching of Jimmy Murphy, I was a professional. Nevertheless, at Preston we played some great football, reached Wembley and almost clinched promotion. I enjoyed my time there. I never looked back after leaving United. Years later, obviously I was upset when I heard about Jimmy. United was his life, he dedicated himself to the club, he gave them his body and soul. He was the driving force, the motivator and communicator. He was a great, great man."

Sputnik

One crisp November night in 1956, 15-year-old Graham Smith made his way from his home in Stockport to the Cliff training ground in Lower Broughton, Salford. Joe Armstrong, United's Chief Scout, had told the lad to ask for Jimmy Murphy or Bert Whalley when he arrived. Full of excitement and enthusiasm, tinged with perhaps a little apprehension, Graham followed Joe's instructions and was told to get changed. When he ran out onto the pitch he was confronted by about 25 players. They were in small groups, kicking a ball to each other and limbering up. Young Graham was stood there wondering what to do, when he became aware of two men approaching him. The first one said: "Hello son, you must be Graham, I'm Bert." Turning to his side, he said: "This is Jimmy Murphy." Graham was in awe of Jimmy and bashfully said "Hello." "I can still remember, some 45 years later, the impression and memory of the man," said Graham, adding, "He instantly put me at ease by welcoming me to, in his words, 'The greatest club in the world - Manchester United'. Jimmy told me how pleased he was that I had agreed to sign for them. This I found difficult to take in. Here was the assistant manager of one of the most famous clubs in the world, making the effort to spend time with a raw inexperienced, and as yet untried youngster."

Very quickly Graham came to recognise that this was the nature of the man. "He was warm, friendly and very approachable, with a passion for the game which never diminished, particularly during the dark and challenging days after Munich." Graham got to know Jimmy much better, particularly after the crash and his memory is rekindled with the memories of Jimmy and the qualities which formed his relationships with the players, securing for him an affectionate and lasting place in the folklore of Manchester United.

Playing at the Cliff, in an evening game for United's 'A' team twelve months later, Graham recalls that although Bert Whalley was in charge on this occasion, Jimmy, not surprisingly, was in attendance. "His appetite for work was prodigious," said Graham. "He would often, after being with the senior players during the day, turn up there, whether it was for a game, or just training, to offer help and support." Although Graham was an orthodox right winger, Jimmy and Bert always encouraged him to move inside if the opportunity arose and during this match, as a cross came in from the opposite wing, he ran in to meet the ball and attempted a volley. Unfortunately, he mistimed the shot and ballooned the ball over the bar. Turning to Bert, Jimmy laughed: "That must have been Sputnik!" a reference to the first man-made satellite launched into space by the Russians a few weeks previously.

From that moment Graham was known as 'Sputnik'. He was, of course, unaware of his nickname until some time later, when, after making his debut at Old Trafford, the Press got hold of it and included it in match reports. The name has stuck and is still used by contemporaries Nobby Stiles and Wilf McGuinness - but it is the association with Jimmy Murphy and Bert Whalley that makes it so special for Graham.

As a part-time professional with United, Graham was pleased to gain a regular place in the 'A' team. He was surprised one day after training when Jimmy called him over to have a chat. As always, he asked Graham how he felt he was progressing. After listening to his views, Jimmy then suggested that, in his opinion, he didn't seem to be playing with his usual confidence. He told him he was moving him down to the 'B' team for a while to help him. Graham was very disappointed, but he trusted Jimmy's judgement implicitly, knowing that he would have good reason for suggesting it and that it was in his best interests. What happened in the following weeks only served to reinforce this belief. During his next few games for the 'B' side he seemed to get his confidence back and playing well.

"It was with a sense of anticipation when I was told Jimmy wanted to see me. His 'meetings' were usually out on the pitch and I can remember walking towards him and seeing the relaxed and friendly grin on his face and feeling totally at ease with him. He put his arm on my shoulder and said he had heard good reports about my form in recent weeks but that he was equally pleased about my attitude and response to being demoted. Then, completely out of the blue, he said that as my confidence was restored, he was going to play me in the reserves against Leeds at Old Trafford." Graham was so shocked and thrilled that he asked Jimmy to repeat what he had just said. "All these years later, I can still remember thinking how skillfully Jimmy had dealt with this situation and how he was a natural talking to players. With the genuine, fair and honest approach that was his trademark, he could always convince us that he had our best interests at heart, whenever he was praising or criticising us. His body language was so expressive, particularly his face and hands, and even if it happened to be strong feedback, he would always respect other views and then focus on the job at hand."

Whenever a United player received an injury during a game, he was instructed to turn up at Old Trafford the following morning to see Ted Dalton, the club physiotherapist, for treatment. After receiving an injury, Graham asked his older brother, Gordon, to drive him to the ground one Sunday morning. Unknown to Graham, and while he was having treatment, Jimmy bumped into Gordon, not knowing who he was, and showed considerable interest in Gordon's job as a PE instructor in the Army.

On the way home the two brothers were discussing the events of the past couple of hours. Gordon told his brother how impressed he had been with Jimmy, telling Graham that Murphy had given him his undivided attention, remarking that "you would have thought that I was an international player he was trying to sign." Graham said that this typified Jimmy Murphy. "He demonstrated a dedication and passion for the game in which he was able to combine a steely resolution and determination with good humour, fun, and a love of people. Above all, he possessed the common touch, a quality that endeared him to all with whom he came into contact. His contribution to the game, and to Manchester United, should never be forgotten."

The Black Prince

Jimmy Murphy was fond of saying that there is no finer sight, or more exciting moment for spectators than a forward racing through a packed defence and blasting the ball into the back of the net. Or, when a high ball is centred, watching a forward shrug off the opposition and, like a phoenix, rise above the crossbar, meet the ball with his forehead and swoosh it into the corner of the goal. These players are like diamonds, hard to unearth and worth millions on the transfer market in these modern times. In the mid-50s, Alex Dawson, nicknamed the 'Black Prince', was one such star. Great things were forecast for the youngster who was referred as United's new goal machine.

A thrilling and exciting centre-forward, Alex stood 5 feet 10 inches tall, tipped the scales at 13st 6lb and was built like Rocky Marciano, with big broad shoulders which looked as if they were permanently on a hanger. He frightened defenders to death with his thick mop of black hair and tough-looking facial features. The world of football was at his feet and he was tipped to eventually join his fellow Aberdonian Denis Law in the full Scotland team.

However, instead of being carefully groomed and guided with tender care into the first team, young Dawson was prematurely thrust into action. He was without doubt a heroic figure in those tension-packed dramas after the disaster. Always an honest trier, even if he was having a lean time, Alex found he was emotionally drained following the events following the crash. He played and scored a phenomenal number of goals for United, scoring on his League and later his FA Cup debut while he still holds the record as the youngest post-war player to have scored a hat-trick in an FA Cup semi-final. Players like Dawson needed skillful players alongside him to supply the ball just where he liked it but when he went into action, the result was usually - GOAL!

Born in the Granite City of Aberdeen in February 1940, Alexander Downie Dawson's father was a Scottish trawlerman. In several books about Manchester United they state that Alex attended the same school as another future goal king Denis Law. This, however, was not the case. Alex and Denis attended different schools, they did, however, play together for Aberdeen Schoolboys. Alex was one of five brothers and two sisters but because of work commitments his father moved the family down to live in Hull, when Alex was just 11.

Like his father, young Alex was destined to be in the business of filling nets, though in Alex's case it wouldn't be fish but goals. He came to Manchester United's attention through a former Liverpool playing colleague of Matt Busby, Eric Patterson. Eric had settled in the Yorkshire seaport after his retirement and watched schoolboy games where he saw Alex play. He phoned Matt Busby and told his friend: "The boy's a natural. I suggest you sign him quickly." Mr Patterson's urgency was because a host of league clubs were extremely keen to secure the signature of the swashbuckling young forward with the cannonball shot in either foot and the ability to leap head and shoulders above most defenders. Jimmy Murphy and Bert Whalley travelled down to Hull to watch Alex play. After just a few minutes Jimmy had a smug look upon his face. At half-time he told Bert: "Come on old pal, I've seen enough." As they walked to Bert's car for the journey back to Manchester, Bert asked Jimmy what he thought about Dawson. "He'll make it," replied Murphy. After that, United pulled out all the stops to sign Alex.

When he reached the school-leaving age of fifteen, young Alex pondered a prosperous football league future - but where? The two Sheffield clubs were hoping to lure him to the Steel City. However, when it came down to it there were only two clubs in with a chance of getting Dawson's signature - United and Preston North End. Alex's father knew that Frank Hill, the Preston manager, was an Aberdonian like himself and he was swayed by this fact. However, he left the choice of club to Alex himself and as far the younger Dawson was concerned, there was only one choice, and that was the star-spangled soccer academy at Old Trafford where he became one of the famous 'Busby Babes.'

Matt Busby and Jimmy Murphy were delighted at their new capture. "Aberdeen's inhabitants have a reputation for being 'stingy'," said Busby, a couple of days after signing young Dawson. "However, I must refute that libel, because it was an Aberdonian, Mr Dawson, who freely gave me a present that every football manager dreams about receiving...an Alex Dawson!"

Dawson came down to Manchester in the summer of 1955, and joined United on the same day as Mark Pearson. When Alex and Mark began training, they were reminded of the achievements of the previous season's Youth Cup team. All three teams had completed the double in their respective leagues and the Youth Team had won the FA Youth Cup for the third year in succession. This was a remarkable achievement that has never been repeated by any other club.

Alex graduated in the traditional Busby-Murphy way by starting his United career with the colts before moving through the 'B' and later the 'A' teams, before he won a place in the club's prestigious, famous and all-conquering FA Youth Cup team. At 16, Alex earned his place in the Central League side and was in the first team aged just 17. When he first joined United, Alex played at outside-right, the position in which he had won his England schoolboy caps. Jimmy Murphy and Bert Whalley worked hard to improve Dawson's all-round ability. The two coaches saw straight away that Alex was difficult for defenders to knock off the ball when he was moving towards goal.

Above all that, Murphy and Whalley were amazed how high Alex could jump from a standing position. The first time they saw him do this was in a practice match. A high ball dropped into the penalty area, it looked like a defender's ball all the way, when all of a sudden Alex leapt upwards and powered a header into the left-hand corner of the goal. They knew they had a jewel. He also had an explosive shot in either foot and a toughness that would prove vital later in his career. However, Murphy and Whalley worked on Dawson's close ball control. They felt he wasn't the ball-player he could become and they drilled him daily.

If you look at some of the Manchester United reports from the time, you will get some idea of Alex's potency as a goalscorer. He was like a shark that had tasted blood when moving towards the opposition's goal. But for an injury to Kenny Morgans, however, he might never have played as a centre-forward. As a contingency plan, Bert Whalley moved Dawson into the middle to lead United's attack. Alex responded by scoring a brilliant hat-trick and caused absolute mayhem in the opposition defence every time he challenged for the ball. The opposing goalkeeper was petrified when Alex shoulder charged him at every opportunity. In the dressing room afterwards Whalley sat down beside Dawson and whispered: "From now on Alex, forget playing on the wing. You're a centre-forward, son."

In his early formative years with United, Bobby Charlton was renowned as a prolific goalscorer for the junior, youth and reserve teams. However, Dawson would emulate his record, regularly knocking in four or five goals a game. For three seasons, Alex tore apart the defences of United's rivals, earning the Scot two FA Youth Cup winners medals and a fearsome reputation.

On April 22nd 1957, United took on Lancashire rivals Burnley at Old Trafford and Alex made his first team debut aged just 17. A few days later, United had their most important game of the season against Real Madrid in the second leg of the European Cup semi-final. Dawson replaced Tommy Taylor, who was nursing an injury. Matt Busby wanted to save Tommy for the crunch game against the Spanish and made eight changes from the team that had beaten Sunderland the previous week: Wood; Foulkes, Greaves; Goodwin, Cope, McGuinness; Webster, Doherty, Dawson, Viollet and Scanlon.

United had already made certain of winning the First Division championship for the second successive year and were now going for the unique treble of League, FA Cup and European Cup. Alex, who had only recently signed professional forms for United, had made his Central League debut against Everton earlier in the season and to this point had scored 21 goals in just 26 appearances - good by any standards.

Before kick-off, the pitch had been liberally watered and the players were slipping all over the place. The 40,000 crowd got right behind young Dawson as he attacked the Burnley goal. He was having a real old tussle with Jimmy Adamson, the vastly-experienced Burnley defender. Dawson went close with a header that went inches over the bar after a beautifully flighted centre from Colin Webster. The Real Madrid players and officials were guests of United for this match and were impressed by the way the depleted United side, especially Dawson, were playing. Dennis Viollet, though not match fit, was encouraging the youngster throughout the game, telling him where to make his runs and when. Viollet was hoping and praying that his groin would hold up - he desperately wanted to play both against the Spaniards and at Wembley in the FA Cup final against Aston Villa in a few weeks' time.

"I was fortunate, very fortunate to have Dennis Viollet playing at inside-left on my debut," recalled Alex. "He was a brilliant player, he wasn't really fit because he had been having treatment for an injury but his passes were inch-perfect. Jimmy Murphy used to tell us that the mark of a good player is that he makes other players play well. Dennis could certainly do that. He encouraged me throughout the game, telling me when to make a run and when to run at the goal from different angles. I thoroughly enjoyed the experience and scored a goal. It was a great feeling when all the lads congratulated me but playing with the kind of players United had in those days was easy for me. They knew where I wanted the ball and they made it simple for me."

Alex kept his place for the trip to Cardiff. Wearing their brand-new Wembley strip, they looked like the champions they were as they ran out onto the pitch. In the opening minutes, Jackie Blanchflower was injured and had to leave the field. Bill Foulkes took over at centre-half and Dennis Viollet moved back to wing-half. United won 3-0 with Colin Webster providing Albert Scanlon with exquisite passes to score twice. Alex got his second goal in consecutive games and played well. His youthful exuberance and aerial dominance nearly resulted in more goals. He was leading the line well and, as always, his heading was superb!

In the final game of the 1956-57 season against West Bromwich Albion at Old Trafford, Alex was again in the goals, scoring for the third successive league game. The newspapers were in raptures about his all-action playing style. They tipped him to become a future Scottish international. Despite all the acclaim and newspaper reports Alex didn't let it go to his head. He knew he had a great deal to learn.

Their Finest Hour

Mark Pearson and Alex Dawson appeared set for stardom until the Munich air disaster decimated England's finest football team. The United coaching staff had been grooming them for the first team but Jimmy Murphy knew that the more success the club achieved while going for the treble of League, FA Cup and European Cup, the more likely the strain on the seniors. Tommy Taylor had already suffered with a dreadful ankle injury for months and was constantly in the thick of the action. As England's first choice centre-forward he was also likely to be called up for international duty at any time. Alex Dawson was Taylor's understudy, but in all honesty the only comparison between them was in their gift for soaring into the heavens for those power-packed headers. The way these two headed the ball was much more powerful than the majority of forwards' best shots. But while Tommy's play had a touch of velvet about it, with nice, neat, deft touches and lay-offs with head or feet and his movement through the middle or out to the wings was silky, Dawson's style of play was all power - all-out effort being his stock-in-trade. Yes, he was fearsome to defenders but he lacked the finesse of Taylor and, as an inexperienced youngster, the ability to conserve his energies for the important moments of a match.

Until the disaster, Alex had scored three times in five senior appearances but from the first game after the disaster until the end of the season, Alex was thrown in at the deep end, his shoulders heavy with the burden of leading the Reds' depleted attack.

Nevertheless, he rose to the occasion as emotional victories over Sheffield Wednesday and West Bromwich Albion took United to the semi-finals of the Cup, where Alex would have his greatest moment in a United shirt. The first game, at Villa Park, had ended in a 2-2 draw and the replay was to be held at Highbury. As compensation the game was televised live so supporters in Manchester wouldn't lose out. The star of the day turned out to be Dawson; all heart, his bruising presence turned the game in United's favour in dramatic fashion.

Before the game Jimmy Murphy had pulled Alex to one side and quietly told him to make his presence felt as early as possible. From the kick-off, United were straight into the attack - both Webster and Brennan crossing the ball into the Fulham box where big Alex. thundered in, shoulder-charging Fulham goalkeeper Macedo, who immediately looked hesitant. In the 15th minute Brennan took a corner kick and delivered a ball to the far post. The Fulham keeper missed the ball completely and Alex, diving full length as if into a swimming pool, found the back of the net. Stevens levelled for the Londoners but ten minutes later United took the lead again as Alex drove the ball straight at Macedo who looked to have it covered but saw it roll agonisingly under his body. There was little doubt that Alex was winning his aerial battle with the Fulham defenders and goalkeeper and despite a Fulham equaliser through Chamberlain, United went in at the break 3-2 up, following another mistake by the hapless Macedo, Shay Brennan nipping in to score a simple goal.

In the second half, Alex Dawson continued to destroy the Fulham defenders' frail confidence and by the 64th minute Alex had completed a record breaking hat-trick. This time he got the ball on the edge of the box and swivelled a rasping shot past poor Macedo. Despite a threatened Fulham fightback United won 5-3, Alex's rampaging performance earning rave reviews from pundits and punters alike.

Alex was understandably on cloud nine after scoring three goals in this never-to-be-forgotten semi-final and though he was singled out as the hero of the semi-final he would have none of it, saying that the whole team were heroes.

"I loved scoring goals," recalled Alex about that never-to-be forgotten afternoon at Highbury, "at every level - school team, England schoolboys, United colts, 'A' and 'B' teams, and reserves, I always wanted to score. If we got beat, a lot of the lads would dwell on it, but I couldn't see any point in that and I used to tell them: 'Forget it, there's always next week and a new game.' I had learned a lot by watching Tommy Taylor play. He was a fantastic centre-forward - the way he would move out to the wing, the positions he took up, his shooting and his heading ability were first-class and he had a heart as big as himself, very courageous indeed. He was such a nice friendly person as well.

"Yes, every opportunity I got I would study his play. He pulled my leg a lot, I didn't mind that because he would always tell me he had watched me play and told me he would have to watch his place in the first team. I know he was only saying that to be kind. A smashing man and a great, great centre-forward."

However, over the course of the coming seasons Dawson's first team opportunities were limited. The signing of Albert Quixall and the return to form of Dennis Viollet, alongside resurgent Munich survivors Bobby Charlton and Albert Scanlon left Dawson in the cold. Despite a hat-trick against Feyenoord in a tour game, the 'Black Prince' was forced to watch the first team from the sidelines for much of the 1958-59 season and it wasn't until Christmas 1960 that he hit the headlines again.

United's first team were struggling in the First Division. It looked as if the aftereffects of the Munich tragedy had finally caught up with them and they were about to be dragged into the relegation dogfight. Then in a three-match winning sequence they pulled clear. It was one of the most thrilling Christmas programmes that United followers could recall. The football the team played was cultured, thrilling and goal-laden. Three games, three victories, with 13 goals scored and only two conceded!

At the time there had been newspaper speculation that Busby was on the verge of signing David Herd from Arsenal and that Dawson would be sold to make room for the Gunner. Alex's close pal, Mark Pearson, was also reputed to be leaving Old Trafford as well. However with Dennis Viollet injured, Alex was back in the number nine shirt again. The first of the three matches was against Chelsea at Stamford Bridge on Christmas Eve. United won 2-1. Big Alex scored one of the goals and gave a very impressive display of good, old-fashioned centre forward play. Then on Boxing Day, the fans were delirious as the Reds thrashed Chelsea 6-0 in the return, after Jimmy Greaves had received all the pre-match publicity.

Before this game, Greaves, who was still only 21, had scored 36 league goals that season and included in this tally were five hat-tricks, and five goals in one game against luckless West Brom. A remarkable striker indeed, however, Jimmy was taking flack from certain critics about his England performances. They called him a poacher and goal grabber. It was said that he just hung up front waiting for colleagues to make goal chances for him, never mind making any for his team-mates.

Walter Winterbottom, talking about the time when Greaves played in the England Youth team said: "Jimmy scored goals in those days but this was thanks to the scheming skills of Manchester United's Mark Pearson!" Alex Dawson had Mark Pearson to thank for helping him score so many goals and Alex it was who outshone Jimmy on this occasion, scoring a brilliant hat-trick.

On New Year's Eve 1960, United were at home to arch rivals Manchester City. There was still speculation that Matt Busby was ready to sell Alex and his close pal, Mark Pearson. City, with Denis Law, Bert Trautmann, Ken Barnes, George Hannah, Gerry Baker and Colin Barlow in the team, were up for the game and it proved to be a thrilling, action-packed spectacle - both sides producing brilliant football and exhibiting wonderful individual skill.

The difference proved to be Dawson as he scored another spectacular hat-trick. Bobby Charlton scored United's first with a low drive after five minutes only for City to hit back with a Colin Barlow header. But United roared their defiance and prompted by Maurice Setters they surged forward. Quixall crossed for Dawson, Trautmann came for the cross but missed it completely, leaving Alex to nod the ball into the net. Just before half-time, the 'Dynamite Kid' struck again, rising majestically to meet a Charlton cross and head another superb goal. Charlton scored his second after the interval and 'Pancho' Pearson scored the last. City were like a beaten boxer staggering around, completely demoralised. Alex was the first United player since Joe Spence, 39 years before, to score a hat-trick in a Derby game and his third was United's 100th Derby goal against City.

"Alex Dawson was Manchester United's ace goal bandit," said David

Meek, the *Manchester Evening News* reporter. "He scored twice in the first half and completed his hat-trick after 65 minutes." David Meek also stated that these goals brought Dawson's goal tally up to nine in six games. "Dawson wrote in big letters that United don't need outside help! Certainly they don't if big Alex can keep this rate of scoring, and his colleagues can continue to create the openings."

"This United was like the 'Red Devils' of old," wrote Frank McGhee. "They were confident, fighting, skillful and deadly dangerous. They all played brilliantly from Bombshell Bobby Charlton to goalkeeper Harry Gregg but I must single out two for extra-special praise: Dawson and right-half Setters. Dawson looks at last like fulfilling all the promise Matt Busby forecast for him so long ago that even the United manager was beginning to wonder if he had been wrong."

"Dawson is a fine player to have in any side," added Tom Finney. "Matt Busby certainly sees the days of greatness at last returning. With Dawson and Pearson he has two youthful and brilliant prospects." Peter Slingsby, writing for the *Manchester Evening Chronicle*, talked about Dawson's terrific form. "Alex Dawson's Scottish ancestors must have had a ball on this New Year's Eve. The Aberdeen-born leader's tremendous hat-trick - his second in successive games - was the cornerstone of United's victory while his energetic leadership was something which City could never counter."

Alex had scored seven goals in three games and although the papers were praising both Mark Pearson and himself, it was clear that Matt Busby was still looking to buy strikers. So was Alex concerned or upset by the rumours and speculation that he might be sold? "Of course I was," he said. "I heard all the talk about Matt Busby making offers for David Herd and other forwards and that I was going to be sold but I just got on with playing, thinking 'whatever will be, will be.' Of course, I wanted to stay at Old Trafford, I had been there since leaving school but I had no control over what the manager wanted to do. All I could do was play as well as I could for whatever Manchester United team I was chosen for."

Dawson's form continued into 1961 as he starred in a heated cup-tie victory against Brian Clough's Middlesbrough. Cloughie was a spectacular striker, averaging 40 goals a season - all in the Second Division admittedly but impressive credentials nonetheless. Middlesbrough were a tough side and pulled out every trick in the book (and some that weren't) in a sizzling encounter that thrilled and sometimes shocked the huge crowd. United deserved their victory because they tried to play open football despite the rugged tackling and fierce body checking handed out by a Boro defence which conceded eleven free kicks in the first half alone. This was United's toughest game of the season. Bobby Charlton was the victim of a great deal of manhandling and intimidation, while referee Mr Alston spent a great deal of time issuing warnings to the Boro hard-men. But could United break down this resolute defence?

The answer comes from the following day's newspaper headlines: "The name is Dawson. The trade - Demolition. The material - Dynamite! That was the advert United's centre-forward could have run in any newspaper... and he could get references to prove it from Chelsea, City and now Middlesbrough. After blasting out the old year by crashing in hat-tricks against the first two, he rocked in the New Year with a two-goal blast against Boro. Noel Cantwell had given the Reds a 1-0 interval lead when he curled a free kick into the top corner of Middlesbrough's net. The Boro team fought for all they were worth in the second-half as Foulkes snuffed out the Brian Clough threat. In the 76th minute, with Middlesbrough looking as if they would snatch an equaliser, Dawson struck. Setters won the ball, delivered a long ball out to Quixall who centred first time for Alex to dart through and glide the ball into the net from close range. This brought a storm of protest from Boro who claimed Dawson was offside. Just before full-time Dawson raced through again to give the Reds a comfortable 3-0 victory. Foulkes, Setters, Brennan and Cantwell hardly put a foot wrong and United also had dynamite Dawson - a player who was being linked in part-exchange deals not long ago and who had been regularly criticised by a section of fans but who now seemed to have a permanent place both in the first team and the hearts of United fans."

"There was something different about Alex - he had an aura about him," said Shay Brennan. "The height he used to get and the way he used to hang in the air for so long. I often wondered how he did it - it was as if he was standing on invisible stilts or on extra-high springs. Nobody could head a ball as powerfully as Alex."

*

George Best is still regarded by many pundits as the greatest player to grace British football and he tells a hilarious story about himself and Alex. In February 1961 George Best was an apprentice at Old Trafford and part of his duties was to clean and dubbin the boots of two senior players. George's two were Harry Gregg and Alex Dawson. "Whenever I look at photographs of players from that period, they all look much older than footballers of today," said George. "Alex Dawson was no exception. He looked as if he had been born 28."

Best spoke highly of both Harry and Alex, saying they were good to him and often gave him a shilling for giving their boots an extra polish and shine. "Alex Dawson was a brawny centre-forward," said Best, "his backside was so huge he appeared taller when he sat down. To me, Alex looked like Goliath, although he was only 5 feet 10. What made him such an imposing figure was his girth. He weighed 13 stone 12 pounds, a stone more than centre-half Bill Foulkes, who was well over 6 feet tall. What's more, there wasn't an ounce of fat on Alex - it was all muscle. You didn't argue with Alex. If he said it was Monday and it was Tuesday you would agree with him," said George laughing.

Best then told of a goal Alex once scored in a midweek game against Bolton. "There were only a few minutes remaining in the game, the scores were level 1-1 when Eddie Hopkinson, the Bolton goalkeeper, muffed a clearance. A United attack had broken down with the ball safe in Eddie's hands and the Bolton defenders and the United forwards turned their backs on him as they made their way back to the halfway line. Hopkinson made a mess of his clearance and instead of booting the ball high into the United end of the field, he miskicked it and the ball shot like a bullet at Dawson who, with his back turned to Hopkinson, was jogging back to the halfway line. Alex was blissfully unaware of anything untoward. The ball hit him square on the back of his head like a missile. His two crowned front teeth flew out of his mouth as he was lifted off his feet and flung forward. When the ball hit Alex, it bounced off him in the opposite direction and sailed over Eddie Hopkinson, stranded on the edge of his penalty area, and flew into the net for a goal. For a split second, the crowd were silent, not believing what they had just seen. Then a deafening roar went up. Alex, meanwhile, was lying flat out, face down in the mud on the Old Trafford pitch, legs and arms spread wide apart. On hearing the roar, he raised his right hand six inches off the ground to acknowledge the cheers of the supporters and his goal!

"The following morning I saw Alex in the boot room at Old Trafford. Normally, when a first team player scores a goal, the apprentices would be telling him how great it was or words to that effect. However, because of the unusual and bizarre circumstances of Alex's fluke goal I thought it better to say nothing and continued my chores.

"'Aren't you going to say "Well done",' Alex asked me and suddenly I felt very awkward. I couldn't say it was a good goal, because in truth it had been completely farcical, especially as they had only managed to find one of Alex's front teeth. The search was still on for the other. But I didn't want to anger him, so I decided to compliment him on his scoring. I said 'Yeah, sorry, Alex. Good goal last night, you took it well.' I expected him to correct me and say what a lucky goal it had been. Alex's face never changed as he replied: 'Yes, well, when you've been a forward in the game as long as I have been, you get an instinct for things. To be truthful, you don't even have to be facing the ball to score!'"

*

From the moment David Herd arrived at Old Trafford in the summer of 1961, 21-year-old Alex Dawson knew his days with Manchester United were numbered. He had played in four first team games and scored two goals. When results went against United, he seemed to be the one who would inevitably be dropped. Had he been burned out because, through nobody's fault, he was rushed into the first team straight after Munich? Had he reached his peak and couldn't go any higher? Well, he continued to plunder goals even after he left Old Trafford.

Alex signed off at Old Trafford with another powerhouse hat-trick, this time against Oldham Athletic in the Lancashire Senior Cup. Still, despite the sadness of leaving the club he had joined as a boy, Alex had scored 45 goals in 80 League appearances for United. In the FA Cup he made ten appearances, scoring eight goals and in three games in the Football League Cup he scored once. In total, he appeared in 93 matches, scoring 54 goals. Alex was far too good a player to be languishing in Central League football and he now had the opportunity to establish himself at another club and prove all the doubters wrong.

On 27th October 1961, Preston North End paid almost £20,000 for Alex. He would give Preston over five years of sterling service. One of the highlights was Alex's performances during Preston's 1962 Cup run. In the fifth round, Preston took on high-flying Liverpool. Under Bill Shankly, they had become a rejuvenated team, heading towards the First Division with the likes of giant centre-half Ron Yeats in their side. Alex gave the massive Yeats a real chasing in all three games and was always dangerous when the ball was in the air. He and Yeats bashed into each other time and again - with no quarter asked or given. Preston's Peter Thompson got the only goal of the match which paved the way for the revenge Alex had been waiting for - a tie against United at Deepdale in the sixth round.

He was beaming. This was what he had been hoping for ever since his move to Preston: to play against his old club and show them how wrong they had been to discard him. Alex was up against United's Noel Cantwell and Preston were without doubt the better team on the day - the Reds could count themselves extremely fortunate not to bow out of the FA Cup competition.

Alex must still be kicking himself for two astonishing misses that led to his old club scraping their way through to a replay they never deserved. Alex was not the only offender. Peter Thompson missed a sitter after only 14 minutes, though he went on to have a great game. Alex tried much too hard. If battling Preston had gone in to their dressing room 3-0 up at half-time there could have been few complaints from United fans. At one point, Alex scored what looked like a good goal but the referee adjudged it offside. "I don't know why the referee didn't allow the goal, it looked a perfectly good one to me," Alex recalled. The replay at Old Trafford in front of over 62,000 people saw another battling performance from Proud Preston. Once again, Alex tried his heart out but Preston had the experienced Willie Cunningham missing through injury and United's extra experience turned the game in their favour - they were victorious 2-1.

The highlight of Dawson's Preston career came when North End reached the 1964 FA Cup Final. It didn't bother Alex that their opponents were red-hot favourites West Ham United, captained by Bobby Moore. In the semi-final, West Ham had thrashed United 3-1 at Hillsborough. The final saw Preston with Nobby Lawton as captain and a young Howard Kendall running midfield, playing beautiful flowing football - they went in 2-1 up at half-time. West Ham pulled it back to 2-2 following a Geoff Hurst equaliser and it looked like heading for extra time until, in the dying seconds, Boyce got the winner for the Hammers.

What the fans remember most, however, was Dawson's brilliant headed goal. Bobby Moore himself was moved to say: "It was a goal to remember. Dawson could get way up high from a standing position, remarkable really the way he jumped. Our centre-half, Ken Brown, was certainly no slouch when the ball was in the air but for Preston's second he was coming down as Dawson seemed to hang in the air for seconds and get his head to the ball and rocket it into our net."

As journalist Steve Curry wrote in *Bobby Moore - A Tribute*: "Preston, painstakingly prepared by Jim Milne, father of Gordon Milne of

Liverpool and England, refused to surrender. Six minutes from half-time they went ahead again with the most memorable of goals from former Manchester United star Dawson whose reputation had flourished at Old Trafford in the wake of the Munich air crash and who had been to Wembley as a teenager in 1958 when United were beaten 2-0 by Nat Lofthouse's Bolton. Dawson's header, from Davie Wilson's corner, was reminiscent of the great centre forwards like Lofthouse, Dixie Dean, Stan Mortensen and Tommy Lawton."

Alex was refused a new contract in 1967 following a Preston career spanning 199 League games and 114 goals - 24 FA Cup games with 13 goals and 14 League Cup games with five goals. Alex later signed for Bury, playing 50 League games and scoring 21 times before moving to Brighton and Hove Albion in the 1968-69 season where he appeared 57 times, scoring 26 goals.

After scoring 214 goals in just under 400 League matches, Alex's career ended after two years playing non-league football for Corby. Alex and his family stayed in the area where Alex found a job in an injection moulding plastic company working shifts. His two sons, Malcolm and Graham both played soccer. Alex was asked if they played centre-forward like him? "You must be joking," said Alex laughing. "They took a long hard look at me and one became a winger while the other played centre-half." Now into his 60s, Alex has no regrets about his life. He still works shifts. The big money players were starting to earn didn't filter down to him so he has to keep working.

Jimmy Murphy always had a soft spot for one of the most courageous strikers he ever coached. "Alex can count himself unlucky not to have won international honours," said Jimmy. "He had been overlooked at the time for the likes of Ian St John and Alan Gilzean, both of whom played for higher publicised clubs in the First Division."

When Alex reached his half-century he discovered the heavy price he paid for every one of his goals. He hadn't made a fortune like modern players. He has had two hip replacements and trouble with other injuries. These injuries were caused by his playing career. Alex was in the forefront as a striker, week after week, averaging a goal every two games throughout his career. In one game playing against Nottingham Forest he leapt up to head the ball and headed the centre-half's head. He broke his nose.

"Whenever I was going to get the nose fixed, I was transferred to another club. In the end I thought 'Oh, damn it, I'll leave it as it is, anyway, people might not recognise me if I had it fixed'," he smiled. He remains unassuming and down to earth. He holds no bitterness toward United for the way he was used and quickly discarded. Could he have made it at the top? Of course he could - check his goal record against the top teams. Sadly, they don't make centre-forwards like Alex Dawson anymore - he would be worth a king's ransom on the transfer market if he were playing today.

The Sixties Revolution

"I've had the best team and squad of players any manager could wish for. This club will become great again. Just mark my words."
MATT BUSBY

Manchester United played beautiful, exciting football in the season following the air disaster, scoring over a hundred goals and finishing runners-up to eventual champions Wolverhampton Wanderers. It was a year that perhaps flattered to deceive in many respects. Both Busby and Murphy knew they had to re-build if they wanted to stay amongst the elite of the First Division. Albert Quixall was bought from Sheffield Wednesday for a record £45,000, while little Warren Bradley won a place in the first team on the right wing and played so brilliantly that he was capped for England. Bobby Charlton continued to progress and was the club's leading goalscorer while Ernie Taylor and Stan Crowther, hasty arrivals following Munich, left Old Trafford for modest fees. Wilf McGuinness regained his fitness and became a first team regular, playing in his hero Duncan Edwards' left-half position. Wilf played so well that, like Bradley, he was also capped by England manager Walter Winterbottom.

Albert Scanlon was another regular out on United's problematic left flank. Albert, who had received severe injuries in the air crash, gave some dashing and thrilling performances and was unlucky not to be selected for England. At one stage, the press were pleading for Walter Winterbottom to select the entire United forward line of Bradley, Quixall, Viollet, Charlton and Scanlon, so majestically were they playing as an attacking unit. Regrettably this never happened.

The following season saw United finish in seventh place in the League table. The highlight of that season was Dennis Viollet's feat in setting the club's single-season goalscoring record with 32 League goals in 36 games. Despite this, Jimmy explained that United were still recovering from the tragedy of 1958. "Many people are disappointed that we only finished seventh. What they don't understand is that we have to re-build and this takes time. We have to be patient."

*

As the last day of 1959 departed and the first day of 1960 came rushing in, Matt Busby and Jimmy Murphy breathed a sigh of relief. While sitting in Matt's office at Old Trafford enjoying a quiet drink as they celebrated a new decade, there was a tinge of sadness as the two friends reflected on the passing of the fifties. The past decade had seen the rise and tragic fall of the 'Busby Babes' - the two men had almost seen all their dreams come true when their young team had developed into the finest this country had ever produced. The youngsters they had coached straight from school had become household names: Roger Byrne, Mark Jones, Duncan Edwards, Eddie Colman, Billy Whelan, David Pegg, Geoff Bent, Jackie Blanchflower, not forgetting Johnny Berry and big Tommy Taylor, the two brilliant players bought to add the final pieces of the jigsaw to their dream of producing not one, but two or even three teams good enough to represent Manchester United in all competitions for the years ahead. That was before the dream ended at Munich. However, the end of that rollercoaster decade offered the pair a chance to rebuild for the future.

What would the sixties hold in store for this great club? They pondered and wondered! They discussed players like Alex Dawson, Mark Pearson and Kenny Morgans to name but three who, as mere teenagers, were thrust into the maelstrom of publicity following Munich. These three lads had been nursed along by Jimmy in the Youth and Central League teams, in readiness to take over when the likes of Tommy Taylor, Johnny Berry, Billy Whelan or Dennis Viollet were injured or had retired. However, as has been explained, they had almost certainly been pushed too soon because of the air disaster.

It had been less than two years since Manchester United had been decimated by the events at Munich and the club and the team were still in a transitional phase. On a personal note, Matt was still having treatment for the injuries he suffered in the crash, but despite this, deep down he was fiercely determined to take his beloved United back to the top of the ladder. He also realised that United's next great team would have to have a strong element of talent bought in from outside. Jimmy and Matt were no longer the keen, relatively young men of the late 40s; a quicker fix was required.

While on a club tour on the continent, Busby and his captain Dennis Viollet went for a stroll together. Dennis, who had also been badly injured in the plane crash but had fought his way back to physical fitness and form, told his manager that he didn't think the club would ever be quite the same again. How could it? Matt looked straight into the eyes of his captain and calmly told him: "I've had the best team and squad of players any manager could wish for. This club will become great again. Just mark my words."

*

Many football fans claim that the heralding of the 1960s brought in the golden age, especially to British football. The £20-a-week maximum wage had been abolished and players could negotiate much higher wages, paving the way for today's millionaires at the top of the game. On the field, England would bring immense pride and prestige to the nation by beating West Germany to win the 1966 World Cup. As is well documented, Matt and Jimmy recovered Manchester United from the ashes and won, as Matt Busby prophesied, the First Division Championship and became Champions of Europe. Bobby Charlton, Bill Foulkes, Nobby Stiles, Denis Law and George Best were the players Busby and Murphy would pin their faith on to resurrect the club.

Looking back on the decade, many pundits paint the sixties as some kind of Shangri-La. The developing rivalries of the northern clubs: Manchester United, Liverpool, Leeds United, Everton and Manchester City, who all won Championships in the sixties, replaced the less glamorous small-town champions and challengers of the fifties: Wolves, Burnley and Blackpool. Part of the reason for this switch of power can be found in the abolition of the maximum wage. The playing field wasn't level anymore. The richer, better- supported clubs paid the better money and got the better players. For the first time in the history of English football, market forces were at work.

The Professional Footballers' Association, led by Cliff Lloyd and the bearded Jimmy Hill, had been instrumental in removing the wage cap. Clubs were now forced to pay their players what they were worth, although it must be pointed out that the Manchester United first team squad were on considerably less money than Fulham's Johnny Haynes, who had become England's first £100-a-week footballer. Although agents had not yet infiltrated the game, many clubs were becoming more cynical and intense - being 'professional' they called it. Club managers and younger coaches were overtaking players in their importance to their particular clubs and gamesmanship and defensive systems were being employed more and more. Jimmy and Matt's theory of 'play it simple' and 'pass it to a red shirt' appeared old-fashioned in this atmosphere of 'win at all costs'.

As a result, the sixties saw many changes in the way football was played and the way people talked about the game. Gone was the old 2-3-5 or 'W' formation which had been pioneered by Herbert Chapman's Arsenal in the 1930s. As a result, wing-halves became midfield players, full-backs were no longer merely defenders but were encouraged to 'overlap' and support their forwards. Inside-forwards became link-men, goalscoring forwards became strikers, while phrases such as workrate, tackling back, centre-back, man-to-man-marking, the professional foul, and playing 'in the hole' became an accepted part of the football vocabulary. This was all new to Jimmy and Matt. They didn't neccesarily like the changes but were determined to counter the new challenges by adapting their own style of attack-minded football.

New faces were brought into the club: Denis Law, David Herd, Maurice Setters, Noel Cantwell, Paddy Crerand, John Connelly and Graham Moore. The expectations of United supporters had increased - they followed United with more passion and fanaticism now. Later on in the decade, fans started wearing team shirts, and this brought more revenue into the club's coffers. Times were certainly a-changing. Throughout the fifties, United fans had always given the Reds loud, sustained, vocal support with their rattles, bells and occasional whistles, without any malice or violent behaviour. By the end of this decade, chanting had gone from being supportive to become increasingly abusive. It was also the decade in which football hooliganism reared its ugly head. The two partners didn't like this one little bit, seeing their beloved club's name tarnished by a small hooligan element masquerading as Manchester United supporters.

During these years, Jimmy Murphy's role at the club changed. He no longer coached the youngsters and newcomers to the club on a daily basis as he had in the past. His role was now closer to Matt Busby and the first team. Jimmy would also scout for prospective players and check on United's opponents. Jack Crompton, another loyal servant of the club, was now in charge of training the first team squad but Jimmy remained enthusiastic and still worked tirelessly to bring the glory days back to Old Trafford. His role now was a complete reversal from his earlier job at Old Trafford. Jimmy, unlike Matt, wore his heart on his sleeve and he was still grieving the loss of his friends in the disaster. Nonetheless, he took great pride in the exciting teams he helped Matt produce in the sixties. He would still pull younger players to one side and give them fatherly and constructive advice about their play or if they had been dropped or done things that would bring them and the club into disrepute. Players like United's flying left-winger, John Aston junior, Tony Dunne, the club's brilliant and loyal full-back, Nobby Lawton, a forward or wing-half and goalkeeper Jimmy Rimmer were thankful for Jimmy's help and advice. If they needed anything he was always there ready to do whatever was necessary. He remained loyal to the core!

*

The decade started badly for United. After finishing seventh in the First Division in 1960-61, the following season saw them drop to 15th in the League table, although they appeared in the semi-final of the FA Cup, losing 3-1 to eventual double winners Tottenham. During these seasons many more stalwarts departed - Dennis Viollet, Albert Scanlon, Alex Dawson, Freddie Goodwin, Ian Greaves, Colin Webster, Nobby Lawton and Ronnie Cope to name but a few. There was also the retirement of Wilf McGuinness, at just 22, following a badly broken leg, sustained while playing for the reserves. New players had been signed such as West Brom's Young England captain, Maurice Setters, West Ham's Noel Cantwell and David Herd from Arsenal. During this transitional stage, Jimmy had been working overtime trying to produce home-bred players and he was reasonably successful when the likes of Jimmy Nicholson, Nobby Stiles, Nobby Lawton, Frank Haydock, Phil Chisnall and Ian Moir were given opportunities. Sadly, apart from Stiles, the other lads quickly moved on to other clubs. As we have seen, Lawton had a successful career as captain of Preston North End, helping them reach the 1964 FA Cup final against West Ham, in which another former United player, Alex Dawson, scored for Preston with a spectacular header during a 3-2 defeat.

However, as the 1962-63 season started, Jimmy was feeling very optimistic. Matt Busby had finally managed to sign Denis Law and shortly afterwards, Paddy Crerand arrived. But while life at United remained pretty much as it had done since the war, football was changing very quickly. The players United signed came from clubs where a blackboard was used as a means of getting points across to players. Players and coaches would spend hours discussing theories and tactics about how their football could be improved. Out on the field, they would work on set pieces, such as corner kicks, free-kicks and throw-ins.

As a little example, the story goes that after signing Noel Cantwell from West Ham Matt Busby was driving the cultured Irish full-back somewhere when Noel matter-of-factly enquired of Matt: "How do you want me to play?" Matt looked surprised by the question and replied: "I've paid a great deal of money for you to play full-back, so just go out there and play," or words to that effect. What Matt Busby meant was that he had bought a very experienced international player and he expected him to fit into United's team pattern and play at full-back. But Noel had been part of the so-called 'West Ham Academy', where Malcolm Allison, John Bond, Dave Sexton and Frank O'Farrell formed a 'think-tank' on the game. These four revolutionised the way players thought about the game as far as coaching and tactics were concerned. They all went on to manage First Division clubs with varying degrees of success but in the early sixties, they would formulate new tactics to counter a particular team's pattern of play.

These new coaches brought in important things like warming up and warming down before and after games. They exchanged hobnailed, toe-capped, dubbined boots for the modern continental, lightweight variety. Big, clumsy shin-pads also bit the dust along with the old baggy shorts and thick, long-sleeved shirts. They would sit down for hours and analyse their game. There was, of course, nothing wrong with that. However, the new players hadn't been brought up in the United tradition and so found it strange that no set coaching or team strategy was in place. Along with everything else in Britain in this period, the times were definitely changing but one thing that hadn't altered was Murphy's coaching philosophy and attitude to individual players. He still believed that football was a simple game made complicated only if you wanted it to be.

Tony Dunne

In early 1960 Joe Armstrong told Murphy that he was going over to Ireland to watch a young left full-back named Tony Dunne. Dunne, who played for Shelbourne, was supposed to join United a few months earlier but Matt Busby had told him to stay a little longer because Shelbourne had reached the Irish Cup final, which they eventually won. Joe told Jimmy that young Dunne, though only 19, had improved dramatically and was a brilliant, potential future Irish international. In fact Tony had already played for Ireland as an amateur. Jimmy told Joe to keep him informed of the situation and within a matter of weeks of their conversation Jimmy and Johnny Aston Senior went to Ringway Airport to meet Tony and welcome him to Manchester.

Tony admits that he was flattered and overawed when meeting Jimmy and John Aston. "They both made me feel welcome and wanted," said Tony. "The way Jimmy greeted me so warmly and enthusiastically you would have thought I was a big star that the club had paid thousands of pounds for, not the £3,000 or £5,000 Shelbourne received for me. I was in awe of everything to do with Manchester United. Like most Irish kids I had followed English football and United's fortunes since that terrible Munich air crash. Billy Whelan was the United player kids my age talked about. Then to be met at the airport by Jimmy Murphy, the man who single-handed kept the club afloat after their darkest hour, well, I couldn't believe it."

Tony was taken to Old Trafford and Jimmy took him into the first team dressing room. Tony, a very shy and quiet lad, blushed. "Tony son," he said, "this is Bobby [Charlton]." As Bobby shook hands with the young Irish lad, Murphy, in his rasping voice, told him: "Mark my words Bobby, this lad is good." Bobby nodded. "Come on son, meet Bill [Foulkes]," he said, introducing the embarrassed youngster to United's longest-serving player. Standing head and shoulders above the diminutive Irish lad, Bill wished him all best. Dennis Viollet gave him a big grin and welcomed him, Nobby Lawton, Alex Dawson and Shay Brennan all shook his hand, patted him on the back and wished him every success.

"John, I want you to say hello to a Dublin lad - Tony here has just joined the club. I know you'll keep your eye on him," said Jimmy, smiling, to Johnny Giles, who was changing into his street clothes. Tony was pleased as punch when shaking hands with the player whose career he had followed closely. A Dublin lad like himself, Giles was talked about in Irish football with reverence. "John Giles was spoken about in glowing terms in Ireland. We were told he was a player who youngsters should model themselves on," said Tony. "I must confess that to me, John was someone I looked up to and dearly wanted to meet." Before going over to Manchester, Giles had played for Stella Maris and Home Farm, two famous clubs in Ireland who had produced good young players. John Giles had been with United since 1956.

After all the introductions were completed, Jimmy showed Tony around Old Trafford. Later, Joe Armstrong took him to his digs in Thornbury Road; a few minutes' walk from the ground. Like most youngsters moving to a new city and a different environment, Tony felt a little homesick. His mother had told him: "If you don't like it, just tell them, and come home." However, he soon settled down in Manchester.

Tony started off in United's youth teams and advanced to the reserves. Jimmy was in charge of him and advised him how to play against certain players and encouraged him to use his great burst of speed and neat, precise tackling. It wasn't long before Jimmy was singing Tony Dunne's praises to the other players and staff.

"One day after training, Jimmy pulled me to one side," recalled Nobby Stiles. "'Nobby son, that young Irish lad we signed, he is good, in fact he's going to become a great player, mark my words.' I had, of course, seen Tony play and had played with and against him in practice matches. He was, as Jimmy said, very talented, and it wasn't long before he was being considered for the first team. I made my first team debut against Bolton on October 1st 1960. Tony made his debut about two weeks later, October 15th, against Burnley. He was a few months older than me and had only joined the club at the start of 1960. I had played in the reserves with Tony, and Jimmy took him with the Youth team for a tournament on the continent, I think it was in Switzerland. He was a good player: fast, a great tackler and brilliant at getting back to retrieve the ball if he lost it. We became close friends and he was a great lad, so quiet. Because of the likes of Best, Law and Charlton, Tony didn't get the publicity his brilliant play deserved. The newspapers only wanted to write about the star names but the three lads mentioned and everyone else in the team appreciated Tony Dunne. What a great left full-back, and I do mean great."

Once he had settled down it wasn't long before he was earning rave reviews for his brilliant play. United had signed Irish international Noel Cantwell in late 1960 and he helped Tony a great deal in his play, advising him when to tackle or jockey the winger.

"There was no coaching at United," said Tony. "Well, not coaching like say, Leeds and other teams did in later years, set pieces, free-kicks, running off the ball, and things like that. Jack Crompton was in charge of first team training and it was mostly fitness work. Matt Busby selected the team he believed would benefit Manchester United and then he let the players get on with it. It would be Jimmy who corrected any mistakes the players made. He was great to me. I'd heard that before the crash, he was always in a tracksuit working with the players out on the training ground. I don't know, because I wasn't at the club then, but he always used to be out with me on the pitch, wearing his tracksuit.

"By then, his role at the club had changed; he was more at Matt Busby's side and together they were great. A couple of days after a game he might be passing in a corridor with a cup of tea in his hand, when he spotted you. 'Hello son, just come here a minute, I want a word with you,' he would say and he would lead me into a room - it might be the tearoom, office or ticket office, it didn't matter. He would break down my game in detail. It was comical really watching him demonstrate the point he was making, the way he sort of did a little hopping and dancing. If I'd played particularly well he would praise my play, pointing out the runs I'd made and the match-saving tackles I'd done - those were Jimmy's words not mine, when describing my play. Afterwards, I would feel a million dollars. He made me believe I was the greatest full-back in the universe. If I'd had a bad game and was dropped from the team, he would pull me to one side and analyse the things I had done wrong or badly. He would snarl, his eyes would light up, and he'd punch the palm of his hand to drive home the point he was making. 'You were brought here because you were good at this or that', he would tell me, pointing out whatever it was. 'Get back to doing the simple things son, you're a great player and you'll soon be back in the team.' After listening to him, I would go out on the field and practise what he had told me, to work on the faults he had pointed out in my play. He was always right!"

Tony gave Manchester United loyal service for 13 years, never causing an ounce of trouble. He played 414 games for United in the Football League, scoring two goals, he made 54 FA Cup appearances, 21 in the Football League Cup and 40 in European games, making a total of 529 appearances. He was also capped 32 times for the Republic of Ireland, making him a dual international having played as an amateur in the Olympic games. Tony never got the publicity given to some of his team-mates in the 1960s team and that his flawless play and sportsmanship deserved. However, he became a highly respected part of the 1960s team in which Law, Best and Charlton were the names everyone spoke about.

It was the decade that saw the team rise from the ashes of Munich and bring glory back to the club. Standing only 5ft 6ins with jet-black hair, Tony was a good-looking lad. United followers appreciated his no-frills play. He was loyal and consistent, he could match the fastest wingers for pace and could play on the left or the right. He became a regular in the 1961-62 season. In the early sixties, Noel Cantwell, for whom Tony had a great deal of respect, was injured and out of action. Jimmy championed Tony's cause with Matt Busby and he took Cantwell's place in the first team and kept his place even following Cantwell's recovery. He won an FA Cup winners' medal in 1963 when United beat Leicester 3-1. Although many believe this was Denis Law's final, and there is no disputing that Denis had a wonderful game, they should watch the video of the match and they would see the masterful full-back display that Cantwell on the left and Dunne on the right gave. It was a fantastic team performance. Tony also won League Championship medals in 1965 and 1967 and was a European Cup winner in 1968. In 1969 he was delighted and proud when he was voted Irish Footballer of the Year. In 1973 the new manager Tommy Docherty gave him a free transfer from United and he joined Bolton Wanderers.

Tony had great respect for Jimmy Murphy. "He and Sir Matt Busby were a fantastic partnership," said Tony. "Brian Clough and Peter Taylor were also a great partnership as were Bill Shankly and Bob Paisley, just to mention a few, but Sir Matt and Jimmy were unique. In my opinion, the club was never the same again after the European Cup victory in 1968. That was because Sir Matt retired from managing and went into the political and administrative side of the club while Jimmy was phased out and treated shabbily. But to be perfectly honest, Jimmy wouldn't have been happy drinking and meeting all the celebrities that used to come to Old Trafford and be entertained in the boardroom or lounge. He was a player's man; he enjoyed being with players and drinking with ordinary people. But like I said, a great, great partnership. I mean, look what they achieved in the sixties. In the ten years after Munich, they won the FA Cup, two First Division championships, the European Cup and had three of their players (Bobby Charlton 1964, Denis Law 1966 and George Best 1968) voted European Footballer of the Year and Matt Busby was knighted. It was a wonderful period, very exciting. And, don't forget, after the 1968 European Cup victory, the club went twenty or so years before winning the League or European Cup again - I know they had a couple of FA cup victories. When Alex Ferguson took charge he turned the club's fortunes around and brought it back to what it used to be when Sir Matt and Jimmy were in charge.

"Yes, they were a wonderful duo. On match days, Sir Matt would come into the dressing room and speak to the team quietly. Everyone stopped lacing up their boots, stretching or whatever they were doing and listened to what he said. He had an air of importance about him, something I believe no other manager had before or since. He was so nice, charming and well-mannered, he never cursed or used profanity, a thorough gentleman who spoke quietly and the respect he engendered was amazing. Nobody wanted to let him down. Mind you, beneath all that charm he could be as hard as nails. He wasn't much of a tactician and seemed to get opposition players' names wrong, but he was more of a psychologist. When he finished talking, Jimmy would take over, and he would physically demonstrate what he wanted certain players to do. He was always charismatic and positive: 'You can beat this lot, you're Manchester United players, this is the greatest club in the world and you're here because you're all great players,' he would say in a non-nonsense type of voice. The players loved it.

"He was so passionate, he spoke with authority and every player respected him like they did Sir Matt, but in a different way. Jimmy would have a drink with us after the game and a laugh and joke. When we lost a game, Sir Matt wouldn't rant and rave, but if we lost and played badly he wouldn't be happy and we would feel guilty we had let him down, but there was no shouting and bawling from him. On the other hand, Jimmy would be agitated and go round explaining to the players where the team went wrong and offering advice. He was so sincere and honest in his analysis of how and why we had lost. He would organise the play and point out to individual players what they should have done etc. And he was right! He would play in the 5-a-sides and it was funny because he took it so seriously. He really was a great person.

"Sir Matt was a very astute man. For instance, he knew each and every one of his players, what made them tick, how to speak to each individual. Sometimes I used to think he knew what we were thinking and what we were going to say or ask him. He was up on a pedestal to me. I had been brought up to respect people, my teachers at school, people like that. I would never, ever get personal with Sir Matt; I never got familiar with him like some of the players did later on. I held him in high esteem - he was like a headmaster to me, or a well-known politician, a very, very important person, someone to respect and look up to, not become familiar with.

"On one particular occasion, after days of plucking up the courage to ask if I could have a word with him privately, I was going to see him in his office to ask him for an increase in my wages. I was informed that he would meet me in his office at a precise time. On the day in question I knocked on his office door. 'Oh hello Tony,' he said as he opened the door. He greeted me so warmly that I began to feel I was being a rascal and impudent for bothering him. He ushered me inside, told me to sit down and make myself comfortable, and asked me if I wanted a drink of anything. As I sat in the chair in front of his desk, I felt nervous and uncomfortable; he looked a great deal bigger, he was sitting in a higher chair while the chair I sat in was lower down and small so I was actually looking up at him. Before I could open my mouth to tell him what I wanted to discuss he looked right at me with that beaming smile. 'Tony, I'm very pleased the way you're playing. You are the best left full-back in the world,' he said. Oh God, I thought, I felt a real rotter, guilty for putting this charming man to all this trouble. How can I possibly be so cheeky and ask him for more money? 'You have been playing really well and I'm giving you a pay increase.' He looked straight at me. This threw me. What do I say to him now, I thought. 'It's in your wages this week,' he continued. 'How's your mother and father? If they ever want to come over for the weekend, let me know and I'll arrange things.'

"After this I felt terrible, bothering this lovely man who had given me a pay rise without me asking him for it. 'Oh, I'm so sorry, what was it you wanted to discuss with me?' See what I mean? Brilliant psychology!

The funny thing was, when I checked my wages that weekend he had given me an increase, but only half of what I was going to ask him for. It was as if he knew I was going to ask him for a certain figure and he halved it. Marvellous! When I told Jimmy this, he burst out laughing!"

When Tony joined United, the club was trying to rebuild after Munich. Players who were there before him had now left and new players were signed. Little cliques formed and some of the new players criticised other players and certain things about the club. This would never have been allowed to happen before Munich. However, Tony paid no attention to the internal politics and set himself the task of gaining a regular place in the first team. Busby, Murphy and all the backroom staff were trying to rebuild the whole foundations of the club. Bill Foulkes, Harry Gregg and Bobby Charlton were the mainstays of the club at that time and had been with the great 1950s team. Jimmy would always be on hand to help, advise or rollick them.

"In 1973 when I was released, I was very upset, heartbroken really. Jimmy called me into his little office. His face was sad and he was near to tears as he said to me: 'Don't be too upset, Tony son. Things are not the same around here anymore. You're still a good player, you're not finished, not at all.' He was so sympathetic and understanding of my situation and yet it was obvious that he had been or was being shunted out of the club like me. The club let me down on a few promises they made to me, I was upset and he understood that and encouraged me to go out and show them how wrong they were. Quite a number of clubs were after signing me after I was released, a few London clubs among them. However, Jimmy told me to join Bolton Wanderers. 'I know they want you son,' he said. It might have been because he knew the manager Ian Greaves, a former player under Jimmy at Old Trafford. 'It's only up the road, your children can stay at their school, you won't have to move house and it won't disrupt the wife and family.' I took his advice and went to Bolton and enjoyed it immensely. I shall always remember Jimmy Murphy with fondness and respect; he helped make me into the player I became at Old Trafford. It was a shame for him the way it all ended but Manchester United were a big business concern by then and in business anyone is expendable, as we know. But Jimmy deserved better treatment. I'll say it again, Matt and Jimmy were the best partnership in football. One without the other seemed impossible, it was like a lost cause but together they were magnificent."

The Rock Upon Which The 1960s Team Depended

When older Manchester United supporters think of the Busby Babes team of the 1950s and appreciate those players, one man's name is never far from their thoughts. That man is Bill Foulkes. Today, although he is now an OAP, Bill remains an impressive figure. Sprightly and tall he looks in wonderful condition - the ideal advertisement for a healthy lifestyle.

Bill helped create the vast empire which his beloved Manchester United has since become. Softly spoken, gentle giant Bill was at the club longer than any other player from the Busby Babes era, starring in the team from the mid-fifties until the 1968 European Cup winning team. Sadly, to many he is a forgotten hero of the club. I think Sir Alex Ferguson would be delighted to be able to call on the services of this man to shore up the present United team's leaky defence. For he was not only an instrumental part of the two First Division championships won by that brilliant, attacking, charismatic Busby Babes team of the 1950s, the forerunners of Alex Ferguson's in the 1990s, but he was also the lynchpin of the 1960s team and its success throughout that decade.

Bill made 679 first team appearances in all competitions for his only club and I was grateful that he spoke to me about his early days at the club, because Bill doesn't often give interviews.

"When I eventually joined United I seriously didn't think I'd make it because the young players Sir Matt and Jimmy had signed were frightening," said Bill whimsically. "Jimmy was always encouraging me. Sir Matt told me that if I became a full-time professional I'd make the grade. I was picked for England while I was still only a part-timer. That was my only cap. We beat Northern Ireland 2-0 and the England captain, the late Billy Wright - a perfect gentleman - said I had played exceptionally well. Jimmy Murphy was always telling me that the England selectors were very short-sighted, because they had overlooked me time and time again. You no doubt have heard it said many times before, but I can vouch for it, that pre-Munich team was unique, a brilliant combination of players who, because of the spirit and loyalty for the club engendered by Sir Matt, Jimmy, Bert Whalley, Tom Curry, Bill Inglis and Joe Armstrong, formed a terrific team spirit.

"Yes, that pre-Munich side was breathtaking. Big Duncan, oh, what a player! Roger Byrne, little Eddie Colman, Mark Jones and Jackie Blanchflower, Tommy Taylor, Dennis Viollet, Billy Whelan and our wingers Johnny Berry, Albert Scanlon, David Pegg and Kenny Morgans. And we had two first-class goalkeepers in Ray Wood and Harry Gregg. I honestly believe that team would have gone on to win the European Cup in the fifties, yes, I'm confident."

Bill Foulkes was among the first recruits to join the youth system, signing for United in 1950 as a teenager while still working down the pit as a miner, and though he made his first team debut in 1952, he was a part-time professional until 1953.

"It was Jimmy who signed me for United," said a smiling Foulkes when reminiscing about how he joined the reds in March 1950. "I was working down the pit and playing football for Whiston Boys Club when I first met him. It seems unbelievable now, could you imagine present day professionals doing that sort of thing? Jimmy was a character, a lovely man, hyperactive, always bubbly and cheery. He badgered me to come to Old Trafford. 'Don't you want to earn some money by playing for us?' he would ask me. What he didn't know was that I was earning a good wage down the pit, better in fact than professional footballers were getting at that time. But he was so persuasive, he told me how he and Matt were building the club into the best in the world. 'We've got players at Old Trafford who are going to be sensational,' he told me. And this was in 1950 before Duncan, Bobby, David and the other Busby Babes had left school. Mind you, the players he was referring to were Jackie Blanchflower, Mark Jones, Dennis Viollet, Geoff Whitefoot, Johnny Scott and Albert Scanlon."

Bill came immediately under the tutelage of Jimmy and Bert Whalley. "Two first class gentlemen and beautiful human beings," says Bill. "They were both extremely knowledgeable about football and players. They were not coaches in the modern sense but brilliant at assessing individuals. They complemented each other wonderfully and were the perfect partnership. Money certainly wasn't Jimmy's God. Jimmy Murphy is more than just a legend in the club's history, he is part of the fabric of Manchester United, a man of deep principles. Younger supporters don't know much about him because he hated all the hype and publicity, it embarrassed him. He dreamed of success for the club, he was always talking about football, great players and wonderful occasions. His hopes and dreams were to make every United player from the juniors to the first team into better players and realise their potential.

"Jimmy Murphy could, and often did, sit a player down or take him out on the pitch and break his game down and put it back together piece by piece like a jigsaw. He analysed your play and worked on your strong points and what he told you made sense. Oh, he could be a terse sort of fellow when the need arose and we all got a tongue-lashing from him at some time other. In my early days at the club he tackled his job with explosive energy that often seemed like an earthquake was about to happen. He didn't have favourites either; everyone was treated equally. In Jimmy's mind if you were a player with Manchester United, be it the juniors or first team, you must have talent or you wouldn't be there, and that was one of the things he worked on, getting the best out of you."

Murphy used to say that in the Busby Babes era, Foulkes was taken for granted by the press and Manchester United supporters because he was so dependable. "There were no frills, fancy flicks, hysterics, waving of arms or arguing with the referee from Bill," said Jimmy, adding, "if he gave away a foul he just got on with the game, no fuss, he was a rock.

Two Murphy Favourites

Renowned as fiesty competitors in the Murphy mould Dawson is pictured **(above)** in full-cry against Middlesbrough in a stormy cup-tie in January 1961. Pearson **(right)** is walking from the pitch having been sent-off in the infamous 'Teddy Boy' clash with Bob Lord's Burnley in March 1958.

Left: Jimmy with Bill Foulkes, Bobby Charlton and new £45,000 signing Albert Quixall.

Left: Matt and Jimmy in the snow before the European quarter-final against Gornik Zabrze in 1968. United lost the game (0-1) but won the tie (2-1).

Below: Jimmy retired as Welsh Manager in the summer of 1963 . His final record read played 43, won 11, lost 19 and drawn 13. Here he is pictured with Welsh titans Mel and John Charles

An original Busby Babe

Dennis Viollet enjoyed a 13 year career at Old Trafford. However his departure in 1962 (just two seasons after setting the club record single season scoring record) heralded the dawn of a new era at Old Trafford. His place as spearhead of United's attack went to his school pal David Herd and later Denis Law.

Bobby Charlton's emergence as a world class performer for United and England gave Matt and Jimmy the basis from which to build their last great team. Following his switch from left-wing to central midfield Bobby became even more influential in United's emotional quest for the European Cup.

A NEW ERA: July 12th 1962 - Law signs for United

As far as Busby and Murphy were concerned this was a red letter day for the club - Busby had been tracking Law since his electric performance against United youths in 1956, giving him his first international cap for Scotland aged just 18 two years later. Murphy declared 'At £115,000 Denis is a bargain' - how right he proved to be.

Johnny Giles

Giles joined United as a teenager in 1956 and later went on to become one of the most influential footballers of his generation at Don Revie's Leeds United. However, his personality did not sit well with Busby and Murphy's concept of 'club spirit'. Giles acrimonious departure in 1963 could be regarded as the dawn of real player power.

Top: Bill Foulkes and Nobby Stiles:
Two of United's unsung heroes of the sixties.

Bottom: Denis Law performs more acrobatics before the Stretford End

Best, Law, Crerand
and Charlton

Four reasons why Murphy and Busby
were able to re-establish United as a
force in the Sixties.

Celebrations

Remarkably Matt and Jimmy's run of success continued throughout the sixties. Here Matt pours a glass for Paddy Crerand as United's 1964/5 championship winning team looks on.

End of an Era: Jimmy accepts Matt's congratulations on his 21st year at Old Trafford in 1967. Unfortunately, within 4 years Murphy had been forced into retirement although he remained a scout for the rest of his life.

James Patrick Murphy 1910 - 1989

Many people thought Bill was a 'sour-puss' but they didn't know him. He was a lovely family man, kept himself to himself. And what a hard feller, when a referee blew his whistle for a foul, he'd just put his hands up as much as to say 'fair enough ref'. He never argued, he'd just run back to his position and get on with the game. He was never in the newspaper headlines because he just got on with playing football, but we knew how valuable he was to the team."

After Munich, Foulkes became club captain but he hated the position and asked Matt Busby to relieve him of this honour so he could concentrate on his own game. After Munich, Ronnie Cope was the first-choice centre-half but in the early sixties he moved to Luton. The club was struggling to find a replacement and tried several candidates including Freddie Goodwin, Bobby Harrop, Frank Haydock, Wilf Tranter, Maurice Setters and Noel Cantwell in the problem position. "We've already got the ideal centre-half at Old Trafford," announced Jimmy. "Bill Foulkes can play there and it will enhance his career. He's dependable, durable, gets up high, is a great header of the ball, a ferocious tackler, strong as a bull, he's a rock." How right Jimmy was. Bill Foulkes went on to give Manchester United loyal and unstinting service, winning four Championship medals and an FA Cup winner's medal as well as that never-to-be-forgotten European Cup winner's medal.

I vividly recall going to Burnley in the early 1960s to watch United play the Lancashire team. Burnley were a classy outfit in this period, having won the League title in 1960 and there was always a little bit of friction at Turf Moor due to their self-opinionated, outspoken chairman, master butcher Bob Lord, who had called United a bunch of 'Teddy Boys' only a few weeks after the Munich disaster. Anyway, Burnley had a big, tough, raw-boned Scottish centre-forward named Andy Lochhead. This player liked to put himself about, charging goalkeepers and defenders and roughing up opposing teams. In this game Bill Foulkes had been moved to centre-half by Matt Busby in a desperate attempt to shore up the Reds' shaky defence.

"I was known as a strong, physical defender," said Bill. "I played the game fairly, or tried to anyway." As usual, big Lochhead did his job of disrupting the opposition from the start by his zealous and physical approach. However, after a few minutes it became quite noticeable that he wasn't having the same effect as usual. The clash between Lochhead and Foulkes was described the following day as 'The Clash of the Titans' and 'The Battle of the Dinosaurs.' Lochhead's physical presence was drastically diminished and in the end he had a very quiet game. However it was in this match that Bill received his only booking from a referee in top-flight football.

Both he and the Burnley player went up for a high ball, Lochhead backheaded it and caught Foulkes full blast in the face breaking his nose. Bill hit the ground with a thud, blood gushing from his face like a fountain. Nobby Stiles ran over to his team-mate and could see he was hurt badly. "Stay down Bill," he told the centre-half. Trainer Jack Crompton sprinted onto the field to administer first aid, he took one look at Bill's face and said: "Sorry Bill, you'll have to come off." As the trainer doused his face with cold water, Foulkes told him to give him ten minutes. A few minutes later the two dreadnoughts locked horns again. Going for another high ball Foulkes ducked and poor Lochhead was injured and was later taken to hospital where he spent three days.

Talking about his defensive partner, Nobby Stiles said: "Bill was a great deal faster than he was ever given credit for. He was a solid, raw-boned, hard-as-nails man. He never gave up, no matter if we were getting hammered, and was a very, very underrated player. The following day, Joe Travis [United's fourth team trainer] and myself were having a pint with Murphy. 'Did you see how Bill [Foulkes] handled that big 'effer yesterday,' said Jimmy smiling and full of enthusiasm at Foulkes' display. 'He kept him quiet and our defence looked solid.'"

Bobby Smith, the Tottenham and England centre-forward of the 1960s, who was no shrinking violet either, said after one particular game against Foulkes: "What a hard man. I was glad to get off the pitch and into the shower. He never left me alone."

Later, following a period of rebuilding at the club, Foulkes reappeared in the successful team of the sixties providing the bedrock from which Best, Law and Charlton could weave their magic. "In 1963 we nearly got relegated, it was a critical time for Jimmy and Sir Matt, we won the FA Cup, but some players left and Sir Matt proved what a great manager he was," Bill recalled. "We won the championship in 1965 and 1967. We should really have won the European Cup in 1966, we had a great team but were hit by injuries at the wrong time and it affected us. George Best, Denis Law and David Herd were injured along with a few others at various times in the season. Of course, we had injuries again in 1968, Denis Law suffered with a long-standing knee problem and I had knee ligament trouble. At times, I thought my career was over; David Sadler took my place at centre-half and did a tremendous job. I hadn't played for four months when Sir Matt brought me back against Real Madrid in the second leg of the semi-final in the Bernabeu. I scored a rare goal in this game. To be honest, I only scored nine goals throughout my career. My knee kept swelling up and I had to keep having the fluid drained from it. We had a chance of winning the League again, but Manchester City beat us to it. During the games I did play during this period, I can't thank Nobby Stiles, Tony Dunne and Shay Brennan enough, they were magnificent covering for me. Paddy Crerand was the playmaker and always looking for the right telling passes to get our forwards on the attack."

Bill continued: "In the final at Wembley against Benfica, it was really emotional. I had been struggling with my knee and doing light exercises. Sir Matt told me I would be playing in the final, and Jimmy would be there constantly encouraging me as I trained alone. My direct opponent Torres was 6 foot four, fantastic in the air, and here I am on our biggest ever night and I've got a ligament injury. But I was inspired, I got the feeling that we were going to win, we had to do it then. It was our last chance and it was Sir Matt's and Jimmy's as well. 4-1, what a relief. Young John Aston was magnificent and Brian Kidd, just 19 on the day, got a goal. A wonderful occasion, great memories."

As far as Matt Busby was concerned: "Bill Foulkes was without a doubt the most wholehearted clubman I've had at Old Trafford in all my time as manager." He continued: "Bill is the perfect example of the classic strong, silent man but when he says something, it means something. Perhaps the greatest quality is his ability to put the requirements of the team - and not himself - first and foremost. He would play anywhere, even in goal, if he thought that by doing so he would be acting in the best interests of the club."

"Sir Matt was more pious and patriarchal," Bill added, "a charming man, he spoke ever so quietly and very seldom lost his temper. However, when he did, he really laid into whoever it was he was upset with. He believed that every player who wore the red shirt was a good player, so he selected the team he believed would win the game. He wasn't a strategist, not in any way, but he wasn't a manager who used smug remarks either, he made playing football so simple. Jimmy was the grafter, the man who all the players approached if they had any kind of problems. His contribution to Manchester United's cause was truly immense. I always got the feeling that he never got the recognition for the great work he did on behalf of the club. Just stop and think about the job he did after the Munich crash, he was incredible."

Our Nobby

Jimmy said Nobby Stiles made the ideal 'sweeper' both in temperament and ability. "Nobby could spot danger coming and immediately nip in to stop it," said Jimmy. "The more I watched and studied Nobby, the more I became impressed with his qualities. When he became a regular in the senior team he gave all the other players confidence. His strengths were in his clean, accurate and powerful tackles. He was always neat and tidy and on the rare occasions he missed a tackle he was so quick to recover. A very underrated player who proved how great he was for both Manchester United and England."

Nobby, from St Patrick's in Collyhurst, joined Manchester United straight from school in 1957. He made 392 first team appearances and scored 19 goals. Nobby was Manchester United to the core. He idolised Eddie Colman and played wing-half like his hero, although in a completely different vein. He won Championship and European Cup medals for United before becoming the hero of the 1966 World Cup Final, helping England to lift that coveted trophy. Nobby was as brave as a commando, as strong as an ox and possessed tremendous stamina. He had the knack of making his team-mates play well. No cause was lost when Nobby was in the team. Not bad for a little baggy-trousered kid from the back streets of Collyhurst.

"When I first went to Old Trafford there was a beautiful warm friendliness about the whole club. Everyone was kind and hospitable from the tea ladies up to Matt Busby and Jimmy Murphy," Nobby recalled. "It was a special kind of magic where everyone cared about each other. There was competition all right. After all, we were all trying to make it to the top. Jimmy took a special liking to me, I don't know whether it was because I was, like him, a wing-half or whether it was because, as a lot of older players told me, I tackled like him - whatever the reason I came in for the full Murphy treatment.

"Jimmy was always telling me about the great fighters who came from Collyhurst, I don't know whether Paddy McGrath had told him about Jackie Brown, another St Patrick's pupil, Johnny King and Jock McAvoy, but he knew all about them. He would often say to me: 'Collyhurst has produced some great fighters and footballers, Nobby, and you can become as great as any of them.' He would have me out on the pitch and the two of us would kick the ball to each other then we would tackle each other. He was always, always encouraging me. 'Go on Nobby, son, you can do that,' he would shout. In practice games he would sometimes play alongside me and tell me when to make a challenge, when to move in and win the ball, how to force the opposing player to do what he didn't want to do. Then he would play against me. His tackling was ferocious. I loved him. His team talks are legendary, yes, brilliant in every respect. Then Munich happened and things changed a little. Manchester United have a lot to thank Jimmy Murphy for in that period just after Munich.

"He was a tireless worker for the club and players. Like I said earlier, he coached me from the beginning. Jimmy taught me how simple the game was. Yes, that's true. He would drum it into me that it was much easier to pass the ball to a team-mate than to try difficult things. Jimmy would explain that all the great players past and present knew when to keep it simple. He never told me what I couldn't do, he always told me what I could do. I'm only 5 feet 5 or 6 but he made me feel a giant with his encouragement. 'Win the ball, Nobby son, and give it early,' he used to tell me. I have no hesitation in saying that it was Jimmy who made me the player I was. When I was selected for England nobody could have been more pleased for me than Jimmy. When England were going through a rough patch before the World Cup I came in for some criticism from certain journalists. Jimmy told me to take no notice of them and just play my normal game. When we eventually won the World Cup he was as pleased as punch for me. A smashing man!

"I was proud to have played for Manchester United and equally proud to have got my early grounding from Jimmy Murphy. He was a strong character with a great sense of humour. He never held a grudge if there was any disagreement during training or a game. He would always listen to your point of view. Jimmy's record of producing and developing young players may never be surpassed. He was a strong character with a good sense of humour - he and Matt Busby formed a fantastic partnership, they were great people."

The Lawman!

In the early 1960s, Matt Busby still suffered from the physical and emotional agony caused by Munich. He was under strict medical supervision and advised to cut down on his workload, even relinquishing his position as the Scotland team manager. In truth, neither Matt nor Jimmy were ever the same again after Munich. How could they be? The whole trauma and the implications of it had to catch up with them sooner or later, quite simply they were mentally scarred. After a long discussion, they both agreed that the club would have to alter the policy of only buying players to complete the team jigsaw, they now had to purchase players from other clubs if they wanted any kind of success.

Although Jimmy was still working eighty hours a week for the club and grooming the youngsters there, the truth was simple, the youngsters were not coming through as they had before the disaster. George Best and Nobby Stiles were working their way through the system but were not quite ready for regular, sustained, first team action.

Matt and Jimmy drew up a list of prospective players who would enhance the team. Both were big admirers of Dave Mackay, a Scottish international while Matt was the national team manager, who played for Heart of Midlothian. Mackay would have been a sensational player for United, he was the type of wing-half the club badly needed. He could move up and down the field and tackle with the best; make and take goals, shoot and he was a real tough-as-nails character. However, Busby was in hospital and United missed out on their ideal man when Tottenham snapped him up.

David Herd joined from Arsenal and, though criticised unfairly by a section of supporters, his goal record over the years proved his worth. West Ham's Irish international left full-back Noel Cantwell also joined the club. The tough-tackling, tenacious West Brom wing-half Maurice Setters came and gave the defence some stability. These signings were very significant but Busby and Murphy knew they needed an inspirational player to lift the team to a higher level, encourage the other players and generate excitement for the hordes of supporters. That man turned out to be Denis Law, the young player whose first Scottish international cap had been awarded by Busby.

Law liked Busby from the first moment he met him and over the coming years thought highly of the United boss. Although he was playing for the Italian club Torino, he let Busby know he was far from happy and wanted to return to British football. There was no doubt in

Jimmy Murphy's mind that in Law, United had a truly great player who would help all the other players at Old Trafford. Jimmy had never been as happy for a long time at the prospect of United adding to their staff.

After long, drawn-out negotiations with the Italians during which, at one stage Matt and United chairman Harold Hardman walked out, deciding enough was enough, United finally got their man. On July 12th 1962, Denis Law signed for United for a British record-breaking transfer fee of £115,000. It would be the third time in a short span of two years that Denis had been the subject of a big transfer. He left his first club Huddersfield Town for Manchester City in March 1960 for the then British record fee of £55,000. Then in June 1961, after just a year with the Blues, he signed for Torino for £110,000, then the biggest fee an Italian club had ever paid for a British player.

There is no doubt that Denis Law was the one player who galvanised Manchester United. He gave the whole club a lift. To people who didn't know him, Law was regarded as arrogant and big-headed - a show-off. He certainly walked with a swagger and with his straw hair bouncing on his head he appeared a cocky, loud-mouthed individual who many critics claimed would rock the boat at Old Trafford and cause resentment among the other players. However, nothing could have been further from the truth. Denis was an easy-going, jovial character who kept his own counsel and within a short time became well-liked by players, staff and supporters. Of more importance perhaps, he was as loyal as could be to the cause of Manchester United.

"At £115,000 Denis Law was a bargain," Jimmy once recalled. "He was great for United. He had this air of confidence about him that rubbed off on everybody and his insatiable appetite for playing swept through the club. Another great attribute he had was that when the going really did get tough, you never found him hiding. Without question, Denis is the most dangerous forward I've ever seen in 30 years of playing and watching football. I've travelled around the world, watched thousands of players, but there is only one Denis Law. Dixie Dean, George Camsell, Tommy Lawton and Tommy Taylor were probably the best all-round English centre-forwards I've seen, the four really great goalscorers. However, these four players could never score the 'impossible' goals that Law gets."

Denis Law was Murphy's type of player to the core. Jimmy likened Law to the great Jimmy Greaves as a striker. "If I had to make a choice I would put Denis slightly ahead of Greaves," remarked Jimmy. "Denis scored a few goals that I firmly believe even the great Brazilian Pele wouldn't have been able to score."

For Denis's part he recognised that Matt and Jimmy formed a unique partnership, "I've always believed that football management is a two-man job. Matt Busby had an extremely good assistant in Jimmy Murphy. Jimmy had tremendous experience, including being the Welsh national team manager. He played a very significant part in making United a successful side. In 1958, his playing staff at that time consisted of two or three survivors from the air-crash, a handful of reserves, and a couple of players hastily signed or borrowed from other clubs. Yet he managed to take them from the fifth round of the FA Cup all the way to the final.

"I was still with Huddersfield Town at the time, but I remember travelling over the Pennines to Manchester on Wednesday, 19 February 1958 to watch their makeshift team take on Sheffield Wednesday. It was just thirteen days after the crash and United's first match since the tragedy. I stood in the crowd at the Scoreboard end and I'll never forget that fantastic atmosphere. It was something you had to witness to understand.

"Jimmy was a superb motivator, full of enthusiasm and positive aggression. Because Busby was not really fully fit after Munich, our training was mostly in the hands of Jimmy Murphy. He wanted plenty of grit, and he didn't like cheats; players who thought they had done enough. Everybody was to help everybody else in the team. He instilled that into the youth and reserve teams, which over the years brought many great players into the side. He was a lot like Bill Shankly, except that he was more fearsome; a fierce competitor.

"We sometimes played better for Jimmy than we did for Matt. He was very popular. I always felt that while Matt Busby gave United their subtlety and sophistication, it was Jimmy Murphy who put a little bite into our play. Together they were a great combination; a real team effort which is exactly what football is about."

*

In 1963 the Pools Panel was set up, following a spell of very cold weather that lasted for six weeks, wiping out football throughout the country. This meant that players were forced into training for matches that were more than likely to be abandoned.

During this period the Pools Panel, in their wisdom, had forecast that United would have had five victories. On one very frosty and snowy Monday morning, as the players were limbering up, Matt and Jimmy came in to talk to the players about a possible friendly game in Ireland. Denis Law, full of mischief, turned to the pair and said: "The Pools Panel have had us down as winning the last five games." With a cheeky smile he enquired: "Will we be getting the win bonuses, boss?"

Busby smiled and coughed quietly but sharp as a tack, Murphy replied: "Good idea Denis. Unfortunately you would have qualified for them but you weren't selected," and with that the rest of the players fell about laughing.

Their Last Great Team

"Although Jimmy was Welsh and Matt was Scots, they were converts, Mancunian converts, like zealots really. They were more Mancunian than born and bred Mancunians"

JOHNNY ASTON JUNIOR

In contrast to Matt and Jimmy's first two great United teams, which cost next to nothing, bar the signing of the occasional Tommy Taylor or Johnny Berry, United's 1963 team had cost more than £300,000. While Denis Law's first season began with great expectations for followers of United, and there was a renewed anticipation and zest about the club, the team struggled for the most part, despite Denis's 29-goal contribution. At one point during 1963 relegation looked a distinct possibility - something unheard of under Busby and Murphy, even in the leanest times.

The main problem seemed to be that while Paddy Crerand, the Scottish international had been added to the squad, the team hadn't clicked - the old rhythm wasn't quite there. Murphy scoffed at suggestions that United were a spent force and that all the money had been wasted. He encouraged the team continuously. He would speak to individual players and boost their confidence. Meanwhile, Busby wasn't really worried and told his players that things would turn around. "We just need a bit of luck," he told them. "Once we turn the corner, everything will fall into place. Keep playing the way you are and it will come right - don't worry."

In January 1963, United were drawn away to Huddersfield Town in the FA Cup. In the team that day was another of Murphy's 'little apples' - Nobby Stiles. As it turned out, United pulverised Law's former club 5-0, Denis grabbing a hat-trick against former United goalkeeper Ray Wood. It looked as if this result might kick-start the team in their quest for League points. Sadly this wasn't the case. In the Cup they beat Aston Villa (1-0), Chelsea (2-1), Coventry (3-1) and Southampton (1-0) in the semi-final to reach Wembley but battled like mad to avoid the drop into Division Two, clinging to First Divsion survival by a mere three points. In the end, rivals Manchester City were relegated while United prepared for a the FA Cup Final against Leicester City on a beautiful, warm sunny day in May.

The Foxes were a very experienced and formidable team with wonderful players such as Gordon Banks, Davie Wilson, Graham Cross, Ken Keyworth and Frank McLintock. They were installed as instant favourites, this being their second visit to Wembley in three seasons. This was where Jimmy Murphy came into his own. He quietly told the United players that they were the better team, he inspired them individually. Luck in the League had deserted them, he said, but it would all come right on the big day. Matt Busby was overjoyed that his team were once again on the big stage, challenging for the big honours and they didn't come bigger than the FA Cup final at Wembley.

"You just watch us click at Wembley," Jimmy told reporters. He was beaming. The team did click and they gave a masterful exhibition of fantastic skill and immaculate passing. It was one of the finest football matches ever played at Wembley. Denis Law had a 'blinder' and the whole team sprayed the ball around like world champions. They fully deserved their 3-1 victory. Jimmy entered United's dressing room after the game. Law was already in the bath and Jimmy walked over to congratulate him. "Well played, son, you had a great game, your goal was a gem, I'm really pleased for you," he told Denis. The 'King' was covered in soap and shampoo - "Great game, are you joking?" he said. "I should have been shot for missing those two easy chances." Jimmy was impressed with Law's honest appraisal of his own performance. Not that he agreed with Denis for a second: "The crowd were still singing and chanting Denis's name and he was pulling himself to pieces. That is the hallmark of a truly great player, a player who's not satisfied with his own performance. One of the chances he was criticising himself for missing was a marvellous leaping header that beat Gordon Banks and bounced off the bar."

Jimmy was full of praise for everyone of the Cup-winning team but gave special praise to Paddy Crerand, claiming that his performance was a lesson to all students of football. Murphy was sure that the winning of this first trophy since Munich was the launch pad for better things to come. The only disappointment was the omission of Nobby Stiles, who had played in every round of the cup. He was upset and he had every right to be - who wouldn't have been disappointed in those circumstances? However, better things were to follow for Nobby in the Red shirt of his beloved United and, later, for England. Murphy's little 'apple' was on his way to becoming a legend!

George Best

Joe Travis, a smashing little man, was another loyal Manchester United servant. As honest as the day was long, Joe looked after one of the United junior teams. We both frequented the Spread Eagle public house, on Rochdale Road in Collyhurst, near Nobby Stiles' home. Obviously our chats would soon turn to football in general and

Manchester United in particular. We had a regular Sunday night ritual. We used to travel to the Whalley Hotel in Brooks' Bar for a drink with Jimmy Murphy. The room was usually quiet - Jimmy liked it that way, no noise or fuss. I would just sit there listening to Joe and Jimmy discussing the previous day's games. I found Jimmy, like Joe, a lovely, warm, friendly person. There was, however, a deep sadness in his eyes, you couldn't fail to notice it.

One day in 1961 the telephone rang at my home and when I answered it, the speaker was Jimmy Murphy. "We've got a kid over from Ireland and I'm told he's a genius," said Jimmy in the kind of tone reserved for something he had heard hundreds of times before. He went on to tell me that this lad had been over once but travelled back home the following day but that his parents had phoned the club to ask if he could go back. Jimmy had set up a practice match in which he was trying out several young players who had been recommended by scouts or had written asking for a trial. Wilf McGuinness was going to referee the game. Jimmy asked if John, my younger brother, could have a try out at full-back. This I quickly arranged.

It was a damp, cold morning when the game kicked off at the Cliff training ground. The pitch was muddy and heavy. I had forgotten about the so-called genius Jimmy had mentioned but after about ten minutes, this frail-looking, pencil-thin kid was running rings around everyone on the pitch. Murphy stood near the dugout and never took his eye off the play. When the match ended, Jimmy, still wearing his suit, strode out onto the muddy pitch and called to the youngster who had scored nine goals. Jimmy draped a fatherly hand over the lad's shoulder and took him to certain parts of the pitch. He was explaining to the lad where he should have run, then he walked to the penalty area and told him what he should have been doing when he was there. This went on for over half an hour. By this time, Murphy's suit was caked in mud but he continued talking to the lad who, it must be said, seemed to be taking heed of what he was being told.

Later, I asked Jimmy if he was the lad he had been told was a future star? "Yes," he replied. "He's got a lot to learn but I'll make him into a player." I asked Jimmy what the lad's name was. "Oh, George Best, I think. And by the way, your brother won't make it," he said with a laugh. Mind you, we teased our John, telling him that his only claim to footballing fame could be that he had played against the great George Best.

Over the following years and months Jimmy worked with Bestie, grooming him into the world-class player he became. In turn, George thought the world of Jimmy and in later years he would always seek out Jimmy when he had problems. They would sit down and Jimmy would put a fatherly arm around George's shoulder and say: "Come on son, what's the problem?" and George would open his heart to his mentor.

Over the years many sceptics have expressed the view that while Matt Busby was arguably the best manager in English football over the past 50 years, his main blemish was his handling of George Best. I disagree. George became a huge star both on the pitch and off it. Matt had never had to deal with a player like Best before. Times were indeed a-changing, it was now the swinging sixties and while Busby tried everything he possibly could to solve George's many problems, his fame was so enormous and the psychological pressures so high that any football manager would have struggled to deal with them. Best's problems were, like his talent, unique. Best was the precedent by which all sporting fame is judged. Like the club, George himself was completely taken aback by his rise from talented winger to international superstar. For a manager like Busby, who relied on the patrician approach to the game in all his dealings with players and staff, this new world of superstardom was an anthema.

More dramatically than the pair had perhaps anticipated, the changes taking place in the game were invading Old Trafford. The warmth and friendliness so prevalent before Munich was not so evident in the sixties. The new players signed from other clubs didn't really understand or appreciate the Manchester United family system. They hardly saw Matt during the week and couldn't understand it. Cliques were forming and there was an unfamiliar attitude in the dressing room; which was something that would most certainly never have been tolerated before Munich.

Then again, Busby and Murphy had been forced into the transfer market to pursue their dream of returning United to the top and with this quick fix came the inevitable problems. New players had to be introduced to the system. The natural family of Manchester United had been so wrecked by the Munich air disaster that a return to the old days, when Jimmy could call on a reserve and know him like the back of his hand had gone, along with rationing and grey demob suits. In this colourful new era, the new boys seemed far from impressed with Busby's ethos and approach to training and tactics. The home-bred players had no complaints because they had been brought up with the United way of doing things.

Nevertheless, United's system was forced to change to cope with the added demands of football in the period. At home and abroad, United were opposed by ever more intricate methods of gamesmanship and preparation. The system which Busby and Murphy had perfected was in its last throes and the sixties glory that followed was as a result of the efforts of these two men. With their departure, the club would struggle in the following decade. Nevertheless it is a testament to both that in this period they maintained an unquenchable thirst for glory and put together a series of results that put the efforts of their more negative rivals in the shade. Bobby Charlton, Denis Law, Bill Foulkes, Paddy Crerand, Nobby Stiles and young George Best were the foundation of that wonderful and exciting 1960s team.

At this point I think it only right and fair to explain the Manchester United approach to football. It's quite true that Matt and Jimmy were never ones for overdoing tactics, either in training or during matches. Before Munich, they had built an exciting team playing simple, attacking football. The reserves and junior teams all played the same way as the first team, so when a player was promoted he knew the system and style of play of the senior players. Many reporters said United played their football 'off the cuff.' In reality, they simply told the United lads to go out and enjoy the game. "Give it to a red shirt," was their pet saying.

Matt reasoned that if he had the right players and if he selected the right team then the other team would be the ones doing the worrying. "Our players knew what to do - they did it as a matter of course," reiterated Jimmy. The new players the Reds signed were obviously not used to this cavalier attitude. However, as a point of interest, move forward a few years to Brian Clough's halcyon managerial era at both Derby and Nottingham Forest. There he signed several players for huge transfer fees: Peter Shilton, Trevor Francis, Colin Todd and Roy McFarland to name but a few. Clough said he was surprised when certain players asked: "When do I pass the ball?" Clough said he didn't expect to spend a fortune on a player and then have to teach him how to play. Now the other extreme of the same era was Leeds' Don Revie who used to supply his players with huge dossiers on tactics and the opposition. That certainly wasn't the Busby and Murphy style of management.]

*

Following the 1963 Cup win, the next season saw the Reds back in European action, making their debut in the Cup Winners' Cup. The team was still not running smoothly, however and after annihilation by Everton in the Charity Shield, Herd, Quixall and Giles were dropped. Johnny Giles moved to Leeds shortly afterwards. New names were appearing in the team as Busby strived for consistency. Lads from Murphy's orchard like Jimmy Nicholson, a big strapping Irishman who the press burdened with the label of another Duncan Edwards; Ian Moir, a brilliant right winger from Scotland, who should have been a huge star; Phil Chisnall, Willie Anderson, David Sadler, Bobby Noble and, of course, Georgie Best. They did well that season in reaching the FA Cup semi-final only to lose to a rampant West Ham 3-1 in atrocious conditions at Hillsborough. They finished runners-up in the League, four points behind champions Liverpool and reached the quarter-finals of the Cup Winners' Cup, losing 5-0 to FC Porto in Portugal.

That summer Jimmy relinquished his job as manager of Wales. The Welsh FA didn't want to lose him but Jimmy explained that he was finding it hard to do both jobs and United needed him more now. His final record as Welsh manager was played 43, won 11, lost 19 and drawn 13.

There remained a lot of discontent within the club. One of the main grouses was money. Most other First Division clubs were paying their players much more than United. Supporters at grounds all over the country could be heard voicing their opinions about so called money-grabbing 'Prima-Donna' players more interested in huge pay packets than football glory. If the United supporters had only known what inappropriate salaries their heroes were receiving they would have been surprised. United's home attendances were the best in the British Isles and better than most European clubs. The players, especially those brought up within the club, loved United but wanted adequate remuneration for their loyalty and service. One thing was crystal clear - they certainly wouldn't end up financially secure for life on the money they were earning with Manchester United.

On the playing side, Busby and Murphy knew more tinkering was needed. By this time Nobby Stiles was a regular, as was George Best. John Connelly, a direct, goal-scoring right-winger was bought from Burnley allowing Bobby Charlton to be moved back into the inside-forward position he favoured. Bobby had played wide on the left wing for quite some time to help the club, now George Best would play there to huge acclaim. Matt and Jimmy broke up the formation of the 2-3-5 system and moved Charlton to an attacking midfield role.

In 1964-65 United reached the semi-final of the European Inter-Cities Fairs Cup, losing to Ferencvaros of Hungary following a play-off. Despite the disappointment of all that, the main focus of the season remained the League championship and, seven years after the Munich tragedy that had robbed United of some of the greatest footballers ever seen, the Red Devils regained the First Division championship. This was indeed a wonderful honour and all the sweeter for the fact that they pipped Leeds United on goal difference.

United also reached the semi-final of the FA Cup, as they had done the previous year, and the Reds lost another FA Cup semi-final (1-0) after an epic and often violent struggle with emerging Leeds United. Johnny Giles had become a dominant player for the Yorkshire team where he remained for many years.

Giles had, of course, been a United player since 1956 but his departure from Old Trafford said much about the changing times in football. Giles disagreed with Busby's and Murphy's assessment of him as a left-winger. In fact, the Irishman saw himself as an inside-forward. Nevertheless, he starred for United in the 1963 Cup Final and looked set to become a regular the following season. But after the FA Charity Shield against champions Everton at Goodison Park, in which United were soundly beaten 4-0, rumours emerged that Giles had fallen out with Busby and that the Irishman had been transfer-listed.

Giles was summoned by Busby in the week following the Charity Shield debacle. Matt was an expert at backing players into a corner and attempted to do the same with his troublesome charge. "How do you think you played?" enquired the United boss. Giles shot back: "Well how do *you* think I played?" The tables had turned. As Giles was leaving, Nobby Stiles was arriving and they crossed in the car park. "It's okay Johnny," reassured Nobby as he neared the Irishman, "don't worry about the transfer list, they'll not let you go." "Well, if they don't want me to go, I certainly do!" and with that, Giles left for Don Revie's Second Division Leeds.

There's no doubt that Giles represented a new breed of professional not content with accepting the wisdom of his elders. Francis Lee did much the same thing when his club Bolton Wanderers refused to sanction a move to Manchester City in 1966. Lee went on strike and soon got his way.

For United's management, however, this lack of 'club spirit' on Giles' behalf must have been baffling. For a man like Jimmy Murphy, who had not only devoted most of his life to Manchester United but also turned down lucrative jobs with Arsenal, Juventus and the Brazilian national team to stay by Matt's side, it must have seemed an anathema. Leeds were a club on the rise in this period and the games between the two clubs have carried an added edge ever since.

English football was changing dramatically and fast becoming a game where cheating, dissent, bad sportsmanship and trouble on the terraces was prevalent. Teams seemed to be paying more attention to physical fitness than skill and football ability. Following their championship triumph, Busby and Murphy would once again be involved in the European Cup. They never spoke openly about it but they both felt they needed to win this particular trophy as a memento to those who had perished striving to win it.

Sadly, it wasn't to be again as United finished fourth in the league and reached their fifth successive FA Cup semi-final, losing 1-0 to Everton. In the European Cup they reached the semi-finals, having beaten a great Benfica team containing Eusebio 5-1 in Portugal. That they went on to lose to FK Partizan Belgrade was a bitter disappointment to Busby and Murphy but the pair remained determined to carry on.

*

Around about this time, Jimmy was asked to travel to Cardiff to appear on HTV's *Lloyd Lewis Sports Round-Up*, a very popular television programme which went out live. Jimmy and his old playing colleague Ivor 'The Engine' Powell were the guests of the programme. Three times Jimmy needed a tot of brandy to help him stop laughing at some of Ivor's stories and remarks. Like Jimmy, Rhondda-born Ivor didn't take any prisoners on the field and always called a spade a spade - unless it happened to be a shovel! Ivor, like Jimmy and Matt Busby, was a wing-half. He had starred with Queens Park Rangers, Aston Villa and Wales. In the early sixties Ivor was player-manager of Southern League club Bath City and had steered them through to the first round proper of the

FA Cup. Bath, with their mercurial Welsh ace, were 'hot news'.

When asked about the secrets of his success Ivor banged the table like a Welsh Chapel Minister and declared: "It's the harmonium in our dressing room!" To emphasise his point, 'Powell the Preacher' repeated: "I'm telling this audience and all the soccer boyos watching that if you haven't got a harmonium in your dressing room, you won't win nothing!" The audience chuckled at Ivor's slip of the tongue, saying 'harmonium' when he meant 'harmony'. Jimmy was nearly in convulsions, his face as red as a United shirt. Fortunately, fellow panellist Ike Powell, the highly-experienced boxing referee, produced a miniature bottle of brandy which Jimmy needed before the happy finale.

When John Lloyd, Welsh Sports Editor of the *Daily Express*, asked Ivor if Bath's FA Cup-tie would be all-ticket, he received this smart reply: "Oh no! Nobody gets into our ground waving bits of paper signed by fools. Everyone has got to pay. We are not Dr Barnado's. Nor Manchester United!" Exit Jimmy laughing all the way back to Manchester.

Alan Gowling

In the middle 1960s Jimmy Murphy waxed lyrical about a tall, gangling teenager who had scored seven goals for Manchester United's 'B' team in a Monday night game. Two days later, on the Wednesday night while playing for the club's 'A' team, the lad scored a spectacular hat-trick, then on the Saturday during his debut for the reserves against Preston North End, he scored the equaliser in a 1-1 draw. He was once termed the 'Galloping Chip' - the lad in question was Alan Gowling!

Jimmy had high hopes that young Alan would turn into a splendid player given time and the right opportunity. This Stockport-born youngster was a big Manchester City fan. He had played for Stockport Schoolboys, Cheshire Schoolboys and for the English Grammar Schools. Despite his devotion to Manchester City, they showed no interest whatsoever in signing him. However Everton, Bolton

Wanderers, Bristol City, Portsmouth, his home town club Stockport County and of course Manchester United were extremely keen in obtaining the lad's signature.

Alan was well educated and didn't fancy going as an apprentice to a club. Wisely, he took his father's advice that football was a precarious occupation and the failure rate was astronomically high. Although he wanted to give football his best shot, he was also determined to continue his education. This Jimmy Murphy thought very sensible indeed.

Alan dreamed of one day becoming another Denis Law. Joe Armstrong had been keeping tabs on him and he was invited to train with the reds on Tuesdays and Thursdays and during the holidays. "Joe was very persuasive," remarked Alan. "After speaking to Matt Busby and Jimmy Murphy, they wanted me to sign as an associate schoolboy, and then become an apprentice. However, I explained that I wanted to take my 'O' and 'A' levels, and they encouraged me to pursue my studies and if things worked out for me, to go to university. I was offered a place at Cambridge University but wanted to stay nearer Old Trafford. I was grateful to them for the encouragement they both gave me on this issue."

In 1967 Alan won a regular place in United's Central League team while he was still studying at Manchester University for an economics degree. After some impressive displays in the reserves, where he scored 20 goals, he made his first team debut on March 30th 1968 in an away game against Stoke City, scoring a goal in United's 4-2 win. He would go on to play in 64 league games for United, scoring 18 goals, six FA Cup games hitting two goals, and seven League Cup matches with one goal before leaving the club for Huddersfield in 1972. In 1971, as a first team regular he scored four goals against Southampton. New manager Frank O'Farrell played him as a wing-half, where he went on to captain England Under-23s. After leaving United in 1972, he played for Huddersfield, Newcastle, Bolton and Preston North End.

"When I began training with United juniors, Wilf McGuinness and Johnny Aston senior were running the coaching. Jimmy was always there doing something or other. He never, ever interfered with what Wilf or Johnny told us, never. He would take me aside and in that strong, grave Welsh voice he would explain the good things I was doing. He would always boost my confidence and I always felt I'd pleased him whenever he pulled me aside. When I made it into the Central League team, Jimmy would often be in or near the changing room. He loved a bit of fun and the older players used to pull his leg in a friendly, respectful manner. Sometimes he would sit in the dugout and we could hear his voice all over the field. Always encouraging and positive and, I might add, very entertaining. His language was colourful to say the least but he was brilliant in the way he got his point across.

"I remember playing at Maine Road for the first team against City, I think it was a 3-3 draw. He came into the dressing room and started talking. It was amazing really to listen to what he said, everyone fell silent as he eulogised about how great we [United] were. He then ripped into the City team, dissecting them man for man. He spoke with firebrand passion; anyone not knowing the situation would have thought this was the most important game in Manchester United's history. He certainly rallied the troops, so to speak. When I finished my university studies and went into full-time training with the first team squad I realised I hadn't been training too hard on my own. Because of my studies, I obviously couldn't train with the squad so I missed out on a great deal. I needed a full twelve months to come up to the level of fitness and sharpness of the other lads. Sadly for me I never got it.

"Frank O' Farrell sold me to Huddersfield for a £60,000 fee. I was sad, but I enjoyed my time at Old Trafford and would not have missed the experience for the world. At Huddersfield, Ian Greaves, the former United full-back, was the manager and he moved me back up front. The three seasons I spent there I was their leading goalscorer. Ian was a wonderful manager."

Alex Stepney

"On the Saturday before United signed me I'd played for Chelsea's reserves against Arsenal. At the end of the game, as I was walking to the dressing room, I looked over to this stairway leading out of the stands. This fellow wearing a hat and a big smile on his face shouted: 'Alex, Alex,' and gave me the thumbs up. I later found out that it was Jimmy Murphy. He had obviously been watching me play. I later learned that Tommy Docherty had told Matt Busby he could choose whichever goalkeeper he wanted to sign; either Peter Bonneti or myself, and he, on Jimmy's recommendation, chose me. If Jimmy had only known he could have saved his breath. I'd have walked up to Manchester to join United. It was funny to hear him selling the club to me.

"I had only been a Chelsea player four months when Tommy Docherty took me to the White House Hotel near Euston station. It was fascinating really because I met these two marvellous people who changed my whole life. It all happened so quickly. I was sitting in the lounge when the great Matt Busby walked over to me and introduced himself. I felt honoured. He excused himself and told me he was just going into another room to speak to Tommy Doc about me joining United; then this chirpy, happy-looking man shook my hand firmly and asked me to follow him. It was Jimmy Murphy and I went into his room.

"Straight away Jimmy charmed me with stories of how great it would be for me if I joined United, the greatest club in the world according to Jimmy. He was so enthusiastic, persuasive and so very passionate about the club. 'You'll be playing with Denis Law, a fabulous player,' said Jimmy before launching into more reasons why I should come to United. 'We have George Best and the great Bobby Charlton and other wonderful players. Oh you'll love it at Old Trafford, don't miss this wonderful opportunity of joining the greatest club in the world.' He was a marvellous character. When Matt came back into the room he started telling me how important it would be for me to be his first choice goalkeeper. They were a fascinating duo. I signed within half an hour of meeting them. How could I refuse?

"When I first arrived at the club, both Matt and Jimmy would come out wearing tracksuits when we had a practice game. Matt had a bright red one and Jimmy's was a baggy old thing. They would walk all around the pitch and their eyes were on you. They never knocked any player, but they would quietly encourage certain individuals. Then they would split up and walk separately around the pitch. I had a great relationship with Jimmy. 'You're the final piece of our jigsaw' he used to say to me.

"I remember after we won the First Division championship we went on a tour to America and Australia. WD & HO Wills, the cigarette makers, sponsored it and we were supplied with as many cigarettes as we liked. On the trip players would play tricks on Jimmy. After a night at the bar where he would regale us with stories about his own playing days, or the Busby Babes team, never boring us, he might sit at the piano or sing - a great man. I recall one night in Christchurch, we stopped in a lovely hotel and outside the hotel room door you could leave your order for breakfast in bed. A few of us players filled in Jimmy's order form and ordered it to be delivered for 6am prompt the following morning. We all set our alarms and peeped out at the scheduled time of his surprise breakfast. Two waiters brought two large trays, knocked on his door loudly. Then we heard Jimmy's husky throated voice. He opened the door and shouted: 'What the effing hell is this lot? You've made a mistake I've not ordered anything,' as the two waiters walked past him and placed the two trays at the end of his bed. We'd ordered kippers, double eggs, fried bread, sausages, you name it and we ordered it. About 10am we went to the dining room for our breakfast and he came in, looked at us and smiled. 'You bloody lot just wait, I'll get my own back,' he said laughing.

"On our last day in Australia, before flying back to Manchester, I was in my room packing my cases when all of a sudden Jimmy opened my door and threw about two thousand packets of cigarettes into my room. A great man! But it was sad the way it all ended for him at United, he loved the place, he really did."

Stepney had been signed from Chelsea in time for the 1966-67 season, while John Connelly was surprisingly sold to Blackburn. Shay Brennan and Bobby Noble, another of Jimmy's youngsters, formed the full-back pairing. David Sadler, a youngster who had played for England amateurs and Maidstone before joining United as a teenager, was prominent in both attack and defence. Later, David was capped by England as a centre-half. More of Jimmy's kids were present in the first team - players such as John Fitzpatrick, Jimmy Ryan, who is currently Sir Alex Ferguson's assistant, Francis Burns and John Aston junior among them. United proved to be worthy First Division champions again and would challenge for the European Cup once more the following season.

Sadly, as far as the League went, this was the last occasion they were crowned champions for some years to come. They would have to wait another 26 years before United colours were on it again when Alex Ferguson achieved this feat after a succession of managers had tried in vain. On the close season tour of Australia Alex Stepney mentioned earlier, Brian Kidd emerged as a new star from Murphy's academy. On the European front, Real Madrid had lost a great deal of their glitter as Portugal's Benfica became the new stars on the European scene - the powerful shooting of their world-class forward Eusebio was attracting all the headlines.

The culmination of a lifetime's work came to fruition on that beautiful, momentous and sun-drenched evening in May 1968. Just over ten years after the Munich air disaster, Manchester United were crowned Kings of European Football. The Holy Grail was won and it represented the conclusion of a dream for two old footballing comrades who had striven for this moment of glory for 22 years.

Many tears were shed and emotions rekindled as the Reds gave English football its biggest boost since England had won the World Cup two years before. The dream had brought the club triumph and disaster and when, in extra time, United scored three goals in a thrilling eight-minute spell to give them a 4-1 victory, the dream was finally a reality. As the band struck up the popular Cliff Richard song *Congratulations*,

Jimmy and Matt, tears streaming down their cheeks, hugged each other amid scenes of hysteria and jubilation. Looking back on that occasion, and being truthful, it has to be said that although the team that lifted the European Cup on that unforgettable night had achieved everlasting glory, it was far from United's greatest-ever team. Be that as it may, that team is immortalised now.

It was a funny old season one way or another. At one stage, the Reds were favoured to pull off a fantastic treble of League, FA Cup and European Cup. However, all the best-laid plans could end in heartbreak with one slice of bad luck, United hit two big obstacles. They lost the services for quite a few weeks of Nobby Stiles, who had been playing out of his skin, with a knee injury that turned out to be quite serious. Nobby's loss was a massive blow to the team at such an important time of the season. Denis Law also suffered badly with injuries, especially to his knee, which saw him in St Joseph's hospital undergoing an operation on the night his team-mates lifted the European Cup.

Jimmy was thrilled to bits that his 'little apples' had won this historic and coveted trophy. The team that beat Benfica contained eight home-grown players out of the eleven who appeared in the final. In fact, Tony Dunne could also be placed as a home-reared player as he had joined United from Shelbourne aged just 18. The other home-bred players in United's team that day were: Shay Brennan, Bill Foulkes, Nobby Stiles, George Best, Brian Kidd, Bobby Charlton, David Sadler and John Aston. All these players will tell you that Jimmy Murphy influenced them throughout their careers.

John Aston Junior

On that glorious occasion when the Red Devils finally lifted the European Cup, who can ever forget the sight of the slimly built, dark-haired youngster flying down United's left wing and turning Adolfo, the Benfica full-back, inside out making him dizzy with his pace and mesmerising him with his trickery for the umpteenth time on that unforgettable night. If there had been a Man of the Match award there would have been no arguments that the unanimous winner would have been John Aston Junior. He was sensational. "This was young Aston's finest game in a red shirt," said Jimmy Murphy. "He was a revelation as he tore the experienced Benfica full-back to shreds. I was especially pleased for him because he had been treated unfairly by a section of so-called fans."

John Aston Junior had played for Manchester and Lancashire Boys before becoming a groundstaff boy in July 1962, turning pro in 1964. John was brought up in a United household; he was the son of John Aston senior who had played for United and England in the early post-war years. After serving his apprenticeship in the junior teams and the successful 1964 United FA Youth team as a wing-half, he made his first team debut against Leicester City at Old Trafford on April 12th 1965.

There was a time when George Best was worried about his future because young Aston was ahead of him for the left-wing position. John was a loyal, whole-hearted player but whenever things went wrong the crowd would turn on him quite unfairly. He made 164 first team appearances and scored 27 goals. In the 1968 Final John was on the left wing while George played on the right.

"Jimmy never drove a car, he couldn't drive," John remembered. "Me and my dad would pick Jimmy up from his house in Whalley Range and take him to either Old Trafford or the Cliff. Every day he would get my dad to stop at the same tobacconists in Trafford Park while he bought his 60 cigarettes. Yes, he bought 60 cigs a day - he smoked like a trooper. He would come out of the shop, shake his head and say to me in that gravel voice of his: 'Don't you take up this filthy habit John, it's terrible.' The thing that struck me about Jimmy and Matt Busby was they both loved living in Manchester. Although Jimmy was Welsh and Matt was Scots, they were converts, Mancunian converts, like zealots really. They were more Mancunian than born-and-bred Mancunians. Jimmy had Manchester in his blood. He loved the city and the club. I remember Bobby Charlton saying that when he signed for United, one of the things that impressed him was when Jimmy told him: 'We've got a railway line right next to the club and you can get home whenever you like.' And it turned out to be true.

"Jimmy was totally honest and straight with players and people. When he was coaching us he could put ideas over so simply, there was never any scratching of heads afterwards. No one would ask: 'What did he say, or mean?' And what he wasn't is in my opinion just as important. Jimmy wasn't a pen and paper man. By that I mean he never pulled out a piece of paper with complicated ideas on it, everything he said and coached was simplified. Another example of Jimmy's brilliance was if Matt Busby asked him about a certain player they were interested in, Jimmy wouldn't write a report, he was a verbal bloke. He would tell him about the player concerned in a way Matt understood.

"As a man, and I think his family will tell you this, he was a very emotional person. To me Jimmy was a very strange mixture. He was a Welsh Catholic with Irish connections. He had all this Gaelic blood running through him. To an outsider he seemed a hard man but underneath it all, he believed in Manchester United. The club was the be all and end all of everything else. A brilliant man!

"You can talk about Jimmy on two levels, what he did for the club and what he did for a player personally. For me he was uplifting. In my first few first team games for United he would wait until I put my kit on and when I came out of the bathroom he would be standing outside waiting for me. He would grab hold of my shoulders and say to me: 'John, I'm not worried about you. I'm worried about one or two in there [meaning other players] but I'm not worried about you.' He would then tell me what great pace I had, how I was the best crosser of the ball in the Football League, had one of the hardest shots, was the best dribbler, etc, etc. He would then pat me on the back turn and go out. I used to feel like a million dollars. This was one of Jimmy's great strengths, instead of pulling me up in front of all the other players in the dressing room he did a one-to-one away from others.

"He was a very honest person - that's why he and my dad got on so well together. You must remember their backgrounds. Whatever has happened at the club now and whatever success they have had it all started from virtually nothing. They had a bombed out ground and Jimmy and Matt Busby started this youth policy. They had seen all the horrors of war, the devastation it had created, friends killed etc, and when they started recruiting youngsters it was like the flower of youth again for them. During my playing days with United my dad never talked about the goings-on at the club, it was only after both my dad and I had retired that we discussed the situation at Old Trafford.

"But in the 1960s, as you know, Jimmy was the assistant manager to Matt Busby. My dad always said that Jimmy was there for when things went wrong. The obvious example was Munich but that's not what he meant. If the team was going through a bad patch, say three or four defeats, Jimmy might be away on scouting missions, Matt Busby would ask him to watch United's next game and tell him where the team was going wrong. Jimmy was the man who could put his finger on exactly what the problem was. Jimmy would analyse the situation. Matt Busby thought, and quite rightly, that if he had a better team than the opposition then United had a better chance of winning, that's a simplistic way of putting it I know but that was Matt Busby's philosophy. If eight of his players were better than eight of the opposition, then United had a better chance of victory. But if things went wrong - and remember during the sixties coaching started to come into football in a big way and teams like Burnley started using a variety of free kicks and practised different methods of throw-ins and things like that - then Jimmy would put his finger on it.

"During our 1968 European Cup run Jimmy was brilliant. 'This is our year, John,' he used to say to me. He believed it was our destiny to win it. Ever the optimist, he never seemed to worry. The players might be a little concerned about playing, say, Real Madrid, but

Jimmy was dismissive of them, not in a malicious or flippant way, but like a schoolboy team. Not derogatory but he would say: 'We'll beat these buggers John, they're bloody nothing,' and we would say to ourselves: 'Yes, we can beat them.' It was Jimmy's homespun philosophy that Manchester United could win and they were the greatest club in the world. He was a real romantic as I have said. He knew how to boost players and relax them.

"Another example of his methods was that he was a lovely pianist and when we were away he would get on the piano and play beautifully, the team felt relaxed at times like this. I remember being on tour and we had no game the next day. On one occasion I was rooming with Shay Brennan. We had been down for our evening meal and then went out for a walk. When we came back to the hotel and went up to our rooms, the door facing our room was Jimmy's and he poked his head out and said: 'Shay, have you got a minute, just a minute.' He dismissed me. The next morning I asked Shay what he wanted 'A minute,' he said. 'I was there till half past three this morning. Mind you, we drank a bottle of whisky and he talked my socks down about football' That was Jimmy!"

There is another forgotten hero of this period - Bobby Noble. This youngster had played for Stockport and Cheshire County Schoolboys before coming to Old Trafford, where he won England Youth caps and captained United's successful FA Youth Cup team. Among his team-mates in the final against Swindon Town Youth were George Best, David Sadler, Jimmy Rimmer and John Aston. Bobby was another one of Jimmy's seeds. A speedy, tough-tackling left full-back who could deliver pin-point passes to his team-mates. He broke through into the first team in the 1966-67 season as United stormed to another championship title. He was being touted as a future England player and an all-time great. Bobby was a tough and wiry character but at 21, with the football world at his feet, his career was curtailed. In April 1967 he was involved in a serious car crash and sustained head and chest injuries that were almost life-threatening, and were most certainly career-threatening. For two years he battled back but he was finally advised by doctors to retire and give up the game. He suffered from double vision and so at 23, a potentially glittering career was over.

The End of an Era

"Jimmy Murphy has never been given the accolade he deserved. He was destined to live in Busby's shadow but there is no denying the debt Sir Matt and the club owed him even though today he is sometimes forgotten by revisionist historians."

MICHAEL PARKINSON

Sadly for Jimmy and all Manchester United fans, the winning of the European Cup signalled the end of an era. A couple of months after the glorious triumph of lifting the European Cup, Matt Busby was awarded a knighthood. Jimmy Murphy? Nothing! To be fair, he didn't expect anything. However, Matt's right-hand man was delighted that his friend had been awarded such a prestigious honour to go along with his CBE and Freeman of the City of Manchester.

With hindsight, which as we all know is crystal clear, it was a great pity that at the same time as Matt was knighted, Jimmy couldn't have been nominated for some kind of honour, such as an MBE or the equivalent, for his sterling work after Munich. Jimmy wouldn't have thanked anyone for nominating him for any such honour, but it would have been a nice gesture. Below are the honours from Jimmy's partnership with Sir Matt Busby:

European Cup Winners: 1968.

Semi-finalists: 1957; 1958; 1966.

First Division Championship:

1951-52; 1955-56; 1956-57; 1964-65; 1966-67.

Runners-up:

1946-47; 1947-48; 1948-49; 1950-51; 1958-59; 1963-4; 1967-8.

F.A Cup Winners: 1948; 1963.

F A Cup Finalists: 1957; 1958;

F.A Cup semi-finalists: 1949; 1962; 1964; 1965; 1966.

Inter-Cities Fairs Cup Semi-finalists: 1965.

F.A Charity Shield Winners: 1952; 1956; 1957.

Joint Winners: 1968.

Runners-up: 1948; 1963.

F.A Youth Cup Winners:

1953; 1954; 1955; 1956; 1957; 1964; 1968.

Over the coming years, Matt's association with Manchester United would continue. He became General Manager, a Director and later President of Manchester United. Matt remained a figurehead until his death in 1994 at the age of 84. Coming to the conclusion of this particular story concerning the Busby-Murphy partnership, I don't wish to dwell too much on the negative things that happened, but I feel it is only right and fair to briefly mention the relationship and the aftermath of Jimmy's retirement.

In the many books and articles on Manchester United over the years there are several mentions of the treatment meted out to Jimmy. For example in the excellent authorised biography on George Best, *Bestie - Portrait of a Legend* by Joe Lovejoy, while describing Best's relationship with Sir Matt, the author writes: "In charge of a first-team squad that was twenty strong, Busby had too many players to concern him to be in a position to devote his full attention to one. And, regardless of his avuncular public persona, he was not the type to play nursemaid to anyone. Wilf McGuinness and Jimmy Murphy, trusty lieutenants and loyal servants, were both dumped and hurt by his [Busby's] ruthless streak. And there is a feeling among the players present at the time that, favourite or not, George Best would have suffered the same fate as Johnny Giles, had he been playing a few years earlier."

Broadcaster Michael Parkinson wrote a touching article in the Daily Telegraph entitled 'Jimmy Murphy's team deserve their place on roll of honour'. Michael, a Barnsley lad through and through and a keen football and cricket follower, wrote about his love affair with his Barnsley team: "One week I was madly in love with Barnsley, the next I had fallen for Manchester United. How's that for an example of the glorious uncertainty of sport." Michael went on to write that he reported the first game United played after the Munich disaster in 1958 against Sheffield Wednesday. He said it wasn't a football match, more a demonstration of grief so profound and resonant it echoes still to this day.

"Outside Old Trafford, countless thousands massed in silence, muffled against the bitter cold, as if awaiting an announcement that there had been a terrible mistake and the disaster had not happened. We didn't realise we were witnessing a resurrection of such consequence that it recruited devotees far afield from the city limits of Manchester and created one of the world's great sporting institutions." While he was watching the midweek game against Wednesday he said he became absorbed by the passion of the crowd, observing the magnificent stadium. "Jimmy Murphy's most significant contribution to the rebuilding of the team - apart from his own tireless energy and fierce will - was to sign Ernie Taylor from Blackpool. There wasn't much of Ernie Taylor. Nowadays he'd probably fail the medical. But what he possessed was the combative spirit of a fighting bull, the cunning of a cat burglar and the kind of skills with a football which made you gibber with delight. He was what used to be called a 'ball-juggling inside-forward.' Once upon a time, every club had one. Nowadays, they are as rare as wingers who can dribble."

Parkinson went on to praise Taylor's skill at unlocking defences with a single pass. Like Johnny Haynes, he had a range-finder in his toe caps, said Parkie, before going on to tell readers that little Ernie was at the end of his career when he joined United from Blackpool but still had enough left in him to orchestrate a glorious finale.

"Jimmy Murphy has never been given the accolade he deserved for enabling Manchester United's revival. He was destined to live in Busby's shadow but there is no denying the debt Sir Matt and the club owed him even though today he is sometimes forgotten by revisionist historians." Michael said it was about time that Jimmy Murphy's team was included on the roll of honour. They might have lacked the glitter of the others but it would be difficult to name another who so courageously battled overwhelming odds. More than that, they were responsible for the special link that exists to this day between Manchester United and a tribal following encircling the world, he said.

Welsh International and former Manchester United player Colin Webster concurs: "If Murphy had not been at Old Trafford, the Busby Babes would never have existed. That's my opinion anyway. Murphy brought in at least 80% of them. He camped outside homes. They used to say families would make their boys sign for United so they could get rid of him. Edwards, Viollet, Taylor, Colman, Pegg, Jones and many more were all Murphy's boys. When I first joined United I had my run-ins with Jimmy, because he wouldn't stand for slovenliness in training or playing. I was usually the oldest player in the reserve team during the early fifties and I was only in my early 20s, so I knew he wanted the younger kids to be set an example. He would rant and rave, but he never held grudges, nor told tales to Matt Busby. And what he achieved after Munich was fantastic. In my own personal opinion I don't think Matt Busby could have done it and to be perfectly truthful neither could many others have done it either. Jimmy Murphy was a special breed of human being, a one off!"

The End of an Era

Retirement 1971

In April 1969, Jimmy's protégé Wilf McGuinness was appointed Chief Coach of Manchester United, Matt Busby became General Manager, while Jimmy remained as his assistant manager. Then, in June 1969, Wilf was promoted to the position of Manager. He had, of course, been with the club as a player and coach for 17 years. His playing career had been prematurely curtailed following a broken leg sustained in a reserve game in December 1959. He was just 22 at the time. To all intents and purposes Jimmy was still officially assistant manager, but assistant to whom?

Jimmy's son, Jimmy Murphy junior, said Matt Busby had promised his dad that: "There will always be a high and honoured position here for Jimmy Murphy. The old partnership will be there in the background to help and inspire the new man [Wilf] in his efforts." Wilf took over Jimmy's office and Jimmy moved in with Joe Armstrong. "Jimmy's life revolved around the dressing room and the training ground. In essence Jimmy was not assistant to anyone, he was not a coach, he was not really a scout, he was in fact really a nobody."

Obviously Jimmy was upset and disappointed with the proceedings but he was steeped in the Manchester United tradition and refused to rock the boat. He was still the loyal and honest person who entered the bombwrecked Old Trafford in 1946. So although he was disenchanted, very hurt and rejected, he carried on going to the ground every single day. "It was his whole life," added his son Nick. "Manchester United was his whole life. He loved the place, loved going there, he couldn't keep away."

On September 30th 1971, Jimmy officially retired from Old Trafford. He didn't want to retire - he felt he still had a great deal to offer the club. It was a sad ending to his 25-year stint at Manchester United, the club he had helped to shape.

Eamon Dunphy wrote in his book *A Strange Kind Of Glory* that Jimmy was offered £20,000, the equivalent of five years' salary, as a retirement settlement and a scouting job which would pay him £25 a week. Eamon also quotes in his book that Shay Brennan was given a free transfer and a pension for life. It would seem that United never repaid the loyalty Jimmy had given them since joining in 1946. Jimmy did not drive and had a regular taxi which picked him up at his home and took him to Old Trafford. The club suddenly ceased paying his taxi fare and stopped paying his telephone bills. Jimmy, according to his son Jimmy, felt very sad, disenchanted and let down by Matt Busby.

"He had turned down lots of good jobs, he had helped make all these great players for United and had saved the club after Munich. He was in limbo, both in his work and financially. Matt blamed the Board but everyone knew Matt was the Board."

However, despite all the rumours over the years Matt and Jimmy never actually had a fall out. None whatsoever! Despite what might have happened, they still had far too much respect for each other. After all, they had been through a great deal together in the cause of Manchester United. So let us be quite clear on this point. There was no blazing altercation or controversy and most certainly no childish name-calling or hysterical headlines in the newspapers. Obviously things were never the same again between the two men, but it's true that Jimmy felt that he was being pushed out by the way things turned out. The two men simply drifted further apart. Matt was busy with his boardroom duties while Jimmy was basically a footballing person, happiest mixing with the players, trainers and coaches.

Even though he was officially retired, Jimmy continued his daily pilgrimage to Old Trafford. He would collect his mail and speak to the scouts and staff. He looked on in sadness at what he saw happening at his beloved club, but he never once interfered with what Wilf McGuinness was doing. That's not to say he wouldn't have helped if he'd been asked. The sad, catastrophic catalogue of managers who were tried after Busby and Murphy retired has been documented in several books and television programmes over the years and it wasn't until 1986 when Sir Alex Ferguson took over the reins that the club found a manager worthy of the role.

However, on a cold, wet day in December 1970, Wilf McGuinness was dismissed as manager of Manchester United. He had taken the team to two League Cup semi-finals and one FA Cup semi-final and though he had tried desperately to turn things around at the club he loved so much, he was deemed to have failed. Wilf was and still is Manchester United through and through and while the younger players such as Brian Kidd responded to his ideas and formations, in the end the level of expcetation was too high; however no man could have tried harder.

Jimmy looked on with a great deal of sadness. He wanted to help Wilf and would gladly have helped if he had been asked but he wasn't. So Jimmy didn't interfere, ever. With the benefit of hindsight, Wilf would most certainly have turned things around if only he had had the ever-faithful and knowledgeable Murphy alongside him. On the day he was dismissed, Wilf sat in the stands at Old Trafford with his head in his hands, hurt and absolutely distraught. Jimmy quietly sat down next to him and they both broke down crying. McGuinness was offered his old job back but so devastated was he, he turned it down and left the club. He took various managerial jobs abroad, mainly in Greece. Within a short time of him leaving United, his hair turned white and fell out, sending him completely bald. This was the aftermath of all the worry at Old Trafford.

"Of course I would have loved it if it had been possible for Jimmy to have worked alongside me when I was put in charge of Manchester United," recalled Wilf. "People need to understand that there were a lot of grey areas at Old Trafford in that period. I was only 31 and Matt was the general manager. If it had been discussed by all concerned and I had been told that Jimmy was to guide me along, I would have welcomed it with open arms, I really and truly would have. But this wasn't the case and I just got on with the job. I loved Jimmy Murphy. He was a very astute man, especially about football. But it was a long time ago and things were a lot different then. Who knows? One thing is certain though and that is that Jimmy Murphy will go down in history as the man who nurtured and developed all those great Busby Babes and the players who followed after the crash. A great man!"

Once again, Sir Matt took charge of the club, coming back as manager for a brief spell after Wilf had been relieved of his job. A new manager wasn't appointed until June 1971, and then it was Frank O'Farrell, a quiet and methodical man who had learned a great deal from the renowned West Ham soccer academy. He brought in Malcolm Musgrove as coach and assistant. Jimmy would still travel to the club every day, still open his mail and have a chat with the staff and the scouts. He still didn't interfere in any way but felt hurt that he wasn't asked for his help or opinion on players.

Then another announcement hit the headlines in December 1972 when O'Farrell, Musgrove and the loyal John Aston senior were sacked. O'Farrell was bitterly upset and felt he had been let down badly. John Aston senior had been a loyal and dedicated servant to Manchester United over the years. His departure was bitter, he also felt let down. He was hurt and angry and asked the chairman, Louis Edwards, why he had been sacked. The chairman, looking distinctly uncomfortable, told him the club were not satisfied with the scouting activities. Aston senior resented this remark and never forgave the club for his shabby treatment.

Shortly after O'Farrell's departure, the controversial, charismatic and flamboyant Tommy Docherty took control as manager. He caused feathers to fly and fell out with several star players along the way but after taking United down into the Second Division, 'The Doc' brought them straight back up with a young, exciting team. In the 1975-76 season they finished third in the First Division and reached the FA Cup Final, losing 1-0 to unfancied Southampton. A year later he took United back to Wembley once again where United beat Liverpool 2-1.

During Docherty's tenure, Jimmy Murphy was brought back into the fold. Talking about Jimmy, the Doc said: "I brought Jimmy Murphy back to help because of his vast knowledge and experience. I used him for scouting and for his judgement about players. Jimmy quickly found Steve Coppell and Gordon Hill, two brilliant wingers. He would say to me: 'Sign' or: 'Don't sign this player.' To be straightforward with you, I never saw Coppell play before he joined United. I just followed Jimmy's advice. I remember him phoning me and telling me to hurry up and sign Coppell. I told him I would go and watch him play. 'You'll be too late,' said Jimmy, 'Liverpool are after him. Sign him now.' Jimmy was different class. He didn't get half the credit he deserved. In my opinion, he was as great as Matt Busby. Matt was wonderful but he would not have been half the man without Jimmy."

Sadly, just after winning the FA Cup, Docherty was sacked following revelations about an affair with Mary Brown, the wife of United's physiotherapist Laurie Brown. After Docherty, United appointed their fourth manager in eight years when the quietly-spoken Dave Sexton took over the managerial reins in 1977. Sexton, whose father Archie had been a famous professional boxer in the 1930s, was a terrific coach, as his later jobs with the England national team proved. At Old Trafford however, he never seemed at ease with all the publicity surrounding the club. He spent a couple of million pounds in the transfer market without success and his teams were perceived by supporters as dour and boring.

In April 1981, after seven successive wins, Dave Sexton was sacked. During his period at Old Trafford, Jimmy had many conversations with Sexton and liked him immensely. He felt a little sorry when he left the club.

In June 1981 Ron Atkinson took over. Ron was flash, bedecked in jewellery and oddly enough, he was the first Manchester United manager since Scott Duncan in the 1930s who wasn't a Roman Catholic. In his first four seasons, United won the FA Cup twice, although he spent millions of pounds in the transfer market. Ron included Jimmy in many of the first team's trips abroad. He valued his wealth of knowledge. The faithful United followers however, were more interested in winning the League and in European glory. In 1986 Ron was shown the door. Alex Ferguson became the new United manager and the Busby-Murphy years were reincarnated. Alex brought back the glory times to Old Trafford. The famous youth system was re-established and the youngsters at last began to hold their own in the first team just as they had in the Busby Babes era and the fabulous 1960s period. Jimmy liked Alex Ferguson; he often said that the club was back in good hands under him. Sadly, Jimmy didn't live to witness those wonderful feats of the 1990s.

*

In March 1978, a testimonial dinner was given for Jimmy Murphy in the United Executive Suite at Old Trafford. Freddie Pye, BBC presenter David Coleman, Sir Matt Busby, Bobby Charlton, United manager Dave Sexton, his assistant Tommy Cavanagh and Cliff Morgan were all present. Bobby Charlton donated one of his treasured England shirts for an auction. He said: "My whole career from the age of 15 was linked with Jimmy Murphy. He was so intense he used to frighten me. He was hell to work for and at times I used to hate him but I owe more to Jimmy Murphy than any other single person in football. Everything he did was for a purpose and I am grateful to him. The success of Manchester United is a testimony to his work."

Sir Matt added: "We had a wonderful and happy relationship. Jimmy was never a 'yes man' which was a good start. Our nature seemed to join to produce common sense. He was straight, honest and loyal." The dinner was organised by admirers under the chairmanship of Tom Henry, the former editor of the *Manchester Evening News*. It was estimated that Jimmy would receive about £4,000. Bobby Charlton's shirt was sold for £500 in an auction that raised £2,000.

*

Harry McShane, the father of film and television star Ian, was a former Manchester United player and scout. Harry and Jimmy would often travel to games together. On one occasion, they went to watch a young centre-half who had been highly recommended for United to sign. Ian took Jimmy and his father to the game in his Rolls-Royce Silver Cloud . As the McShanes settled down in their seats, the players were kicking in before the referee blew his whistle to start the game. Jimmy suddenly stood up and said: "Right, come on, let's go." Harry was puzzled and wondering what was wrong, asked Jimmy what the matter was. "I thought you wanted to check out the centre-half," said Harry. "I've seen enough," replied Jimmy, "we don't need him."

Talking a few years later about the player he and Jimmy had gone to look at, Harry said: "Jimmy was right, spot on in fact in his assessment, the lad never amounted to anything. Just from watching the player kicking in, Jimmy knew he wouldn't make the grade at the top level. And, to be fair to him, the lad never did anything of note. It was fascinating the way he could tell whether a player would make it or not, especially with United."

Stuart Pearson was spotted and recommended by Jimmy and so too was a young player Jimmy went to watch play in Leicester City's reserves, a player who really thrilled him. It was ironic really, going to check on a lad playing in Leicester's second team, but the young Leicester forward caught his eye immediately. Jimmy urged United to sign him at the earliest opportunity. Gary Lineker was the player's name. Jimmy had watched him as an unknown who had yet to play first team football and thought he was a certainty to make the top grade. Alas, Jimmy's report was never acted upon.

United's scouting in the early eighties left something to be desired. On one occasion, Jimmy went to Old Trafford and spoke to one of United's newer scouts, who shall remain nameless. Jimmy asked if he was checking on any particular player. The scout looked a little bemused and told Jimmy he had looked at a young Scottish player eight or nine times. Jimmy didn't say anything at this, but you could see what he was thinking. "Well, have you decided what to do about this lad?" Murphy asked. The scout replied that he would go and have another look before making a recommendation. United never followed up their interest.

The player concerned? Gary McAllister. As Johnny Aston senior said when he heard this: "Eight or nine times? It would have taken Jimmy no more than three or four visits at the most to decide one way or the other whether he was a player for United."

*

In November 1978 Jimmy was discussing modern-day coaching with some friends. His view was that although he firmly believed that coaching was a very important part of football it had been taken to extremes. When he started as a youngster he had to stand on his own two feet and he received precious little help from anyone "It was a man's world and professional soccer was the survival of the fittest," he said. He was of the opinion that there was far too much talking and over-coaching was confusing the players. "They are filling the players' heads with too much theory and complicated tactics. We are in danger of stifling their individuality. I can see it at international level and in club matches. It stems from too many people doing too much talking. The damage done by the talkers is to young players," he said.

His method, he explained, was to let youngsters play with freedom for the first four or five months after they joined United. This gave the lads time to develop their own talents. He used George Best and Bobby Charlton as examples. "These two were great players but as different as chalk and cheese in temperament and everything. I knew that it was important to let George develop naturally. The training staff were told not to try and change his style. We knew that George was immature at times in his football and even when he became experienced there were times when I wished he'd have passed to other players more often. He scored goals, made up his own moves, frequently out of nothing because of his fantastic skill with the ball and if he had been forced to play to a rigid plan he might well have been a failure. So it was important to let him develop naturally as a boy. He held on to the ball too much but that was his style. If George Best was starting out in football today I wonder how he would have got on with the systems and whether it would have been so easy for him to reveal his genius to the world. I wonder how many George Bests are being destroyed at this very minute by coaches who fail to appreciate that a pennyworth of skill is worth a pound of theory any day?"

He went on to say that people shouldn't run away with the idea that when he was coaching he just sent players out to play and that was that. He mentioned Bobby Charlton as another example. Jimmy said that like Best, Bobby was blessed with wonderful ability but that there were aspects of his game that he had to work on.

"Bobby did so many things as a boy instinctively, but we had to tell him that he must first master the short game before becoming the great long ball player that helped him win 106 caps for England," said Jimmy. "We didn't set about coaching Bobby with too much talk and theory. We showed him the practical way, which was always my approach. I used to play with or against him regularly to show him what I wanted. Bobby was an excellent pupil and I think he would be the first to agree that he couldn't have managed without the practical kind of coaching and encouragement that he received at Old Trafford in his early days. We didn't kill him with talk though because coaching for me has always been practical work rather than blackboard theory."

So who was the Greatest Of Them All?

"He could play anywhere and I do mean in any position. In present day football he could have played until he was 50."
JIMMY MURPHY

"Who was the greatest player you ever saw?" This was a question Jimmy was forever being asked by journalists and fans. It was a difficult question for him to answer because over the years he had played with or against many of the greatest names in soccer before the war and groomed many of the best modern players for United and Wales.

Before giving his answer he would try to divide the players into pre-war and post war. Peter Doherty, the great Irish international inside-forward, was one of Jimmy's all-time favourites, as was Raich Carter. Murphy's definition of a great player was one who played the game in his own time. Technique, spirit, constructive ability and fitness all contributed. However, the quality that lifted a great player from the ordinary was of playing the game at his own speed, thus controlling the pace of the entire game.

Johnny Carey was another of his favourites. Jimmy believed that

So who was the Greatest Of Them All?

Carey was one of the greatest full-backs of all time and said he had a wonderful football brain, was cool under pressure and had brilliant ball control. Carey's greatest gift though, was his positional sense. Other points that Jimmy thought Carey had were his versatility and captaincy. Roger Byrne was described by Jimmy as the best left-back he had ever seen in all the years he had spent in the game. Danny Blanchflower was also high on Murphy's list of all-time greats. Jimmy said the Irishman had no rivals as an attacking wing-half. He was an outstanding schemer who had revitalised Irish football. He also had an high opinion of the Tottenham player Ron Burgess, who, said Jimmy, was not as good as Blanchflower when attacking but a much better all-round player because of his defensive technique. Burgess, said Jimmy, was as strong at the end of a game as he was at the start.

Fellow Welshman Roy Paul also featured high on Murphy's list. Paul was a dominating figure, especially in defence. According to Jimmy, he was one of the greatest captains of all time and a source of tremendous inspiration. He also mentioned players of the calibre of Billy Wright of Wolves, Bobby Johnstone, the little Manchester City player and Jimmy McIlroy, the Burnley and Northen Ireland inside-forward. He also mentioned a player he thought would have been sensational at Old Trafford, his fellow Welshman Ivor Allchurch. Jimmy always maintained that if Ivor had been with Manchester United or another more fashionable club, he would have been regarded as a truly great player.

"I well remember years ago, as a player with West Brom we played Stoke at their ground and Stanley Matthews tore us to pieces," said an enthusiastic Murphy. "He is a 'must' on anyone's list of all-time greats. He was the only player with a completely personal style that can never be imitated or hardly even analysed."

When the name Tom Finney cropped up Jimmy's eyes lit up. He regarded the 'Preston Plumber' as one of the two or three greatest players he had ever seen. Jimmy said Finney could play in any forward position and he would even play him as a wing-half. "Yet," said Jimmy, "I was privileged to be associated with John Charles - he was a colossus.

He was easy to handle. The 'Gentle Giant' they called him, and that just about summed him up. Many times I used to say to him: 'John, don't let other players push you around son.' He always replied by saying: 'But Jimmy, they're so much smaller than I am.' John Charles, is, I think, the best of all. Yes, even better than Tom Finney. Charles had everything; strength, scheming ability, a shot in either foot, ball play, a superb physique. He's the best header of a ball I've ever seen, and he could truly play anywhere."

Jimmy had fond memories of the pre-Munich side but whenever the name Duncan Edwards was brought into a conversation he would go silent for a few seconds, lower his head and tears would stream down his cheeks. Duncan was indeed a young colossus who lost his life before reaching his prime. "I was very instrumental in bringing all those young Busby Babes through the different levels up to the first team and for many international honours," he said, "and believe me, it was a thrill to see them win Junior Leagues, Youth Cups, and in 1954, the International Youth Tournament in Switzerland. But seeing them mature from bright-eyed schoolkids was just as thilling and satisfying as managing a cup-winning team at Wembley or winning the Championship.

"However, I don't really like selecting one individual but I feel I must mention one player in particular. And I know the likes of Wilf McGuinness, Bobby Charlton, Bill Foulkes and Nobby Stiles will agree with me wholeheartedly. Duncan Edwards is the lad's name! I was privileged to have been closely associated with this lad, who, without a doubt was the greatest-ever English player. Duncan and my fellow Welshman John Charles, were two giants of world football. I have no intention of being drawn into any argument as to who was the greatest between these two brilliant, world-class footballers.

"Dunc's record speaks for itself. At 15 he played in United's first team. He was in the England team at 17 years and eight months. He won 19 full caps and collected two League championship medals before he was 21. That's some record isn't it? Dunc's transition from playing in our youth and junior teams was so easy because even at a young age, he had the temperament of a mature player. He was christened 'Boom-Boom' by the Germans after he scored a truly breathtaking goal against them in Berlin in 1957. If pushed into a corner for a decision then, yes, Duncan Edwards was the greatest player of them all. He had no weakness, I know that's hard to stand by, but he didn't. He could play anywhere and I do mean any position. In present day football he could have played until he was 50. And he was a player who never, ever moaned or groaned."

Full-Time

On Tuesday November 15th 1989, Jimmy Murphy passed away. He was 79.

A little story to end this book. And it's perfectly true and typifies the kind of man Jimmy Murphy was. In October 1989 Fred Eyre, the former Manchester City player was, at over 40, still playing competitive soccer. On this particular day Fred was playing, unbeknown to him, Jimmy was standing on his own in a quiet corner of the pitch watching the game. "I was huffing and puffing, but still enjoying playing," said Fred, who is now a brilliant after-dinner speaker and compere, besides being a very astute businessman and author. At the end of the game, Fred spotted Jimmy walking away and he shouted: "Jimmy, Jimmy!" Jimmy immediately stopped and looked around and saw Fred running over to him. Fred shook his hand and asked how he was keeping. "I was caked in mud and absolutely knackered," recalled Fred. "I expected Jimmy to say: 'What the bloody hell are you doing still trying to play football, or words to that effect.' Instead a big beaming smile came across his face. He seemed genuinely pleased and said: 'Well done Fred, son, you're still enjoying playing. Good on you.' Then he made my day when without any sign of in-sincerity or aloofness he said to me: 'I only wish I'd have got hold of you when you were 15, Fred lad, I'd have made a great player out of you. Good luck to you son and keep playing if you're enjoying it.'

Those few words coming from this great man who had coached thousands of players, meant more to me than Jimmy could ever imagine. He made me feel important. The great Jimmy Murphy telling me he could have made a great player out of me. He knew the right things to say to boost one's confidence. When I played for City's juniors and met United's kids if Jimmy was in charge we knew we were in for a tough game. Yes, even at Maine Road, Jimmy Murphy was highly respected."

The Bronze

On the evening of the February 2nd 1999, in the Manchester United Museum at Old Trafford, a bronze bust of Jimmy Murphy was unveiled. For years, old-time supporters had written, phoned, cajoled and implored the club via newspapers and local radio stations to honour Jimmy Murphy in some form for the unstinting work he had done for Manchester United. It was a magical evening and a wonderful occasion despite being a little late. It was a night the Murphy family will treasure, especially for the in-laws and his fifteen grandchildren; some of whom had never met Jimmy or were too young to remember him. Sir Alex Ferguson was present and they heard Wilf McGuinness, Shay Brennan and Nobby Stiles speak of Jimmy Murphy with such warmth and loving affection. The only regret was that Jimmy's wife Winnie did not live long enough to see this recognition.

Speaking on behalf of the family, Jimmy Murphy junior told the assembled audience: "On behalf of the Murphy family may I say a few words of thanks. To the directors of Manchester United for commissioning the bust of our father Jimmy Murphy. To the ex-players' Association for their support in this matter. To Ben Panting for his wonderful creation. To the fans who have written to the newspapers and phoned radio programmes over the years supporting a memorial to our father."

Clearing his throat Jimmy continued: "One of Dad's many qualities was his humility. He was a humble and straightforward man, who never forgot his roots in the Welsh mining community. He had no interest in big houses, fancy cars, exotic holidays, restaurants and clubs. As long as Mum was happy, the family healthy and he had enough money for a pint and a cigarette, then he was contented. He hated fuss and, if alive today, would be waiting in one of the local pubs for someone to pick him up on the way home from this function. To Dad, Manchester United was not about Matt Busby. It was not about Busby and Murphy. It was about the whole club. Everyone was important to him. He tried to find time for everyone. He never forgot the important work done by Walter Crickmer and Les Olive; by his great pal Bert Whalley and the other coaching staff; by the lovely Joe Armstrong and the other scouts; by everyone connected to Manchester United. We would like to think this bust represents not just Jimmy Murphy but is a symbol for all the backroom staff - the family that was Manchester United."

Although Jimmy didn't live long enough to see the success that Sir Alex Ferguson eventually brought to Manchester United, he was always confident that given the time and support of the board he would make a success of his job as manager of Manchester United. Jimmy had spoken to Sir Alex and the new manager listened intently to what the still passionate Murphy told him. Jimmy was still in love with Manchester United and he expressed his hopes and dreams for his beloved club. For the record, Jimmy thought Sir Alex was warm-hearted, knowledgeable and had the passion needed to bring the glory years back to Old Trafford. How right he proved to be.

Index

Index

Index

Yeats, Ron 188.
Youth Policy 2, 28.

Zurich International Youth
Tournament 56-7.

Other Books from Empire

Merseyside Maestros
The 100 best Everton & Liverpool footballers
by Dean Hayes
£9.99 - 210 pp - Paperback
From Aldridge to Yeats, Ball to Young Merseyside's greatest footballing heroes since the war and the careers that shaped their clubs' history.

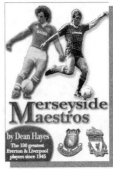

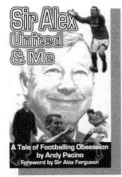

Sir Alex, United & Me
A Tale of Footballing Obsession
by Andy Pacino
Foreword by Sir Alex Ferguson
Sir Alex Ferguson is one of the most respected and successful characters in British sport today but were it not for the support of die-hard supporters like Andy Pacino he may have been lost to United before he had a chance to weave his managerial magic.

Roger Byrne
Captain of the Busby Babes
by Iain McCartney
£16.95 - Hardback
"A good old-fashioned book about a good old-fashioned player" Daily Telegraph

Morrissey's Manchester
the essential Smiths Tour
by Phill Gatenby
Foreword by Mick Middles
£5.99 - Paperback
"A tour of the people and places that influenced the most influential of bands"

To order call 0161 273 7007
or send a cheque (payable to Empire Publications) to
1 Newton St., Manchester M1 1HW